The use of technology for the management of the EU/US Immigration and Asylum Policy- possible risks for fundamental rights protection

STUDIES IN EUROPEAN INTEGRATION, STATE AND SOCIETY

Edited by Magdalena Góra, Zdzisław Mach and Katarzyna Zielińska

VOLUME 8

PETER LANG

Marta Kołodziejczyk

The use of technology for the management of the EU/US Immigration and Asylum Policy– possible risks for fundamental rights protection

PETER LANG

Bibliographic Information published by the Deutsche Nationalbibliothek
The Deutsche Nationalbibliothek lists this publication in the Deutsche Nationalbibliografie; detailed bibliographic data is available online at http://dnb.d-nb.de.

Library of Congress Cataloging-in-Publication Data
A CIP catalog record for this book has been applied for at the Library of Congress.

Printed by CPI books GmbH, Leck.

ISSN 2193-2352
ISBN 978-3-631-80819-1 (Print)
E-ISBN 978-3-631-81719-3 (E-PDF)
E-ISBN 978-3-631-81720-9 (EPUB)
E-ISBN 978-3-631-81721-6 (MOBI)
DOI 10.3726/b16758

Peter Lang – Berlin · Bern · Bruxelles · New York · Oxford · Warszawa · Wien

This publication has been peer reviewed.

www.peterlang.com

To my Dearest Parents Renata and Alfred
Last but not least,
to my lifelong medicine
dr-Maciej Wojtacha

Between Knowledge and Power - the use of technology for the management of the EU/US Immigration and Asylum Policy: possible risks for fundamental rights protection.

by Marta Kołodziejczyk

Acknowledgments

This book is the result of my scientific investigation done between 2010–2019 during which I have been supported by a number of prominent intellectualls whom I would like to mention in chronological order:

Professor Zdzisław Mach- founder of the Institute of European Studies at the Jagiellonian University; an open-minded and inspiring personality; always ready to support young ambitious researchers;

Professor Adam Daniel Rotfeld-with whom, while serving as His assistant at the Polish Institute of International Affairs (Warsaw), I had the privilege to exchange on daily basis my personal views on various scientific concepts;

dr Jorrit Rijpma-passionate researcher who while conducting His splendid seminar on „Smart borders" at the European University Institute (Florence), inspired me to approach this phenomenon from my own perspective;

Professor Kazimierz Lankosz- who shared with me His numerous insights, inspiring thoughts and encouraged me in the process of doing my research.

Contents

Introduction

It used to be a passport, both as a means to identify and sort people and as a requirement for the legitimate movement across territorial spaces that allowed states to assert their sovereign prerogative to regulate the entry and exits of persons[1]. Nowadays, in the age of globalization when innovative means of transport and telecommunication have increased people's 'capabilities and aspirations to migrate', Western countries (European Union & USA) attempt to reinforce their power over the cross-border movement of people by constructing databanks[2] equipped with modern technological tools such as: bone scanners, speech-recognition utilities and last but not least biometrics-defined as technologies that measure and analyze human body characteristics, such as fingerprints, eye retinas and irises, voice or facial patterns and hand measurements or DNA for authentication purposes. As our existence is being translated into more inputs and outputs of data to be processed and embed technology everywhere, self-governed, independent human being, capable of mastering his/her own freedoms and rights-as privacy theory presupposes - is on a collision course with the human being subjected to and affected by more and more complex Information & Communication technologies (ICT). This process is to be observed in the framework of the European Union's area of Freedom Security and Justice where information sharing, including the exchange of more complex and sensitive personal data is a common practice[3]. Whenever Member States' authorities take decisions in the realm of migration policy-issuing a passport to its nationals, deciding on the responsibility of a particular member state for an asylum claim or determining whether an individual is legally staying on territory of the European Union-their actions are governed by the European legislation that at the same time provides politicians and governmental bodies with the plethora of technological tools allowing them, for instance, to check personal data including biometric data and exchange relevant information through secured EU networks

---

1 J. Torpey, *The Invention of a Passport: Surveillance, Citizenship and the State*, Cambridge University Press 2000, p. 35.

2 *Migration and the New Technological Borders of Europe*, H. Dijstelbloem A. Meijer (ed), Palgrave and Macmillian, New York 2011, pp. 1–15.

3 F. Boehm, *Information Sharing and Data Protection in the Area of Freedom, Security and Justice. Towards Harmonized Data Protection Principles for Information Exchange at the EU level, Springer Berlin Heidelberg* 2012, pp. 321–368;

of communication[4]. Personal data are therefore constantly exchanged, not only between Member States and with third countries, but also between EU bodies[5]. On the practical level, this cooperation is carried out by a network of European agencies, bodies and Member States authorities exchanging information between each other as well as with third parties based on EU initiatives, administrative agreements or international treaties[6]. The number of these established throughout the years has recently caused concerns over - on the on hand - interoperability between EU information systems in the area of borders and security - on the other - fundamental rights infringements linked to the right to private life (Article 7 of the EU Charter of Fundamental Rights (the Charter) and the protection of personal data (Article 8 of the Charter). In a state of mass surveillance, personal rights and freedoms are severely limited, as clearly predicted in Orwell's book „1984". Furthermore, the actual broader availability of data can in itself have additional implications-positive or negative-on, for instance, the right to an effective remedy (Article 47) or the prohibition of torture and inhuman or degrading treatment or punishment (Article 4), liberty and security of person (Article 6) integrity of the person (Article 3) the right to asylum (Article 18) and prohibition of collective expulsion (Article 19) rights of the child (Article 24) and equality before the law (Article 20)[7].

---

4 Jorrit J. Rijmpa, *Brave New borders: The EU's Use of New Technologies for the Management of Migration and Asylum*, (in:) *New Technologies and EU Law*, M. Cremona (ed.), Oxford University Press 2017, pp. 197–237.

5 In this context, it is worth to mention that one of the most important tools for the achievement of the AFSJ provided for in the Title V TFEU is a reinforced police and judicial cooperation (Articles 82–89 TFEU), which is carried out in no small part by sharing and exchanging personal data. Furthermore, article 87 TFEU clarifies that the EU shall establish police cooperation involving all the Member States' competent authorities, including police, customs and other specialized law enforcement services.

6 For example: the Treaty of Prüm (signed in May 2005) by seven Member States (Belgium, Germany, Spain, France, Luxembourg, the Netherlands and Austria) outside of the framework of the EU and contains provisions about enhanced cross-border cooperation, particularly in combating terrorism and cross-border crime related to the exchange of DNA profiles, fingerprints and vehicle registration data; meanwhile the provisions of the treaty have been transposed to the EU law by the Council Decision 2008/615/JHA of 23 June 2008 on the stepping up of cross-border cooperation, particularly in combating terrorism and cross-border crime, OJ 2008, L-210/1.

7 *Fundamental rights and the interoperability of EU information systems: borders and security, European Union Agency for Fundamental Rights,* Vienna 2017, p. 7.

In a reality where opportunities for surveillance are constantly growing along with technological developments, research questions of this book are focused on „knowledge versus power" scheme. A common suggestion here is the idea of finding the balance between - on the one hand- knowledge- understood as minimal personal information obtained for a particular purpose by an administrative body and-power-interpreted here as competences and restrictions, e.g. data minimization, purpose/storage limitation imposed on executive bodies by the EU Data Protection Law in the context of the EU immigration and asylum policy as well as exchange of data with third countries, for instance the United States of America. As far as the term balance is concerned, it is defined as „a state of equilibrium"; Aristotle called this point „the golden mean" (i.e. the middle ground between extremes). The so-called balancing idea is to be found in the European Convention on Human Rights case law, stating that „inherent in the whole of the Convention is a search for a fair balance between demands of the general interest of the community and the requirements of the protection of the individual's fundamental rights"[8]. Hence, bearing in mind the so called trade-off model according to which it is not possible to increase one of the values without decreasing the other this research investigates if the privacy and security concerns are appropriately balanced on the both sides of the Atlantic (EU/USA) in the framework of the digitalized migration policies. Hence, this book is structured in the following way: 1) Privacy and data protection - history and current state of law; 2) European Union Competence & Technology appliance in the field of Asylum and Migration Policy in the area of Freedom, Security and Justice; 3) Possible risks of fundamental rights infringements posed by the digitalization of the EU immigration and asylum policy; 4) Between knowledge and power – use of technology for the management of migration policy: European Union versus United States of America.

8 Soering v. the United Kingdom, No. 14038/88, 7 July 1989, § 89.

I Privacy and data protection-history and current state of law

Privacy and data protection as a specific field of law have been elaborated over the last four decades, notably in the context of the Council of Europe and the European Union, stimulated by the growing impact of information and communication technology. The concept of the 'right to privacy' emerged however in international law after the Second World War. The dangers of the misuse of science were a concern of the UN already in the 1940s and later anticipating several issues that occupy the front pages today (2020). This was illustrated in the Article 12 of the Universal Declaration of Human Rights (UN General Assembly, Paris 1948) according to which no one shall be subjected to arbitrary interference with his privacy, family, home or correspondence. Furthermore, the International Conference on Human Rights of 1968 adopted the Proclamation of Teheran predicting that, "*[w]hile recent scientific discoveries and technological advances have opened vast prospects for economic, social and cultural progress, such developments may nevertheless endanger the rights and freedoms of individuals and will require continuing attention*". In a follow-up resolution, the General Assembly agreed that "*recent scientific discoveries and technological advances ... may ... endanger the rights and freedoms of individuals*" and requested a study on four issues of concern with regard to human rights arising out of science and technological advancement, namely, (1) respect for privacy "*in light of advances in recording and other techniques;*", (2) protection of physical and intellectual integrity due to advances in biology, medicine and biochemistry; (3) limits on the use of electronics to protect the rights of individuals; and (4) "*generally, the balance that should be established between scientific and technological progress and the intellectual, spiritual, cultural and moral advancement of humanity*". The voices of concern seemed to be heard in Germany where the state of Hesse adopted in 1970 the first law on data protection, which only applied on its territory. In 1973, Sweden passed the world's first national data protection law. Consequently, by the end of the 1980s, several European states (France, Germany, the Netherlands and the United Kingdom) had also enacted legislation on data protection. Furthermore, in 1993 the World Conference on Human Rights (1993) proclaimed the Vienna Declaration and Program of Action, which noted "*that certain advances, notably in the biomedical and life sciences as well as in information technology, may have potentially adverse consequences for the integrity, dignity and human rights of the individual, and call[ed] for international cooperation to ensure that human rights and dignity are fully respected in this area of universal concern*". This declaratory level of protection became later lawful in Article 8 of the European Convention on Human Rights (ECHR) according to which everyone has the right to respect for his/her private and family life, home and correspondence, and no interference by a public authority with the exercise of this right is allowed except in accordance with the law and where necessary in a democratic society for certain important and legitimate interests. The above mentioned definition has been reflected in the series of judgments, e.g.: Leander v. Sweden (26.03.1987); Kopp v. Switzerland (25.03.1998); Amann v. Switzerland (16.02.2000), issued by the European Court of Human Rights (ECtHR) in Strasbourg. However, in about 1970 the Council of Europe came to conclusion that Article 8 ECHR had a number of shortcomings, e.g. the uncertain scope of 'private life', the emphasis on interference by public authorities, as well as lack of a more proactive approach against the possible misuse of personal information by companies or other organizations in the private sector. As a result, the Data Protection Convention, also known as Convention 108 (Strasbourg 1981), had been adopted and has been ratified by 47 Member states of the Council of Europe, including all EU Member States. Parties to this convention guaranteed every individual, whatever his nationality or residence, respect for his/her rights and fundamental freedoms; in particular right to privacy, with regard to automatic processing of personal data relating to him/her ('data protection'). In addition, the concept of 'personal data' was defined as "any information relating to an identified or identifiable ('data subject')". Let us now consider some of the key provisions of the above-mentioned Data Protection Convention known as the Convention 108; personal data are to be "*obtained and processed fairly and lawfully*" and "*stored for specified and legitimate purposes and not used in a way incompatible with those purposes*". Personal data should also be "*adequate, relevant and not excessive in relation to the purposes for which they are stored*", "*accurate and, where necessary, kept up to date*". Other crucial principles expressed in the text of the Convention are: "*appropriate security measures*", "*additional safeguards for the data subject such as the right to have access to his or her own personal data, the right to obtain rectification or erasure of such data, and the right to remedy if such rights are not respected*". To conclude, the Convention's philosophy is not that processing of personal data should always be considered as a breach of privacy; however, in its interests as well as other fundamental freedoms, any processing must always observe certain legal conditions. In this context, the core elements of Article 8 ECHR, such as interference with the right to privacy only on adequate legal basis, and where necessary for a legitimate purpose, have been transferred into a broader context. Since 2013, however, the Committee of the Convention 108 has been working on modernization proposals related to such issues as: proportionality (so far implicit and concerning only the data), in particular data minimization; accountability, in particular of data controllers and processors; privacy by design; obligation to declare data breaches; transparency of data processing; additional safeguards for the data subject such as the right not to be subject to a decision solely based on an automatic processing without having his or her views taken into consideration, the right to obtain knowledge of the logic underlying the processing, and the right to object; possibility for International organizations to accede to the modernized Convention. In September 2016 a draft amending protocol was referred for discussion and adoption to the Committee of Ministers of the Council of Europe, the executive body of the organization where the 47 member states are represented. As a result, the data protection Convention of the Council of Europe which had for the past four decades been the only international legally binding instrument on the protection of private life and personal data open to any country in the world has finally been, after 7 years of intense work and negotiations, modernised.[9] Convention 108+, aims to ensure that the transfer of personal data across borders is done with appropriate safeguards, and that it is compatible with normative frameworks across the world, including the European Union's legislation. Some of the innovations can be summarized as follows: a) Stronger requirements regarding the proportionality and data minimization principles and lawfulness of the processing; b) Extension of the types of sensitive data, which will now include genetic and biometric data, trade union membership and ethnic origin; c) Obligation to declare data breaches; d) Greater transparency of data processing; e) New rights for the persons in an algorithmic decision making context, which are particularly relevant in connection with the development of artificial intelligence; f) Stronger accountability of data controllers; g) Requirement that the "privacy by design" principle is applied; h) Application of the data protection principles to all processing activities, including for national security reasons, with possible exceptions and restrictions subject to the conditions set by the Convention, and in any case with independent and effective review and supervision; i) Clear regime of transborder data flows;

9 Thorbjørn Jagland, Secretary General of the Council of Europe, *"Convention 108: from a European reality to a global treaty"*, Strasbourg, 17 June 2016.

J) Reinforced powers and independence of the data protection authorities and enhanced legal basis for international cooperation.[10]

To conclude, the right to respect for private life and the right to the protection of personal data are closely related. Both strive to protect similar values, i.e. the autonomy and human dignity of individuals, by granting them a personal sphere in which they can freely develop their personalities, think and shape their opinions. They are thus an essential prerequisite for the exercise of other fundamental freedoms, such as freedom of expression, freedom of peaceful assembly and association, and freedom of religion. The two rights, however, differ in their formulation and scope. The right to respect for private life consists of a general prohibition of interference, subject to some public interest criteria that can justify intervention in certain cases. To contrast, the protection of personal data is viewed as a modern and active right[11], putting in place a system of checks and balances to protect individuals whenever their personal data are processed. What is more, the act of processing must comply with the essential components of personal data protection, namely independent supervision and the respect for the data subject's rights.[12]

Although the Data Protection was put on the agenda of the Council of Europe and, as a result, exposed in the binding Conventions, this intergovernmental organization was less successful in terms of ensuring greater consistency across the EU. Some Member States were late in implementing the Convention, and those who did so arrived at different outcomes, in some cases even imposing restrictions on data flows with other Member States. Concerned that this lack of

10 Opened for signature in 1981, the Convention for the Protection of Individuals with regard to Automatic Processing of Personal Data currently has 55 State Parties: the 47 Council of Europe member states, Argentina, Cabo Verde, Mauritius, Mexico, Marocco, Senegal, Tunisia, and Uruguay. Burkina Faso was invited on the 23 March 2017 to sign and ratify the Convention 108; the invitation is valid till 24 March 2022, See: Non-member States of the Council of Europe; five years validity of an invitation to sign and ratify or to accede to the Council's of Europe's treaties (status as of 16 March 2020), at: https://rm.coe.int/CoERMPublicCommonSearchServices/DisplayDCTMContent?documentId=09000016806cac22 (Accessed: March 2020);See also: Chart of signatures and ratifications of Treaty 108 at: https://www.coe.int/en/web/conventions/full-list/-/conventions/treaty/108/signatures (Accessed: March 2020).

11 Advocate General Sharpston described the case as involving two separate rights: the "classic" right to the protection of privacy and a more "modern" one, the right to data protection. See CJEU, Joined cases C-92/09 and C-93/02, *Volker und Markus Schecke GbR v. Land Hessen, Opinion of Advocate General Sharpston*, 17 June 2010, para. 71.

12 Hustinx, P., EDPS Speeches & Articles, *EU Data Protection Law: the Review of Directive 95/46/EC and the Proposed General Data Protection Regulation*, July2013.

consistency could hamper the development of internal market involving a circulation of people and services, where the processing of personal data was to play an increasingly important role, the European Commission submitted a proposal for a Directive to harmonize the national laws on data protection in the private and most of the public sector[13]. After four years of negotiations the Directive 95/46/EC on the protection of individuals with regard to the processing of personal data and on the free movement of such data has been adopted. It specified the basic principles of data protection already included in the Convention 108 of the Council of Europe. In the first place, it required all Member States to protect the fundamental rights and freedoms of natural persons, and in particular the right to privacy with the respect to processing of personal data, in accordance with the Directive. In this context, the data could be processed only if the data subject has unambiguously given his/her consent, if processing was necessary for the performance of a contract to which the data subject was party, or for compliance with a legal obligation, for the performance of a government task, in order to protect the vital interests of the data subject, or to protect the legitimate interests pursued by the controller, except where such interests were overridden by the interests of the data subject. Furthermore, the Directive committed the controller to always inform the data subject about the purposes of the processing and other relevant matters in order to guarantee fair processing in respect of the data subject. In case of not fulfilling this condition, the data controller might become liable for committing an offense. Responsibility for compliance with national legislation on data protection belonged to supervisory authorities. Secondly, the Directive applied to the processing of personal data carried out "in the context of the activities of an establishment" of the controller on the territory of an EU Member State. In other words, where the controller was not established in the EU, the applicable law was that of the Member State in which the equipment used for processing was located. Thirdly, according to the Directive personal data could only be transferred to third countries that ensured adequate level of protection.

To conclude, the Directive 95/46/EC required the Member States neither to restrict nor prohibit the free flow of personal data between them for reasons connected with such protection. This provision aimed at achieving an equivalent high level of protection in all Member States and as a result assured a balanced development of the internal market. This goal has not, however, been entirely fulfilled due to the fact that the above-mentioned Directive allowed Member States

13 V. Reading, *The European Data Protection Framework for the twenty-first century*, in: *"International Data Privacy Law"* 2012, vol. 2, No. 3, pp. 119–129.

fairly broad discretion on its transposition. Furthermore, the need for reform of the current EU data protection legislation can be also explained by the rising impact of IT technologies on our lives. Specifically, at the time when the Directive was adopted the Internet barely existed; in nowadays reality, on the contrary, the data processing is taking place on the web sites, by search engines or social networks. This has been reflected in the European Commission's official comment focused on such challenges for the protection of personal data in the future as: the astounding capabilities of modern technologies; the increased globalization of data flows; and access to personal data by law enforcement authorities that was greater than ever. Another crucial reason for the review of the Directive 95/46/EC has to do with the new institutional framework of the EU. The Lisbon Treaty (December 2009) emphasizes fundamental rights[14]; Article 16 provides for comprehensive data protection in all policy areas, regardless of whether it relates to the internal market, law enforcement, or almost any other part of the public sector. Not to mention about the separate right to the protection of personal data laid down in Article 8 of the Charter of Fundamental Rights that became legally binding on the EU institutions and national governments with the entry into force on 1 December 2009 of the Treaty of Lisbon amending the Treaty on European Union and the Treaty establishing the European Community; the latter being renamed the Treaty on the Functioning of the European Union (TFEU)'[15].

1 The choice of new legislative instruments

In the context of the reform of the EU data protection framework there had been a great deal of discussion as to whether the new instrument should take the form of a directive or regulation[16]. Article 16 (2) TFUE mandates the European legislators to adopt 'the rules relating to the protection of individuals with regard to processing of personal data', without, however, specifying the type of legislative act to be chosen. As a consequence, in line with Article 289(1) TFEU on the ordinary legislative procedure, the rules can be laid down in a regulation, a directive, or a decision. Let us note that the regulation has general application being

14 G. Fuster, *The Emergence of Personal Data Protection as a Fundamental Right of the EU*, Springer 2014, pp. 3–33.

15 *Reforming European Data Protection Law*, Serge Gutwirth, Ronald Leenes, Paulde Hert (Eds.), Springer 2015, pp. 3–15.

16 *Executive summary EDPS Opinion of 7 March 2012 on the data protection reform package*, at: the https://edps.europa.eu/sites/edp/files/publication/12-03-07_edps_reform_package_summary_en.pdf (Accessed: January 2020)

at the same time directly applicable (it does not require implementation by EU member states), whereas the directive sets forth the results to be achieved, but leaves the means for achieving them largely up to implementation into national law by the members states. That is why one of the major complaint with the data protection directive 95/46 has been the lack of harmonization caused by the distinctive features of this particular legal act. It is worth to mention that by now the Commission has launched several legal actions for improper implementation of the Directive; in March 2009, the Court of Justice in Luxembourg ruled (case against Germany) that the requirement of 'complete independence' for a supervisory authority means that it should be free from any external influence. This has been also recently confirmed and elaborated in a case against Austria. On the contrary, regulation leads to a greater degree of harmonization, since it immediately becomes part of a national legal system, without the need for adoption of separate national legislation; in other words, regulation has legal effect independent of national law and overrides contrary national laws[17]. That is why the choice of regulation would according to the European Commission reduce legal fragmentation among member states in respect to different national data protection laws. This would lead e.g. to a net savings for companies of about €2.3 billion a year in terms of administrative burden alone. But even the regulation cannot result in complete harmonization of all legal provisions affecting data protection or totally eliminate the need to amend national laws. This fact may confirm that the type of legal instrument used is not determinative with regard to harmonization; for example it is also possible for a directive to leave little margin for member state implementation (e.g. EU Consumer Rights Directive 2011/83/EU).

2 Territorial scope

Let us now concentrate on the most significant provisions of the two legislative instruments that form the core of the data protection reform package: in the first place, the Regulation, setting out the general EU framework for data protection; secondly, the Directive for the police and criminal justice sector which is due to replace Framework Decision 2008/977/JHA which covers the protection of personal data processed by police and judicial authorities in criminal matters. Article 3 of the proposed Regulation contains the rules governing its territorial scope. In spite of innovation in this respect there is a lot of continuity which is evidenced

17 P. Craig & G. de Búrrca, *EU Law: Text, Cases and Materials*, Oxford University Press 5th ed. 2011, pp. 105–106.

in the concept, already reflected in the Directive 95/46, of *"the processing of personal data in the context of the activities of an establishment"* in the EU as the basic test for determining when the EU data protection law applies (Article 3(1)). However, at the same time, under Article 3(2) of the Regulation, data controllers not established in the EU may become subjects to the EU law when their processing activities are related to *"the offering of goods or services"* to data subjects residing in the EU, or to the monitoring of the behavior of EU residents. The goal of these changes is to bring more non-EU-based companies offering services over the internet liable for data protection breaches under EU law. On the other hand, the proposed Directive aiming at achieving greater harmonization of EU member states' rules on data protection in the area of police and criminal justice sector applies to domestic processing operations. This is necessary as neither article 8 of the EU Charter of Fundamental Rights nor Article 16 TFEU makes a distinction between domestic and cross-border processing operations, but refers to processing activities that fall within the scope of EU law and the free movement of personal data. In addition, both the proposals for the Regulation and for the Directive are addressed to member states only, and therefore do not apply to the processing of personal data by the Union institutions, bodies, offices, and agencies, that will continue to apply Regulation (EC) No 45/2001.

In the context of the above-described two legislative instruments, regulation and directive that form the core of the data protection reform package, it is worth to mention the opinion of the European Data Protection Supervisor (EDPS) on the Commission's proposal. In the first place, EDPS welcomed the proposal for Data Protection Regulation as *"a huge step forward"* towards more effective and consistent protection of personal data across the EU[18]. However, the architecture of the package in itself – a Directive and a Regulation – signals that there might be a problem with its comprehensiveness. The main weakness of the package is that the level of protection in the proposed Directive is substantially lower than in the Regulation.

In the first place, police and justice are the areas where the use of personal information inevitably has an enormous impact on the lives of private individuals. That is why it is difficult to understand why the Commission, instead of proposing comprehensive legislative framework, has decided to frame the data protection into two separate, unequal in terms of data protection guarantees, legislative acts; namely, the regulation and the directive. Moreover, the choice for a self-standing instrument is regrettable and constitutes a missed opportunity

18 *Executive summary EDPS Opinion of 7 March 2012 ...*, Op. Cit.

to clarify and ensure the consistent application of rules related to situations in which activities of the private sector and of the law enforcement sector interact with each other and borderlines are becoming increasingly blurred. Examples of these situations are the transfer of Passenger Name Record (PNR) data and data on financial transfers to law enforcement authorities. This risk is especially visible in the context of the European Union management of immigration and asylum that relies heavily on the use of technology, biometrics and the exchange of information between national and EU authorities, including through large-scale databases that are to be described in the next chapter of this book. It is undeniable that appliance of technology for the regulation of immigration and asylum poses risks for the protection of fundamental rights. That is why it is necessary that the European Union comes to conclusion on the biometric identifiers and data approach that is coherent harmonized and at the same time equipped with fundamental rights safeguards. However, the proposed Directive fails to include important elements regarding the retention of personal data, transparency towards individuals, keeping personal data up to date, and ensuring it is adequate, relevant and not excessive. Similarly the European Data Protection Supervisor regretted in particular that "the Commission did not propose stricter rules for the transfer of personal data outside the EU; data protection authorities were not given mandatory powers to effectively control the processing of personal data in this area; the possibilities for the police to access data processed in the private sector were not regulated. To conclude, the proposed directive might cause fragmentation in the EU Data Protection System, rather than introducing consistency."[19]

3 Reinforcement of the rights of data subjects

In a recent survey, more than two-thirds of Europeans-72 per cent- expressed their concerns connected to uncontrolled usage of their personal data by companies on the Internet. That is why the aim of the new legislative acts proposed by the Commission was to strengthen individuals' rights by improving the ability to control their data[20]. In this context, the requirement of consent as one possible

19 *EDPS welcomes a "huge step forward for data protection in Europe", but regrets inadequate rules for the police and justice area, Press release* 25 January 2012.

20 *Proposed EU Data Protection Regulation One Year Later: The Albrecht Report,* in: *"Privacy & Security Law Report"*, 12 PVLR 99, 01/21/2013, pp. 1–7.

ground for lawful processing of personal data has been clarified[21]. It is worth to mention that the 'consent' is currently defined in Articles 2(h) and 7(a) of Directive 95/46/EC as *'any freely given specific and informed indication'* of a data subject's wish to agree to the processing of his/her personal data. In addition, this agreement must be 'unambiguously' given in order to make the processing of the personal data legitimate. However, national laws have transposed this concept quite differently. Consequently, national supervisory authorities tend to apply variable interpretations of consent. Furthermore, the meaning of 'unambiguously' given consent is interpreted in a differentiated manner: in some member states consent has to be given 'expressly' and in some cases even in writing, while other member states also accept some forms of implied consent. As a consequence, valid consent in one member state may not be legally valid in others, therefore creating uncertainty amongst controllers operating in several member states on whether a data processing operation is lawful or not. Hence, in the proposed Regulation the definition of 'the data subject's consent' of Article 4(8) is remedied by adding the criterion 'explicit' which allows to avoid the confusing parallelism with 'unambiguous'. Moreover, where consent is the legal ground for data processing, Article 7 states that the controller must be able to demonstrate that the consent has taken place. A the same time, the Regulation reaffirms that the data subject may withdraw his or her consent at any time, bearing in mind that this will only take full legal effect for future processing. Furthermore, consent is excluded in Article 7(4) as a ground for processing in specific cases of significant imbalance between data controller and data subject, for example in the framework of an employment relationship. Similarly, Article 8 sets out further conditions for the lawfulness of consent for processing of personal data of children below the age of 13 years in relation to services offered to them on-line.

As regards the context of reinforcing the rights of data subject, it is worth to emphasize that the Regulation enhances administrative and judicial remedies in case data protection rights are violated. In particular, Article 76 (1) enables certain associations, for example, consumer protection associations whose statutory aim includes the protection of personal data, to bring actions, on behalf of one or a group of data subjects whose rights may have been violated, to court. Similarly, article 73 (3) of the proposed Regulation provides that these data protection NGOs, in cases of personal data breaches, may address a supervisory

21 E. Kosta, *Consent in European Data protection Law,* Martinus Nijhoff Publishers, The Hague 2013, pp. 261–381.

authority in any member state in their own right; without obligation to obtain data subject's authorization to act on his behalf.

As far as the national authorities responsibilities for data protection are concerned, the proposed Regulation strengthens their potential for initiating legal actions by: a) clarifying the conditions for the establishment and for ensuring the complete independence of supervisory authorities in member states (Articles 46–50); b) providing for fully harmonized provisions for the competences, duties, and powers of the supervisory authorities (Articles 51 to 54); and as a result, c) creating legal basis and conditions for an efficient cooperation between supervisory authorities established in EU Member States (Articles 55 to 56); d) introducing the 'one-stop-shop rule that gives companies operating in more than one member state, a single supervisory authority responsible for monitoring their personal-data processing activities in the EU, rather than force a company to deal with multiple bodies in different countries.

4 Right to be forgotten

The "*right to be forgotten and to erasure,*" is likely to be one of the most controversial provisions of the Regulation. In theory, this right addresses an urgent problem in the digital age: it is very hard to escape your past on the Internet now that every photo, status update, and tweet lives forever in the cloud. Although the right to request the controller to delete unlawfully processed personal data is already guaranteed in the Directive 95/46/EC it is difficult, according to the European Commission, for an individual to enforce this right in the online environment. Especially that the way in which these rights can be exercised is not harmonized, and therefore enjoying the so-called 'right to be forgotten' is actually easier in some Member States than in others. That is why, in order to strengthen the level of protection guaranteed to individuals the European Commission published on the January 1, 2012 the Proposal for a Regulation on the Protection of Individuals with Regard to the Processing of Personal Data and on the Free Movement of Such Data ("GDPR"), which updated the former Data Protection Directive. Hence, the unified regulation is due to give all European Union citizens a right to be forgotten online, in other words the right for an individual user to have his or her personal online data removed from the web. It is worth to mention in this respect that this legal rule has been officially acknowledged in the judgment Google Spain SL and Google Inc. v. Agencia Española de Protección de Datos (AEPD) and Mario Costeja González issued by the Court of Justice of the European Union (CJEU) as renamed by the Treaty of Lisbon in 2009. The case concerned a reference for a preliminary ruling made by the Spanish High Court to the CJEU, which arose out of a dispute between Google Inc and Google Spain on the one hand, and Mr. Costeja González and the Spanish Data Protection Agency on the other. Let us now dwell on the facts of the above mentioned case; in 2010, Mario Costeja González, a Spanish national, filed a complaint with the Spanish Data Protection Agency ("Agencia Española de Protección de Datos", "AEPD") against La Vanguardia Ediciones SL, a large publisher of daily news in Spain, as well as Google Spain and Google Inc.[22] González, the data subject seeking erasure, contended that whenever a Google search of his name was carried out, the top results listed linked the Internet user to two property auction notices for the recovery of social security debts that Mr Costeja González had owed 16 years earlier, which still appeared on La Vanguardia's website. Furthermore, the applicant claimed that these articles "although truthful, injured his reputation and invaded his privacy."[23] That is why, González demanded that the Spanish newspaper erased them because they were no longer relevant, since the proceedings had been concluded more than a decade ago[24]. The newspaper publisher refused to erase the articles because the Ministry of Labour and Social Affairs had ordered their publication[25]. Next, the plaintiff demanded that Google remove the link to those stories and thereby eliminate any association to his name. In other words, an order was demanded to the effect that the newspaper should alter, delete, or protect this information, and that Google should either delete or conceal the links to those pages. As far as the procedural history of Google Spain v. AEPD is concerned, the Spanish Data Protection Agency (AEPD) ruled that Google was responsible, as a data controller, for removing results about the plaintiff from its search engine.[26] After the AEPD's decision, Google brought action before the Audiencia Nacional, Spain's highest court, which referred the case to the Court of Justice

22 Case C-131/12, Google Spain SL. v. Agencia Española de Protección de Datos (May 13, 2013), http://curia.europa.eu/juris/document/document.jsf?text=&docid=152065&doclang=EN, (Accessed: January 2018); See also: Michael L. Rustad & Sanna Kulevska, *Reconceptualizing the Right to be Forgotten to Enable Transatlantic Data Flow,* in: "Harvard Journal of Law & Technology", Volume 28, Number 2 Spring 2015, pp. 350–416.

23 Dave Lee, What Is the "Right To Be Forgotten"?, BBC (May 13, 2014), at: http://www.bbc.com/news/technology-27394751, (Accessed: May 2018).

24 Google Spain SL, Case C-131/12, § 15.

25 Opinion of Advocate General Jääskinen § 19, Google Spain SL v. Agencia Española de Protección de Datos (May 13, 2014) (Case C-131/12), at:http://curia.europa.eu/juris/document/document.jsf?text=&docid=138782&doclang=EN, (Accessed: January 2018).

26 Google Spain SL, Case C-131/12, § 17.

of the European Union. As a consequence, on June 25, 2013, Advocate General Niilo Jääskinen issued his advisory opinion, finding that Google had no responsibility to remove any links on its search engine based on a privacy claim[27]. He reasoned that suppressing legitimate and legal information already in the public domain would interfere with freedom of expression and undermine the objectivity of information on the Internet.[28] However, the CJEU rejected the Advocate General's argument and recognized a broad right to be forgotten under Spain's implementation of Directive 95/46/EC. The court found, in the first place, that Google, as an indexer of information, was processing personal data and therefore subject to the Directive's obligations for data controllers.

Secondly, the court drew upon Articles 12(b) and 14(a) of the Directive to hold that Google owed a duty to erase information from its search index (Google Spain SL, Case C-131/12). Thirdly, the CJEU rejected Google's argument that imposing a duty to remove personal data violated the principle of proportionality, and that such removal must be addressed to a publisher of the website because the publisher was responsible for making the information public[29]. Furthermore, court reasoned that search engines make access to this information effortlessly available, because they enable users to obtain *knowledge* about a data subject by simply typing the subject's name.[30] What is more, due to their preeminent role in organizing data, search engines like Google are far more likely to interfere with the data subject's right to privacy than the original website publisher. However, as the British House of Lords observed the judgment of the Court is unworkable due to the fact that it does not take into account the effect the ruling would have on smaller search engines that, unlike Google, rarely have at their disposal resources to process thousands of removal requests, they may receive. In addition, the House of Lords sub-committee, noted that the expression, 'right to be forgotten' is misleading because information can be made more difficult to access, but it does not just disappear. Furthermore, it was argued that it is 'wrong in principle' to leave it to search engines to decide whether or not to delete information, based on 'vague, ambiguous and

27 Opinion of Advocate General Jääskinen, § 138.

28 Id. § 120–34.

29 Google also argued that the least cost avoider for removing access to the information was the website and not the search engine. Furthermore, they argued that to require a search engine to remove content from its index "would take insufficient account of the fundamental rights of publishers of websites of other internet users and of the operator itself."

30 Google Spain SL, Case C-131/12, § 80.

unhelpful' criteria[31]. To conclude, according to the recent judgment (ECJ Ruling C-131/12) of the Court of Justice of the European Union where the information is inaccurate, inadequate, irrelevant or excessive for the purposes of the data processing (§ 93 of the ruling) individuals have the right - under certain conditions - to ask search engines to remove links with personal information about them. In this vein, in case of giving consent as a child not being aware of risks by envisaged processing, the new law allows this individual to remove any such data that were made public on Internet at that time. Simultaneously, the Court explicitly clarified that the right to be forgotten is not absolute but will always need to be balanced against other fundamental rights, such as the freedom of expression and of the media (§ 85 of the ruling). It is also worth to mention that, according to the judgment of the European Union Court of Justice, 'the right to be forgotten' cannot amount to a total deletion of history (Joint Cases C-92/09 and C-93/09 Volker and Markus Schecke and Eifert (2010) ECR 1-000, § 48). Hence, a case-by-case assessment is needed considering the type of information in question, its sensitivity for the individual's private life and the interest of the public in having access to that information. The role the person requesting the deletion plays in public life might also be relevant. Moreover, the traditional right to erasure ('right to be forgotten') expressed in the Regulation is further strengthen in such a way that the controller who has made the personal data public is obliged to inform third parties processing the data that the data subject has requested the controller to erase any links to, or copies or replications of that personal data. However, appreciating this provision the European Data Protection Supervisor (EDPS) recognized that it may be in some cases a huge effort to inform all third parties who may be processing such data, as there will not always be clear understanding of where the data may have been disseminated[32]. To conclude, "the right to be forgotten and to erasure" are likely to be one of the most controversial provisions of the Regulation that came into force across the European Union on 25 May 2018. Especially if compared to USA standards of data protection. While in Europe the intellectual roots of the right to be forgotten can be found in French law, which recognizes le droit à l'oubli-or the "right of oblivion"—a right that allows a convicted criminal who has served his time and been rehabilitated to object to the publication of the facts of his conviction and incarceration. In America, by contrast, publication

31 European Union Committee-Second Report EU Data Protection law: a 'right to be forgotten'?, 23 July 2014 at: https://publications.parliament.uk/pa/ld201415/ldselect/ldeucom/40/40.pdf (Accessed: May 2018)

32 European Data Protection Supervisor 2012, Op. Cit., pp. 24–25.

of someone's criminal history is protected by the First Amendment, leading Wikipedia to resist the efforts by two Germans convicted of murdering a famous actor to remove their criminal history from the actor's Wikipedia page[33].

5 Right to access and right to data portability

In line with the current state of EU data protection law, any person must be able to exercise his right of access to personal data relating to him/her, so that he/she can verify the accuracy of the data and the lawfulness of the processing. However, in a reality of the vast amount of personal data being processed in the on-line environment, the easier access to one's own personal data must be further assured. That is why article 15 of the Regulation adds new elements, such as the controller's obligation to inform the data subjects about the applied storage period, and of the rights to rectification, to erasure and to lodge a complaint with the competent supervisory authority. Moreover, the Regulation introduces a new right; the data subject's 'right to data portability'. Hence, article 18 provides the right to obtain from the controller a copy of the personal data ' in a structured and commonly used electronic format', allowing for any further use by the data subject, in particular allowing the data subject, in particular allowing to transfer his/her personal data from one automated processing system of the controller to and into another, without being prevented from doing so by the controller.

6 Enhancing the responsibility of controllers and processors

In the first place, it is crucial to define the above terms; controller is characterized as natural or legal person, public authority, organization, agency or any other body which alone or jointly with others determines the purposes and means of the processing of personal data. Processor, on the other hand, is the natural or legal person, public authority, agency or any other body that processes personal data on behalf of the controller. Secondly, as far as the controller's responsibilities are concerned (article 22 of the Regulation) in the framework of data protection reform, the new legislative acts (regulation, directive) focus on controllers' obligation to be able to 'demonstrate' compliance with the Regulation by adoption of internal policies for ensuring such compliance. The effectiveness of such mechanisms must be verifiable either by internal or external data protection specialists or by data protection certification mechanism envisaged under Article

33 J. Rosen, *The right to be Forgotten*, in: 64"Stanford Law Review" 88, February 13, 2012, pp. 88–92.

39. In addition, in order to give data subjects greater control over their personal data, the Regulation sets out further obligations for the controller by requiring him to apply the principles of 'data protection by design' and 'data protection by default' (Article 23).

Consequently, data protection by design means that controllers of data – whether companies or public bodies – take a positive approach to protecting privacy, by embedding it into both technology (for example hardware like computer chips or services like social networking platforms) and into their organizational policies (through, for example, the completion of privacy impact assessments). Furthermore, privacy by default means that when a user receives a product or service, privacy settings should be as strict as possible, without the user having to change them. In this way, everyone feels comfortable to consciously choose the privacy setting within which he feels most comfortable with. Rather than allowing the service provider making a guess about what he might prefer. In addition, service providers should support their users in this regard by providing user-friendly methods to change privacy settings. Not to mention about the need for transparency enshrined in data processing practices.

7 Responsibility of controllers and processors in the European case law

In order to exemplify the general parameters for liability of internet users as well as internet data providers in the context of data protection law in the on-line environment, this section discusses the following judgments: Italian Google case, Google Spain SL, K.U. v Finland judgment, Linqvist judgment.

The European jurisprudence has set some general parameters for liability of internet users as well as internet providers in the context of data protection law in the on-line environment. Among many judgments referring to the judicial development of the data protection law, one may distinguish Italian Google case. The facts of the case look the following, on September 8, 2006 a video was posted in Google Videos showing a disabled student being bullied and insulted by three of his colleagues (while another student was recording with her mobile phone, and ten more were watching the scene without intervening). More precisely the disabled student, suffering from autism and impairment in hearing and sight, was the object of both verbal and physical abuse. In particular, he was called a "mongolo" (a derogatory term used for people affected by Down syndrome) and in this connection, a reference was made to the "Associazione Vivi-Down", a charity providing assistance to persons affected by the Down syndrome. The video, which had duration of about 3 minutes, was viewed by a high number of people (more than 5000 downloads). At a certain point, it was the most popular one in the category of "video divertenti" (funny videos). Users of Google video posted various messages commenting on the video (starting on 4 October); some flagged it as being inappropriate and some e-mailed Google requesting for the video to be removed. However, evidence existed only for the flagging on 5 November 2006 and an email request on the following day (Google stated that it was unable to provide documentation of all comments and flagging). On the 7th of November, the Italian Postal Police, after a communication from a citizen, requested Google to take down the video, which was removed on the same day. Thus, the video remained available for about two months after it had been initially made public in Internet. As a result, the publishing of the video gave rise to three distinct lawsuits: 1) the first concerned the four students having an active role in the video (the three abusers and the moviemaker). They were identified, thanks to the information on their identities provided by Google, and were condemned by the Tribunal of Turin with a one year sentence (work in social services), for assault and slander. The second lawsuit concerned the teacher and the school (for failing to prevent the offence). The third lawsuit, which is the one considered here, concerns Google, namely its Italian partner company (Google Italy) and its executives. The charges brought against them consisted of criminal defamation and violation of data protection rules. With regard to defamation the indictment was of "concorso in diffamazione aggravata" (co-participation in aggravated defamation), that is of contributing to the defamation of the disabled teenager. With regard to data protection the indictment was that Google Italy was processing personal data, and in particular health data, illicitly, for the purpose of making a profit. The case was decided on 24 February 2010 by the Italian Judge Oscar Magi: all four Google executives were acquitted with regard to the charge of defamation, and three of them were sentenced to a six-month suspended jail sentence for violation of data protection law. The decision occurred to be controversial; by many, it was perceived as an attempt to initiate censorship in the internet. However, on the other hand, there were also some voices heard advocating the need to intervene in Italy against the publication of insults and threats against politicians and other public persons in the months preceding the Google incident (internet bloggers in particular were accused of having instigated an aggression against the Prime Minister, Silvio Berlusconi). That is why commentators openly approved the decision, finding it immoral that Google could be exempted from any liability for the damage suffered by innocent people as a consequence of Google's commercial activity (providing user-generated contents), from which it draws huge profits, in particular by collecting advertising (in 2009 USD$22 billion of advertising revenue). Especially that Google was considered to possess technical means to control content and exclude offending postings, however, it refrained from such controls for the sake of cutting costs (by savings on personnel) and maximizing profits (by attracting the vast audience interested in prurient, lurid or offending contents). Interestingly, the conviction of the three Google executives on charges of violating Italian privacy laws has been overturned on December 21, 2012 by the appeals court in Milan; this verdict was hailed by the Google as a victory for Internet freedom.[34]

Let us now dwell on the charges brought against Google executives: defamation and breaching data protection law. In the former, according to the Italian judge the executives had the legal obligation to prevent the defamation by exercising a preventive control over contents uploaded on Google Videos site, but they had not taken such action. That is why the criminal liability of the Google executives for defamation did result from their failure to act: the executives had the legal obligation to prevent the defamation by exercising a preventive control over contents uploaded on Google Videos site, but they had not taken such action (according to Art. 40 of the Italian Criminal Code, failing to prevent an event which one has the legal obligation to prevent, amounts to causing it). In addition, according to the prosecutors, Google was no mere host provider, but rather a content provider, who had the obligation to correctly process the personal data contained in the uploaded videos and had the duty to avert those crimes that may be prevented by correctly processing the data. Since the failure to correctly process the personal data (i.e. the failure to ensure that only data that could be legally processed were uploaded and made available through the internet) caused the defamation to happen, Google executives in charge of the processing of personal data were liable for defamation. However, the judge did affirm that even though he wished that a law were issued making internet providers liable for negligence, this had not yet been the case. Given the state of the Italian law, there was no general obligation for hosting providers to monitor the contents of postings on their platforms[35]. Thus, he dismissed the charge for defamation: since Google had no obligation to prevent the upload of offensive materials, it was not criminally liable for defamation subsequent to the upload of such materials. It is worth to mention in this context, that this reasoning mirrors the Art. 15 of the EU Directive on Electronic Commerce, which forbids EU Member States to "impose a general

34 Italian Appeals Court Acquits 3 Google Executives in Privacy Case by Eric Pfanner, at: „The New York Times" December 21, 2012, at:https://www.nytimes.com/2012/12/22/business/global/italian-appeals-court-acquits-3-google-executives-in-privacy-case.html (Accessed: February 2020).

35 "it does not exist, at least until today, a legal codified obligation which imposes on internet service providers to exercise prior control over the uncountable series of data

obligation on providers, when offering the services covered by Articles 12, 13 and 14, to monitor the information which they transmit or store, nor a general obligation actively to seek facts or circumstances".

The liability of the internet search engine operators has been already acknowledged in the judgment Google Spain SL and Google Inc. v. Agencia Española de Protección de Datos (AEPD) and Mario Costeja González that can be summarized as follows: internet search engine operator bears responsibility for the processing that it carries out of personal data which appear on web pages published by third parties. Thus, if, following a search made on the basis of a person's name, the list of results displays a link to a web page which contains information on the person in question, that data subject may approach the operator directly and, where the operator does not grant his request, bring the matter before the competent authorities in order to obtain, under certain conditions, the removal of that link from the list of results.

However, in the above mentioned case the Court was not asked to determine whether search engines also processed special categories of personal data that was the key issue of the judgment in the second of two cases concerning the 'Right to be forgotten'. The first, Google v CNIL, focused on the territorial scope of the right. In the second, GC, AF, BH, and ED v Commission nationale de l'ínformatique et de Libertes (CNIL), Premier ministre, and Google LLC (hereafter: GC), the Court addressed a request for a preliminary ruling after the French data protection authority (CNIL) refused to require Google to dereference various links to third party websites in the list of results displayed following searches of their names.

As regards the former, the circumstances of the case looked the following: Google Inc. having been given formal notice by the CNIL on 21 May 2015 to apply the de-referencing to all the extensions, had refused to do so and had confined itself to removing the links in question from only the results displayed following searches conducted from the domain names corresponding to the versions of its search engine in the Member States. As a result, the Commission nationale de l'informatique et des libertés (French Data Protection Authority, France-„the CNIL") in its adjudication of 10 March 2016 imposed a penalty of €100 000 on Google Inc. that in turn requested the Conseil d'État (Council of State, France) to annul the adjudication of 10 March 2016 by stating that the right to de-referencing does not necessarily require that the links at issue

---

that pass every second through the network of the managers or owners of websites (...)." Sentenza n. 1972/2010. Tribunale Ordinario di Milano in composizione monocratica. Sezione 4 Penale. p. 103.

are to be removed, without geographical limitation, from all its search engine's domain names. Consequently, the Conseil d'État has referred several questions to the Court of Justice for a preliminary ruling seeking to ascertain whether the rules of EU law relating to the protection of personal data[36] are to be interpreted as meaning that, where a search engine operator grants a request for de- referencing, that operator is required to carry out that de-referencing on all versions of its search engine or whether, on the contrary, it is required to do so only on the versions of that search engine corresponding to all the Member States or only on the version corresponding to the Member State of residence of the person benefiting from the de-referencing.

The Court inaugurated the announcement of its judgment by recalling that it has already held in the Case: C-131/12,Google Spain SL and Google Inc. that the operator of a search engine is obliged to remove from the list of results displayed following a search made on the basis of a person's name links to web pages, published by third parties and containing information relating to that person, also in a case where that name or information is not erased beforehand or simultaneously from those web pages, and even, as the case may be, when its publication in itself on those pages is lawful. Furthermore, while adjudicating on the case C-507/17 Google LLC, successor in law to Google Inc. v Commission nationale de l'informatique et des libertés (CNIL)[37] the Court pointed out that Google Inc.'s establishment in French territory carries on activities, including commercial and advertising ones, that are inextricably linked to the processing of personal data accomplished for the purposes of operating the search engine concerned and, second, that that search engine must, in view of, inter alia, the existence of gateways between its various national versions, be regarded as carrying out a single act of data processing in the context of the activities of Google Inc.'s French establishment. Such a situation therefore falls within the scope of the EU legislation on the protection of personal data. It is worth to mention in this context, that in a globalised world, as the Court emphasized, internet

36 Directive 95/46/EC of the European Parliament and of the Council of 24 October 1995 on the protection of individuals with regard to the processing of personal data and on the free movement of such data (OJ 1995 L 281, p. 31) and Regulation (EU) 2016/679 of the European Parliament and of the Council of 27 April 2016 on the protection of individuals with regard to the processing of personal data and on the free movement of such data and repealing Directive 95/46 (General Data Protection Regulation) (OJ 2016 L 119, p. 1, and Corrigendum OJ 2018 L 127, p. 2).

37 Judgment in Case C-507/17 Google LLC, successor in law to Google Inc. v Commission nationale de l'informatique et des libertés (CNIL),Court of Justice of the European Union PRESS RELEASE No 112/19 Luxembourg, 24 September 2019, at: https://curia.europa.eu/jcms/upload/docs/application/pdf/2019-09/cp190112en.pdf (Accessed: March 2020).

users' access — including those outside the EU — tothe referencing of a link referring to information regarding a person whose centre of interests is situated in the EU is likely to have immediate and substantial effects on that person within the EU itself, so that a global de-referencing would meet the objective of protection referred to in EU law in full. However, it has been also stated that numerous third States do not recognize the right to de- referencing or have a different approach to that right. Not to mention that the right to the protection of personal data is not an absolute right, but must be considered in relation to its function in society and be balanced against other fundamental rights, in accordance with the principle of proportionality. In addition, the balance between the right to privacy and the protection of personal data, on the one hand, and the freedom of information of internet users, on the other, is likely to vary significantly around the world.

Summarizing, it has been concluded by the Court that currently, there is no obligation under EU law, for a search engine operator who grants a request for de-referencing made by a data subject, as the case may be, following an injunction from a supervisory or judicial authority of a Member State, to carry out such a de-referencing on all the versions of its search engine.

However, EU law requires a search engine operator to carry out such a de-referencing on the versions of its search engine corresponding to all the Member States and to take sufficiently effective measures to ensure the effective protection of the data subject's fundamental rights. Thus, such a de-referencing must, if necessary, be accompanied by measures which effectively prevent or, at the very least, seriously discourage an internet user conducting a search from one of the Member States on the basis of a data subject's name from gaining access, via the list of results displayed following that search, through a version of that search engine 'outside the EU, to the links which are the subject of the request for de-referencing. Whether the measures put in place by Google Inc. meet those requirements is to be ascertained by a national court. In addition, it has been also pointed out that, while EU law does not currently require a de-referencing to be carried out on all versions of the search engine, it also does not prohibit such a practice. Accordingly, the authorities of the Member States remain competent to balance, in the light of national standards of protection of fundamental rights, a data subject's right to privacy and the protection of personal data concerning him or her, on the one hand, and the right to freedom of information, on the other, and, after weighing those rights against each other, to order, where appropriate, the operator of that search engine to carry out a de-referencing concerning all versions of that search engine.

Considering the latter, namely the case GC, AF, BH, and ED v Commission nationale de l'ínformatique et de Libertes (CNIL), Premier ministre, and Google

LLC (hereafter: GC) its circumstances looked the following; a claimant known as GC wanted a link to a satirical photomontage depicting her in an illicit relationship with a politician removed from Google's search returns; AF demanded that search results that identified him as a public relations officer for the Church of Scientology, a position he no longer held, to be removed; BH claimed deindexing of articles linking him to contemporaneous investigations into the funding of political parties, but that did not reveal their outcomes; ED had requested the de-indexing of articles that mentioned a prison sentence of seven years and ten years judicial supervision for sexual assaults on children under the age of 15. The common thread between all of the parties was that the links included special categories of personal data within the meaning of Article 8(1) and (5) of the now repealed Data Protection Directive 95/46/EC (similar provisions can now be found in Article 9 of the European Union's General Data Protection Regulation). In response to the above mentioned claims, the French data protection authority (CNIL) concluded that these requests were to be denied and closed their files. Hence, the parties brought an action before the Conseil d'Etat asking the Court to serve notice on Google to carry out the dereferencing request.

As a result, the Court determined whether, "having regard to the specific responsibilities, powers and capabilities of the operator of a search engine, the prohibition on the processing of special categories of data (now Article 9 GDPR) imposed on other controllers of processing data caught by Article 8(1) and (5) of Directive 95/46, subject to the exceptions laid down there, also apply to this operator as the controller of processing by means of that search engine?" In other words, the referring court wanted to know, in the first place, whether Google was a data controller for the special categories of data it was processing. If the answer is yes, then, secondly, must Article 8(1) and (5) of the Directive be interpreted in a way that requires search engines, subject to exceptions in the Directive, to grant the requests for de-indexing links to web pages that contain that type of data?

Before answering the above questions, the Court reminded that Article 52(1) of the European Union's Charter of Fundamental Rights (hereafter: Charter) permits limitations on the exercise of rights, as long as they are provided for by law, respect the essence of the rights and freedoms found in the Charter, and are proportional, especially when balanced against other rights. The erasure right now found in Article 17(1) of the GDPR ("the right to be forgotten") does not apply when processing is necessary for one of the grounds found in Article 17(3)(a) of the Regulation – one of which is the exercise of the right of expression and information, guaranteed by Article 11 of the Charter.

As regards the first question, the Court answered affirmatively. Namely, „the provisions of Article 8(1) and (5) of Directive 95/46 must be interpreted as meaning that the prohibition or restrictions relating to the processing of special categories of personal data, mentioned in those provisions, apply also, subject to the exceptions provided for by the directive, to the operator of a search engine in the context of his responsibilities, powers and capabilities as the controller of the processing carried out in connection with the activity of the search engine, on the occasion of a verification performed by that operator, under the supervision of the competent national authorities, following a request by the data subject."

Secondly, the Court started its justification with a reminder that Article 52(1) of the European Union's Charter of Fundamental Rights (hereafter: Charter) permits limitations on the exercise of rights, as long as they are provided for by law, respect the essence of the rights and freedoms found in the Charter, and are proportional, especially when balanced against other rights. The erasure right now found in Article 17(1) of the GDPR ("the right to be forgotten") does not apply when processing is necessary for one of the grounds found in Article 17(3)(a) of the Regulation – one of which is the exercise of the right of expression and information, guaranteed by Article 11 of the Charter.

The Court then examined the conditions when a search engine is required to accede to a deindexing request to delete links to web pages which contains special category personal data that follows a search for a data subject's name. Of note is the Court's reference to Article 14 of the Data Protection Directive, which provides data subjects with the legal basis to obtain erasure of data does not comply with the Directive. Furthermore, the Court refers to instances (examples provided in Article 7(3) and (f)) wherein a data subject can object at any time on compelling legitimate grounds to the processing of personal data relating to him or her, unless provided for in national legislation.

At Paragraph 52, the Court lays out its reasoning for determining that a search engine is "obliged to remove from the list of results displayed following a search on the basis of a person's name links to web pages, published by third parties… even, as the case may be when its publication in itself…is lawful."

To conclude, like Google Spain, the described above judgment is due to have potentially serious implications for the search giant. By stating that Google is processing special categories of data, the Grand Chamber has put Google in an akward position. Google will have to rely on either article 85 GDPR (Processing and freedom of expression and Information)or prove that is has a 'substantial public interest' in processing special categories of data in each case, lest its processing be incompatible with GDPR[38]. To put in words of Sylvia de Conca, search engine operators are confirmed to be controllers with regard to the processing necessary to create the search result list and the structured overview present under each result.

38 See europeanlawblog.eu, at: https://europeanlawblog.eu/2019/11/20/ gc-others-vs-cnil-and-google-this-is-a-special-case/, (Accessed: February 2020).

In their quality as controllers, search engine operators are subject to the prohibition and exceptions concerning sensitive data as per Article 8 of Directive 95/46/EC and 9 of the GDPR, since no specific derogation exists. However, the extent of their obligations as controllers is peculiar in the case of sensitive data and is limited to assessments following the request of the data subjects, due to the nature of the technology involved which would make an a priori evaluation impossible. In complying with the right to be forgotten, search engine operators must carry out a balancing of the right to personal data protection with the freedom of expression and information. In this regard, the importance of the role of search engines in making information available is stressed. Furthermore, the right of the general public to research is deemed to be not only limited to current information but also to the past, although in this case the search engine operator should evaluate whether, due to the time passing, the information concerning offences and criminal convictions no longer reflect reality and the web pages reporting outdated information should either be de-listed or listed only after those pages reporting more updated circumstances[39].

Another landmark judgment, namely the K.U. v Finland delivered by the European Court of Human Rights (EtCHR) limits the duty/right to confidentiality of Internet service providers (and the protection of the privacy of their users), for enabling the protection of the rights of third parties and the prosecution of wrongdoings. The applicant was a 2-year-old boy, who complained that an unknown person had, without his knowledge, placed an advertisement in his name on a dating site. The announcement contained personal information of the applicant (name, phone number, link to personal page with photo, and description of physical aspects) and had a sexual connotation. The applicant became aware of the advertisement when somebody contacted him for a meeting. The Internet service provider refused to reveal the identity of the IP address-holder, as it was bound by a duty of confidentiality according to Finnish telecommunications law. Consequently, the Helsinki district court refused to oblige the service provider to disclose identification data in breach of professional secrecy, since there was no explicit legal provision authorizing the disclosure. More precisely, according to that court, malicious misrepresentation was not an offence authorizing the police to obtain telecommunications identification data. Other domestic courts upheld this position. The final result was that the applicant never got access to the identity of the person in question, and the managing director of the Internet service provider could not have

39 De Conca, S. GC et al v CNIL: Balancing the Right to Be Forgotten with the Freedom of Information, the Duties of a Search Engine Operator (C-136/17 GC et al v CNIL), European Data Protection Law Review Volume 5, Issue 4 (2019), pp. 561 - 567, at: https://doi.org/10.21552/edpl/2019/4/17 (Accessed: February 2020)

been prosecuted. However, the Strasbourg court found that this outcome violated the right to private life, as defined in Article 8 of the ECHR, 'a concept which covers the physical and moral integrity of the person'. The right protected by Article 8 does not lead merely to a negative obligation on the state, but might also entail a positive obligation 'inherent in an effective respect for private or family life'. According to the European Court of Human Rights, 'these obligations might involve the adoption of measures designed to secure respect for private life even in the sphere of the relations of individuals among themselves'. While States have a margin of appreciation in fulfilling the obligation arising from the Convention, the latter nevertheless places limits on this margin. The Court, while acknowledging that 'freedom of expression and confidentiality of communications are primary considerations and users of telecommunications and Internet services must have a guarantee that their own privacy and freedom of expression will be respected, such guarantee cannot be absolute and must yield on occasion to other legitimate imperatives, such as the prevention of disorder obligation on the state, but might also entail a positive obligation 'inherent in an effective respect for private or family life'.

While considering the liability of internet users in the on-line environment, it is also worth to mention the Lindqvist judgment of 2003 that addressed the application of the Data Protection Directive (DPD) to personal data posted on Internet websites. Ms. Lindqvist, who worked as catechist for a parish in Sweden, set up Internet pages for parishioners preparing for a sacrament. In those pages, she provided information about herself and 18 fellow parishioners-catechists, indicating full names, jobs, hobbies, phone numbers, and other matters. Ms. Lindqvist posted among others health related information about a person who had injured her foot and consequently worked half time on medical grounds. As a result, the Court of Justice of the European Union held that the act of mentioning, on an Internet page, individual persons, identifying them by name, and giving information about them, constitutes processing of personal data. Moreover, according to the CJEU 'the processing of personal data consisting in publication on the Internet so that those data are made accessible to an indefinite number of people is not covered by the exception provided for by Article 3(2) of the DPD (currently article 2 § 2 GDPR), which only excludes from data protection the data-processing activities carried out in the course of the private or family life of individuals. Furthermore, the judgment also addressed the relation between the DPD and the general principles of the EU law, in particular, the fundamental rights enshrined in the European Convention of Human Rights, such as freedom of expression in particular. The CJEU stated that member states had a margin of maneuver in implementing the DPD, and emphasized the role of national jurisdictions, stating that 'it is for the national courts to ensure a fair balance between rights and interests in question, including the fundamental rights protected by the European order.' The Lindqvist judgment provides a useful framework for understanding how data protection rights can be applied even when no economic activities are involved. Undoubtly, excluding charitable and religious activities from data protection would have made the application of the DPD very uncertain, depending on the qualification of the concerned activity. What is more the narrow interpretation given to the private or family life exception is particularly relevant, since it implies the application of data protection to individual users posting online information. To conclude, we then need to establish how to apply the same data protection rules to two very different kinds of data controllers: on the one hand bone fide individuals, namely, users processing personal data for their individual purposes, and, on the other hand organizations processing personal information on large scale for commercial purposes.

To conclude, the reform of the EU data protection framework constitutes a huge step forward for data protection in Europe, considered by some as "Copernican revolution". It is to be expected that the proposed rules would strengthen the rights of individuals and make controllers more accountable for how they handle personal data. Especially that, the online publication of user-generated content including personal data directly concerns a conflict between the user posting the information and the data subject, and thus a conflict between the user's freedom of expression and the data subject's privacy and data protection rights. However, it also involves the Internet Service Provider, on whose platform the content is published and distributed. As we have seen above, the role of the Internet Service Provider (ISP) can be construed in different ways. On the one hand, the ISP may appear to be co-responsible for the violation of privacy: the ISP contributes to the means through which the privacy violation is committed, and does that for a profit (Google Italy case; K.U. v Finland judgment of the ECtHR). Moreover, by making the information easily accessible and searchable the ISP enhances its illicit circulation. On the other hand, the ISP has the role of an enabler, rather than that of an author, of the violations. In fact, by providing users with the possibility of free and uncensored use of its platform, the provider contributes, while aiming at a profit, to the free development of citizens' personality, to the growth of civil and political debate, and to the creativity of the Internet. However, the ISP may also be ordered to remove an individual's personal data from the web (Google Spain SL and Google Inc. v Agencia Española de Protección de Datos (AEPD) and Mario Costeja Gonzalez). Thus, it is undeniable that the multifaceted role of Internet service Providers (ISPs) and the different legal values involved in their activity, explains why there is an on-going debate over whether and to what extent they should be liable for illegal user-generated contents, the debate that is likely to continue in the future.

Summarizing, in EU law two conditions are required for the provider to block or remove illegal content (so preventing the violation or its continuation): first of all, the provider must be aware that the user has carried out a certain activity, and secondly, he must obtain knowledge that the content generated by that activity violates someone else's rights (in particular privacy rights). However, while considering whether to limit the liability of providers it has often been affirmed that the provider cannot be made responsible since the provider is unable to reasonably control all user-generated content. However, it has to be also taken into consideration that, in fact, establishing that user-generated content is illegal often involves an uncertain balancing exercise: the legality of the distribution of the content depends on whether, under the particular conditions of the case, the uploader's civil rights (and in particular his or her freedom of expression) should prevail over the third party's privacy rights. By making the ISP responsible for the illegal content hosted in its platform, even without a request by a competent authority, we put the burden of establishing whether the content is illegal on the Internet Service Provider[40]. Thus there is a risk of favoring an excessively cautious attitude by the provider, who, to prevent possible liability, would indulge in censorship whenever there is the smallest risk of a judicial decision in favor of privacy, thereby unduly restricting freedom of expression. Not to mention about the risk that those who want to prevent the distribution of information about themselves will threaten to sue providers for privacy violation, to induce the providers to censor the concerned content, even when it expresses legitimate criticism. This is the fundamental legal and political issue that underlies the more specific and apparently technical questions involved in this subject matter, namely the issues of whether the provider or the user is the data controller, of when online distribution can be considered to be a private activity (to which data protection is inapplicable) having limited accessibility, of whether and to what extent the liability exemption for host providers also concerns violations of privacy. Current rules limiting the liability of host providers with regard to user-generated content give the most appropriate balance between the interests and the rights involved. This conclusion does not exclude the need for providers to take initiatives concerning the education of their users with regard to data protection. In particular, platform providers should be urged (by the competent data protection authorities) to provide their users with better information about the need for other people's privacy rights to be respected, as suggested by the Article 29 Working Party's Opinion 5/2009. These precautionary measures would be fully consistent with the limitation of the provider's

40 *Peer-to-peer privacy violations and ISP liability ...*, p. 17.

liability, since they do not impose any censorship on users, but are only meant to make them aware of their pre-existing data protection duties.

To conclude, the key changes with the General Data Protection Regulation (GDPR) can be summarized as follows: 1) Extra-territorial applicability: GDPR applies to the processing of personal data by controllers and processors in the EU, regardless of whether the processing takes place in the EU or not. However, the GDPR applies also to the processing of personal data of data subjects in the EU by a controller or processor not established in the EU, where the activities relate to: offering goods or services to EU citizens (irrespective of whether payment is required) and the monitoring of behavior that takes place within the EU. In addition, non-EU businesses processing the data of EU citizens are obliged to appoint a representative in the EU; 2) Right to Access-defined as the right for data subjects to obtain from the data controller confirmation as to whether or not personal data concerning them is being processed, where and for what purpose. Furthermore, the controller shall provide a copy of the personal data, free of charge, in an electronic format. It is to be acknowledged that this change is thought to be a dramatic shift to data transparency and empowerment of data subjects; 3) Right to be Forgotten-entitles the data subject to require a controller to delete their personal data if the continued processing of those data is not justified. The conditions for erasure, as outlined in article 17 of the General Data Protection Regulation, include the data no longer being relevant to original purposes for processing, or a data subjects withdrawing consent. It should also be noted that this right requires controllers to compare the subjects' rights to "the public interest in the availability of the data" when considering such requests; 4) Data Portability- the right for a data subject to receive the personal data concerning them, which they have previously provided in a '*commonly use and machine readable format*' and have the right to transmit that data to another controller; 5) Privacy by Design-has existed as a concept for years now, but it has just become part of a legal requirement with the GDPR. At its core, privacy by design calls for the inclusion of data protection from the onset of the designing of systems, rather than an addition. More specifically - '*The controller shall..implement appropriate technical and organisational measures..in an effective way.. in order to meet the requirements of this Regulation and protect the rights of data subjects*'. Article 23 calls for controllers to hold and process only the data absolutely necessary for the completion of its duties (data minimization), as well as limiting the access to personal data to those needing to act out the processing; 6) Data Protection Officers-under Directive controllers were required to notify their data processing activities with local DPAs, which, for multinationals, could be a bureaucratic nightmare with most Member States having different notification requirements. Under GDPR, it is not necessary to submit notifications/registrations to each local DPA of data-processing activities, nor will it be a requirement to notify/obtain approval for transfers based on the Model Contract Clauses (MCCs). Instead, there will be internal record keeping requirements, as further explained below, and Data Protection Officer appointment will be mandatory only for those controllers and processors whose core activities consist of processing operations that require regular and systematic monitoring of data subjects on a large scale or of special categories of data or data relating to criminal convictions and offenses[41].

41 GDPR Portal, at: https://gdpr.eu/ (Accessed: January 2020)

II European Union competence in the field of Asylum and Migration Policy (The area of freedom, security and justice)

1 Introduction

Today's Area of Freedom, Security and Justice regulated in the Treaty on the Functioning of the European Union (TFEU) in the form of policies on border checks, visas, asylum and migration (Part Three, Title V TFEU, chapter 2) dates back to the mid-1970s when an increasing number of informal cooperation structures developed at ministerial level, among them: TREVI: Terrorisme, Radicalisme, Extremisme, Violence Internationale which gathered EU Member countries' justice and internal affairs ministers who decided on the 29th November 1991 to establish European Police Office (EUROPOL). Europol was originally foreseen as a European law enforcement organization established on the basis of Europol Convention (1999–2000) accompanied by an assortment of legal provisions progressively extending Europol's competences. This organization aimed at improving the cooperation of the competent authorities in the Member States by collecting, storing, analyzing and exchanging information.[42] Europol prepares threat assessments, strategic analyses and general reports based on information provided by the Member States (MS)[43] while also offering expertise and technical support for investigations and operations carried out within the EU that take place under the supervision of the EU member countries.[44] What is more,

42 Article 88 TFEU and Article 5 (1) lit. a of the Council Decision of 6 April 2009 establishing the European Police Office, OJ 2009, L-121/37; for a deepened understanding of Europol and its tasks see: F. Boehm, *Information Sharing and Data Protection in the Area of Freedom, Security and Justice*, Springer Berlin-Heidelberg 2012;

43 Article 5 (1) lit. f Council Decision of 6 April 2009 establishing the European Police Office, OJ 2009, L-121/37; see for instance the threat assessment relating to organized crime: *European Union Serious and Organised Crime Threat Assessment 2017*, at: https://www.europol.europa.eu/newsroom/news/crime-in-age-of-technology-%E2%80%93-europol%E2%80%99s-serious-and-organised-crime-threat-assessment-2017 (Accessed: July 2018).

44 Article 5 (1) lit. f Council Decision of 6 April 2009 establishing the European Police Office, OJ 2009, L-121/37; see for instance the threat assessment relating to organized crime: *European Union Serious and Organised Crime Threat Assessment 2017*, at: https://www.europol.europa.eu/newsroom/news/crime-in-age-of-technology-%E2%80%93-europol%E2%80%99s-serious-and-organised-crime-threat-assessment-2017 (Accessed: July 2018).

one of the goals of Europol's work is the harmonization of investigative techniques in the MS. Bilateral cooperation principally occurs through the establishment of Europol national units in each Member State while each one seconds a liaison officer to Europol.[45] Additionaly, direct contacts between competent national authorities and Europol may be also allowed.[46] The Europol Convention was, however, replaced in January 2010 by a Council Decision intended to be more "flexible" by reducing the duration of the ratification process for potential changes to it in comparison to the process provided for in the former Europol Convention and also by transforming Europol into an agency.[47] Furthermore, Europol also became more "communautarised" and thus more independent from the contributions of Member States. Thus, in contrast to the Europol Convention, the funding of Europol is to be financed by the Community budget. Hence, Europol's staff is subject to EU staff regulations. According to the new Council Decision, Europol has the following principal tasks[48]: 1. To collect, store, process, analyze and exchange information and intelligence; 2. To notify the competent authorities of the Member States without delay via the national unit, referred to Europol's Decision Article 8, of information concerning them and of any connections identified between criminal offences; 3. To aid investigations in the Member States, in particular by forwarding all relevant information to the national units; 4. To ask the competent authorities of the Member States concerned to initiate, conduct or coordinate investigations and to suggest the setting up of joint investigation teams in specific cases; 5. To provide intelligence and analytical support to Member States in connection with major international events. Furthermore, according to Article 5 (3) of the Europol Decision, Europol has additional tasks including developing specialized knowledge of the investigative procedures of the national authorities and providing advice on investigations and strategic intelligence. It shall also assist the Member States by providing support, advice and research in the training of members of national authorities, organizing and equipping those

45 Article 8 and 9 Council Decision of 6 April 2009 establishing the European Police Office, OJ 2009, L-121/37, note that currently 121 liaison officers work at Europol, compare Europol Review, annual general report on Europol activities 2009, p. 6.

46 Article 8 (2) Council Decision of 6 April 2009 establishing the European Police Office, OJ 2009, L-121/37.

47 Opinion of the EDPS on the proposal for a Council Decision establishing the European Police Office (Europol) – COM(2006) 817 final, OJ 2007, C-255/13, point I.(2); Den Boer et al. (2008),p. 111.

48 Article 5 (1) Council Decision of 6 April 2009 establishing the European Police Office, OJ 2009, L-121/37.

authorities as well as promoting crime prevention and forensic methods and analyses. It is to be acknowledged that the Europol Decision was hastily adopted before the entry into force of the Lisbon Treaty in order to avoid inter alia the mandatory participation of the European Parliament in the adoption process required by the Treaty's new provisions.[49] The consequence of this rushed timing was that the legal effects of the TEU and the TFEU on Europol have been delayed for a five-year period regarding the jurisdiction of the Court of Justice[50] (no infringement procedures and references only from 17 national Courts) and the powers of the Commission to bring a matter before the Court of Justice.[51] So far, parliamentary scrutiny is restricted to two areas: general informational duties in the form of a general report forwarded to the European Parliament after endorsement of the Council, and consultation requirements concerning the adoption of implementing rules dealing with details of Europol's data processing systems in cooperation with third states.[52] To conclude, article 88 TFEU regulates Europol's future mission and tasks including its competence to coordinate, organize and

---

49 See House of Lords Europol report, European Union Committee, 29th report of session 2007–2008, "Europol: coordinating the fight against serious and organised crime", published 12 November 2008, p. 15, paragraph 23 and Article 88 TFEU.

50 As Europol's judicial control was one of the most discussed issues since its establishment, a protocol on the interpretation, by way of preliminary rulings, by the Court of Justice of the EC of the Convention on the establishment of a European Police Office was introduced in 1996 (Council Act of 23 July 1996 drawing up, on the basis of Article K.3 of the Treaty on European Union, the Protocol on the interpretation, by way of preliminary rulings, by the Court of Justice of the European Communities of the Convention on the establishment of a European Police Office, OJ 1996, C-299/1), but its acceptance by the Member States depended on an additional declaration accepting the Court's jurisdiction in case of preliminary rulings on the interpretation of Europol Convention which made at least a partial judicial control of Europol subject to the political choice of the Member States,

51 Articles 9 and 10 of the protocol no. 36 on transitional provisions, annexed to the Lisbon Treaty, OJ 2010, C-83/201, to the details see Chap. A III 1 d. However, regarding future amendments of the Europol Decision under the new Lisbon Treaty, it has to be taken into account that upcoming measures in the field of police and judicial cooperation in criminal matters will now be subject to the usual effects of EU law (direct effect and supremacy) and legislative acts will have the form of Directives and Regulations adopted by using the so called "ordinary legislative procedure" which combines the decisions of the Council and the European Parliament and forms the basis of the jurisdiction of the Court of Justice.

52 Articles 37 (10) (c), 14 (1), 26 (1) or 28 (1) Council Decision of 6 April 2009 establishing the European Police Office, OJ 2009, L-121/37.

implement "investigative and operational action carried out jointly with the Member States' competent authorities or in context of joint investigations teams, where appropriate in liaison with Eurojust".[53] As far as the Europol's processing of data is concerned, it undertakes it in three ways: within its Information System (EIS), by analyzing work files and the index system. In addition, a secure information exchange tool, SIENA (Secure Information Exchange Network), connects the Member States via the Europol national units and the Europol liaison bureaus but does not routinely involve Europol. SIENA has been in use since 2009, replacing the information exchange application (Info-Ex) that had been in use since 1996. In 2016 the number of objects stored in the EIS, used by the all 28

53 Article 88 (2) (b) TFEU. These tasks relate to "serious crime affecting two or more Member States" as well as "forms of crime which affect a common interest covered by a Union policy". The focus therefore remains on supportive tasks. Article 88 (3) TFEU stipulates that the application of coercive measures remains the exclusive responsibility of the competent national authorities. Therefore, Article 88 TFEU has improved democratic control over Europol that is exercised on one hand by the European Parliament and on the other by the national parliaments that "contribute actively" to the AFSJ by being "involved in the political monitoring of Europol". However, to come back to the current legal framework, the scope of the Europol Decision does not yet cover crime affecting a common interest covered by a Union policy, but organized crime, terrorism and "other forms of serious crime" affecting two or more Member States (See: Article 3 Council Decision of 6 April 2009 establishing the European Police Office, OJ 2009, L-121/37).An annex to the Europol Decision lays down 24 wide ranging forms of crime which Europol is competent to deal with: unlawful drug trafficking, illegal money-laundering activities, crime connected with nuclear and radioactive substances, illegal immigrant smuggling, trafficking in human beings, motor vehicle crime, murder, grievous bodily injury, illicit trade in human organs and tissue, kidnapping, illegal restraint and hostage taking, racism and xenophobia, organized robbery, illicit trafficking in cultural goods, including antiquities and works of art, swindling and fraud, racketeering and extortion, counterfeiting and product piracy, forgery of administrative documents and trafficking therein, forgery of money and means of payment, computer crime, corruption, illicit trafficking in arms, ammunition and explosives, illicit trafficking in endangered animal species, illicit trafficking in endangered plant species and varieties, environmental crime; illicit trafficking in hormonal substances and other growth promoters. Six legal definitions of specific crimes, such as "illegal immigrant smuggling" and "motor vehicle crime" are provided to substantiate the content of some of the listed crimes (See: Annex to the Council Decision of 6 April 2009 establishing the European Police Office, OJ 2009, L-121/37; for an overview of the databases, refer to Engel (2006), pp. 46–54). The existence of an organized criminal structure, as was the requirement for Europol's actions in the Europol Convention, is no longer a limiting element.

Member States as well as EUROPOL on behalf of the third parties, was 395 357 (an increase of 34 % compared to 2015); among them data of 103,796 suspected and convicted criminals were processed (an increase of 20 % compared to 2015).[54] In this context it is worth to underline that according to Article 12 (1) of the Europol Decision, the data introduced in the EIS must be necessary for the performance of Europol's tasks and relate to persons who are suspected of having committed, taken part in or have been convicted of criminal offences pursuant to the national law of the Member State which provided the information concerned and in respect of which Europol is competent. Additionally, even in case of "factual indications or reasonable grounds" under a Member State's law "to believe that a person would commit criminal offences", entry in the EIS is possible. As F. Boehm underlines the wording of Article 12 (1) lit. b of the Europol Decision constitutes a remarkable broadening of the requirements to be fulfilled in order to enter personal data into the EIS, compared to the more restrictive formulation of Europol Convention Article 8 (2) which required "serious grounds" for entering personal information in the EIS. To the extent the wording in subparagraph 1 of Article 12 of the Europol Decision has been widened, the maximum quantity of particulars of persons whose data may be entered into the EIS has also been considerably extended.[55] Added to the list of basic personal information (name, place of birth, nationality and sex), allowed under the Europol Convention are particulars concerning social security data (social security number, driving license, identification documents, passport data), the whereabouts, profession and "where necessary", biometric information such as fingerprints and DNA profiles. When exactly it seems to be necessary to input biometric data is not clarified more precisely. According to the current Europol Decision, it is possible to store data for a three-year period regarding individuals who potentially will commit a crime in the future, based on factual indications. Considering that data stored in the EIS could be investigated, accessed by all 28 Member States[56] and liaison officers from third states, as well as transmitted to third parties the entry of data from individuals based on factual indications that this person might one day

54 See: EUROPOL Annual Review 2016–2017, at: https://www.europol.europa.eu/europol_review (Accessed: July 2018).

55 It is more than likely that such wide-ranging extensions of Europol's competences and data processing possibilities would not have passed the European Parliament without fundamental amendments.

56 On January 31th 2020 Britain formally exited the European Union; as a result the number of the EU Member States has been changed to 27, See: Press Send for Brexit: E.U. Seals U.K. Withdrawal by Email by HYPERLINK "https://www.nytimes.com/by/

commit a crime, seems to be extremely far reaching. As a consequence of the entry, investigations against the persons might be instituted. It is worth to mention that this situation fundamentally challenges ECtHR's foreseeability criterion to be observed in its jurisdiction in *Weber and Saravia v. Germany and Association for European Integration and Human Rights* and *Ekimdzhiev v. Bulgaria* in which the ECtHR tolerated data transfer to other law enforcement authorities only under the condition that specific facts – as opposed to mere factual indications – aroused the suspicion that someone had committed one of the offences. While the German solution in Weber and Saravia v. Germany (requiring specific facts – as opposed to mere factual indications) might constitute only one possibility to limit the circle of persons concerned by surveillance measures and governmental data mining, the ECtHR leaves no doubt that the collection of personal data in absence of any suspicion would certainly contradict the guarantees of Article 8 ECHR. Besides challenging ECtHR case law, the far reaching entry possibilities are also in contradiction to principle 2 of Recommendation R (87) 15, which limits data collection for police purposes to the extent necessary for the prevention of a real danger or the suppression of a specific criminal offence.[57] Unless the law clearly authorizes wider police powers to gather information. Real danger is thereby explained as "not being restricted to a specific offence or offender but includes any circumstances where there is reasonable suspicion that serious criminal offences have been or might be committed to the exclusion of unsupported speculative possibilities". The latter sentence obviously excludes data collection due to mere "factual indications" that an individual might become a criminal in the future. Furthermore, the storage of data of criminals and possible criminals in the same database also opposes to principle 3.2 of Recommendation R (87) 15 specifying that data based on facts should be distinguished from data based on opinions or personal assessments. When analyzing whether or not an individual represents a

---

matina-stevis-gridneff" Matina Stevis-Gridneff, "International New York Times Jan. 30, 2020, at: https://www.nytimes.com/2020/01/30/world/europe/eu-brexit-decision.html?searchResultPosition=2 (Accessed: January 2020).

57 Point 43 of the explanatory memorandum of Recommendation R (87) 15 of the Council of Europe Committee of Ministers to member states regulating the use of personal data in the police sector, (Adopted by the Committee of Ministers on 17 September 1987 at the 410th meeting of the Ministers' Deputies) indisputably clarifies that this rule attempts to prohibit an open-ended and indiscriminate collection of data by the police. In this context, Recommendation R (87) 15 refers to the wording of Article 5 (c) of Convention No. 108 and Article 9 (2) lit. a of Convention No. 108 which allows for a derogation from the principle that personal data must be adequate, relevant and not excessive in relation to the purpose for which they are stored in regard to the "suppression of criminal offences".

possible criminal, an assessment based on evaluations of several facts has to be made. By its very nature the results of this assessment are the outcome of an opinion made by analysts, but these data are not stored in a separate database. Article 12 (5) of the Europol Decision at least stipulates that in case Europol entered the information itself and gives filing reference, it has to specify the source of the information and that the entries have to be deleted, if proceedings against the person concerned are "definitively dropped or if that person is definitively acquitted"; however, most importantly, Europol Decision Article 12 does not include a provision protecting the data related to possible criminals who have never committed a crime and may never be subject to investigations or court proceedings. Once more, it is extremely questionable whether the processing of the data, including biometric information, on a 3 years basis complies with the presumption of innocence and the guarantees of Article 8 ECHR which provides for a difference of treatment of the data of criminals and that of possible suspects (compare S. and Marper v. the United Kingdom).

Gradually this informal cooperation in the realm of policies on border checks, visas, asylum and migration was transformed into institutional one, especially by signing the Schengen Agreement (1985) by Belgium, France, Germany, Luxembourg and the Netherlands and, as a result, applying the first Schengen Information System (SIS) two years later. This information system was made operable for the purpose of registering persons and goods that should be refused entry into Schengen area without internal borders or that are searched for by one of the Schengen Member States. In addition, it applies to all EU countries with the exception of the United Kingdom, Ireland, Bulgaria and Romania but including Iceland, Norway and Switzerland. It is worth to mention that the main stimulus for the creation of an area without internal borders was the free movement of goods, persons, services and capital as ensured in the provisions of the Treaties where the project of internal market was conceptualized. The abolishment of internal borders, however, was a very contentious issue at that time what has found its expression in the famous Margaret Thatcher's Bruges Speech (1988), in which she emphasized that "*[…] it is a matter of plain common sense that we cannot totally abolish frontier controls if we are also to protect our citizens from crime and stop the movement of drugs, of terrorists and of illegal immigrants*"[58]. In this vein, since the late

58 R. Harris, The collected speeches of Margaret Thatcher, Harper Collins Publishers, London1997, p. 322.

1980s immigration has largely been construed as a societal security threat[59]. The phenomenon of so-called securitization was to be observed either at the level of political discourse[60] or policy praxis[61]. In the course of time, the number of Schengen member states have grown; Austria, Finland and Sweden became EU members on 1 January 1995. Consequently, in 1999 the Schengen Convention was integrated into the European Union acquis, implying that all EU Member States needed access to SIS. In 2008 by means of Council Regulation (EC) No 1104/2008 and Council Decision 2008/839/JHA the new system was further developed, testing and transfer of data from SIS 1+ to SIS II was announced. For the meantime, the first generation SIS was expanded first into SIS 1+ (2001) and later cloned into SISone4all (2007) in order to cope with the new Member States. The above-mentioned legal arrangements were concluded within the changing political architecture of the European Union; the Treaty on European Union signed in Maastricht (1992), introduced a three-pillar structure: the European Community and intergovernmental Common Foreign and Security Policy as well as Justice and Home Affairs. As a result, different rules existed in EU law for the protection of personal data; Directive 95/46, Regulation 45/2001 and Article 286 EC Treaty (after entrance into force of Lisbon Treaty in 2009; Article 16 TFEU) guaranteed data protection rules in first pillar matters. Data processing in second and third pillar matters was excluded from the scope of these instruments which, due to the fact that in areas related to law enforcement and judicial cooperation, such as Area of Freedom, Security and Justice (AFSJ) horizontal information sharing, including the exchange of personal data, has become an essential tool in the internal security policy of the EU, constituted a potential threat of fundamental rights infringements. Under such circumstances, data processing in these areas was governed by the public international law instruments of the Council of Europe[62]. In November 2008,

59 H. Grabbe, The Sharp Edges of Europe. Extending Schengen Eastwards, 2000,in: "*International Affairs*", Volume 76, Issue 3, 1 July 2000, pp. 519–536. J. Huysmans, *A Foucaultian view on spill-over: Freedom and security in the EU*, 2004, pp. 294–318.

60 B. Buzan O. Waever J. De Wilde, *Security. A new framework for analysis*, Lynne Rienner Publishers 1998, p. 18.

61 D. Bigo, *Security and immigration: Toward a critique of the governmentality of unease*, in: „Alternatives" 27 (2002), pp. 63–92.

62 Convention No. 108, the ECHR standard: Recommendation R (87) 15 of the committee of ministers to member states regulating the use of personal data in the police sector, adopted on 17 September 1987.

the Data Protection Framework Decision 2008/977/JHA on personal data processed for police and judicial cooperation in criminal matters (FDPJ) was finally adopted with the intention of covering data processing in third pillar matters[63]. It is however important to note that its scope was very restricted and did not cover data processing of Europol and Eurojust[64].

A major change, understood as the acquisition by the Community powers for the regulation of its external borders, was brought with the Treaty of Amsterdam of May 1st 1999, as a result of which asylum matters were shifted from intergovernmental fora under the Third Pillar of the Treaty establishing the European Union (EU) to the supranational under the Title IV of the Treaty establishing the European Community (EC) and the transformation of the Schengen *acquis* into European law. In addition, article 62(2) (a) EC confered upon the Council the power to adopt measures on the crossing of the external borders of the Member States, establishing standards and procedures to be followed by MS in carrying out checks on persons at such borders. Furthermore, on the basis of Article 66 EC, the Council could take measures to ensure cooperation between the relevant departments of the administrations of Member States in the areas covered by Title IV EC, and also between these departments and Commission[65]. The transfer of powers in the JHA to the First pillar has been both partial and gradual; in line with the article 67 EC that provided for transitional period of five years (the period ended on 1 May 2004) in which the Commission shared its rights of initiative with Member States[66]. During that transitional period, decision-making in the Council was unanimous, with the right of consultation for Parliament. On the basis of the second intent of Article 68(2) EC, the Council extended, as of 1 January 2005, the co-decision procedure

63 Council Framework Decision 2008/977/JHA of 27 November 2008 on the protection of personal data processed in the framework of police and judicial cooperation in criminal matter, OJ 2008, L-350/60; the processing refers to automatic and non-automatic processing of personal data: Article 2 (a) FDPJ, OJ 2008, (L-350/60).

64 „A Council Framework Decision on the protection of personal data processed in the framework of police and judicial cooperation in criminal matters will be applicable to the transfer of personal data by Member States to Europol. The relevant set of data protection provisions in this Decision will not be affected by that Framework Decision and this Decision should contain specific provisions on the protection of personal data regulating these such as the SIS or the CIS".

65 No agreement was reached on the legal basis for the Schengen Information System (SIS) and consequently it was brought under the Third Pillar on the basis of Article 2, paragraph 4 of the Schengen Protocol.

66 J. Rijmpa, EU Border Management after Lisbon Treaty, „Croatian Yearbook of European Law and Policy" (2009) 121–149.

to Article 62(2)(a) EC[67]. As far as the role of the Court of Justice of the European Union in the AFSJ is concerned, its competency was restricted; only national courts from which no further judicial remedy is possible, have a duty to refer preliminary questions to the CJUE which, in the area that touches directly upon the civil liberties of EU citizens, might be perceived as anomaly[68].

On the basis of these new legal arrangements enshrined in the Amsterdam Treaty "Title VI" of the TEU and "Title IV" of the TEC the European Council adopted under the auspices of the Finnish Presidency in October 1999 the first multi-annual program on the EU's AFJS - the Tampere Programme (SN 200/99, Brussels). It constituted the first occasion in which the European Council officially endorsed a multi-annual program outlining the policy guidelines for the implementation of the European Union's Area of Freedom Security and Justice. The Tampere Programme[69] contained an agenda (the Tampere milestones) for the development of a Union for Freedom, Security and Justice during the years 1999–2004 and called for a common EU policy and approach to be gradually introduced on issues such as labor, immigration, integration of Third Country Nationals (TNC), external borders controls and asylum. What is more, the formal communitarization of immigration and asylum policies could be observed in establishing such measures as: European Refugee Fund (Decision 2000/596/EC); rules concerning temporary protection of displaced persons (Council Directive 2001/55/EC); minimum standards for giving temporary protection in the event of a mass influx of displaced persons and on measures promoting a balance of efforts between Member States in receiving such persons and bearing the consequences thereof (Directive 2001/55/EC); criteria for determining the member state responsible for examining an asylum application lodged in one of the member states by a third-country national (Regulation (EC) 343/2003); an action program for

67 Council Decision 2004/927/EC providing for certain areas covered by Title IV of Part Three of the Treaty establishing the European Community to be governed by the procedure laid down in Article 251 of that Treaty (2004) OJ L396/45. In accordance with Protocol No 35 on Article 67 EC, the Council has acted since 1 May 2004 by qualified majority on a proposal from commission and after consulting the European Parliament in order to adopt the measures referred in Article 66.

68 Further restriction of the Court's jurisdiction is contained in the Article 68(2), excluding the Court's jurisdiction over measures taken under Article 62(1) EC (the legal basis for measures related to the abolition of internal border controls) in so far as they relate to the maintenance of law and order and the safeguarding of internal security.

69 *"From Tampere 20 to Tampere 2.0: Towards a new European consensus on migration"*, Philippe De Bruycker Marie De Somer Jean-Louis De Brouwer (eds.), European Policy Center 2019, at: http://odysseus-network.eu/wp-content/uploads/2019/12/Publication-Final-3.pdf (Accessed: March 2020).

administrative co-operation in the fields of external borders, visas, asylum and immigration (Council Decision 2002/463/EC). Furthermore, the Tampere Agenda dedicated to the creation of an area of freedom, security and justice in the European Union, based on solidarity and on the reinforcement of the fight against trans-border crime by consolidating cooperation among authorities, foreseen the establishment of Eurojust- a judicial coordination unit composed of national prosecutors, magistrates, or police officers of equivalent competence, detached from each Member State according to their own legal systems.[70] Its mandate and especially its data processing provisions and control mechanisms were changed in 2009 by the Council Decision 2009/426 which specified Eurojust's main objectives as: in the first place, stimulation and improvement of the coordination between the competent authorities of the MS during investigations and prosecutions in those States, taking into account any request emanating from a competent authority of a Member State and any information provided by anybody competent by virtue of provisions adopted within the framework of the Treaties; secondly, cooperation advancement between the competent authorities of the MS, in particular by facilitating the execution of requests for, and decisions on, judicial cooperation, including those regarding instruments giving effect to the principle of mutual recognition; thirdly, providing the competent authorities of the Member States with support in order to render their investigations and prosecutions more effective. Furthermore, according to the amended Eurojust Decision, Eurojust's mandate refers to "the types of crime and the offences in respect of which Europol is at all times competent to act".[71] Thus, the far-reaching list of crimes for which Europol is responsible and which is laid down in Article 3 of the Europol Decision as well as in its annex expressly applies additionally to Eurojust. It is noteworthy that since the entry into force of the Lisbon Treaty, Article 85 (1) TFEU has significantly reinforced the role of Eurojust by enlarging its future functions from merely those of a coordinative mission to the initiation of criminal investigations and dispute settlement as regards conflicts of jurisdiction.[72] However, before Eurojust's tasks[73] are extended, a further important provision of Article 85 TFEU relates to the

70 Council Decision 2002/187/JHA of 28 February 2002 setting up Eurojust with a view to reinforcing the fight against serious crime, OJ 2002, L-63/1, in the following: Eurojust Decision 2002; the first steps to establish Eurojust were already taken in 1999 at the Tampere summit, but Eurojust's final legal framework was not adopted before 2002.

71 Article 4 (1) Eurojust Decision.

72 Article 85 (1) (a) TFEU.

73 See: EUROJUST: Consolidated Annual Activity Report 2016, at: http://www.eurojust.europa.eu/doclibrary/corporate/CAAR/Consolidated%20Annual%20Activity%20Report%202016/EUROJUST-CAAR2016_EN.pdf (Accessed: June 2018).

legislative procedure establishing Eurojust's legislative framework and restricts overambitious changes in Eurojust's competences; namely, participation of the European Parliament, by using the ordinary legislative procedure (comparable to the provisions concerning future modifications in Europol's legislative framework), is mandatory when adopting future changes in the legislative framework concerning Eurojust. However, before the European Parliament became capable of exercising its control functions over the former third pillar body, similar to Europol, Eurojust's legal basis had been hastily adopted in the end of 2008 and entered into force in June 2009 shortly before the Lisbon Treaty[74] took effect, a fact which delayed the full application of important changes such as the judicial control by the European Court of Justice[75] or parliamentary scrutiny. An additional significant change arises through the integration of the former third pillar in the TFEU. Thus, Eurojust became a body of the European Union to which the provisions of general application of the TFEU, in particular Article 16 TFEU, fully apply. Additionally, the possibility to transform Eurojust into a European Public Prosecutor's Office, an intensely disputed topic during the last years, was provided for in Article 86 TFEU[76]. Its establishment would further clarify Eurojust's relation to the European

74 *"The Lisbon Treaty 10 years on: Success or Failure?"*, Kelemen R. Daniel, Södersten Anna, Spaventa Eleanor, Thies Anne, van Middelaar Luuk, Sieps – Swedish Institute for European Policy Studies, at: http://www.sieps.se/en/publications/2019/the-lisbon-treaty-10-years-on-success-or-failure/ (Accessed: March 2020).

75 To the question of limited judicial control of the European Court of Justice, see case C-160/03 Spain v. Eurojust, judgment of 15 March 2005, were the Court dismissed the action as inadmissible as it did not find itself competent to judge over a call for applications issued by Eurojust and concluded that this call could not be the subject of an action for annulment under Article 230 EC (whereby the Court did not follow the alternative opinion of AG Poiares Maduro).

76 On 17 July 2013, the European Commission issued two legislative proposals on the basis of Articles 85 and 86 TFEU. The proposal for a Regulation on Eurojust seeks to improve its governance and accountability framework and, ultimately, to strengthen the operational work of Eurojust in the fight against cross-border crime. The European Commission further issued a Proposal for a Regulation on the establishment of a European Public Prosecutor's Office (EPPO), a novel European actor that would specifically investigate, prosecute and bring to judgement perpetrators of crimes affecting the financial interests of the EU (so-called PIF crimes). Negotiations on the Regulations in the Council and European Parliament are ongoing. See also: "Towards a European Public's Prosecutor's Office (EPPO), Study for the LIBE Committee 2016", at: http://www.europarl.europa.eu/RegData/etudes/STUD/2016/571399/IPOL_STU(2016)571399_EN.pdf (Accessed: July 2018).

Anti-Fraud Office (OLAF)[77] that partially has an overlapping mandate that consists of: 1) conducting (external and internal) independent investigations into fraud, corruption and irregularities involving EU funds; 2) investigating serious misconduct by EU staff and members of the EU institutions, thereby contributing to strengthening citizens' trust in the EU institutions; and 3) developing EU policies to counter fraud. Hence, OLAF can bring added value to Eurojust by: a) Specialist knowledge with cases involving the EU budget; b) Internal/EU staff investigations; c) Digital forensics; access to databases managed by OLAF; d) Coordination between the national administrative authorities; e) Expertise provided to judicial authorities; and f) Evidence from an OLAF investigation to be used in a criminal case. Eurojust, on the other hand, manages the so-called Case Management System (CMS) which involves Eurojust's temporary work files and an index system, both containing personal data.[78] The CMS is intended to support and coordinate investigations and prosecutions including Eurojust's participation, "in particular by cross-referencing of information".[79] Additionally, it shall facilitate the Member States' access to information on ongoing investigations and prosecutions. The data elements contained in the CMS were subject to significant changes in the Eurojust Decision amended in 2009.[80] A good example is the modification of Article 15 (1): in contrast to the former Eurojust Decision of 2002 according to which only data of persons who were already subject of criminal investigations or prosecution could be processed, the amended Eurojust Decision allowed to process personal data in Eurojust's CMS from individuals suspected of having committed or having taken part in a criminal offence.[81] Furthermore, in addition to the already quite elaborate list of data elements,[82] which could be processed by Eurojust, new types of information, such as DNA profiles, fingerprints or data related to internet

77 *Report from the Commission to the European Parliament and the Council- 30th Annual Report on the Protection of the European Union's financial interests—Fight against fraud* - 2018 COM/2019/444 final, at: https://eur-lex.europa.eu/legal-content/en/ALL/?uri=CELEX:52019DC0444 (Accessed: March 2020).

78 Article 16 Eurojust Decision.

79 Ibid, Article 16 (2).

80 See EDPS opinion on the Council Decision concerning the strengthening of Eurojust and amending Decision 2002/187/JHA of 5 December 2008, OJ 2008, C-310/1, p. 3, para 13, which makes references to Articles 9 (4), 9a, 12 (15), 13a, 15, 26 (1) (a) and 27a Eurojust Decision.

81 Compare amendment of Article 15 (1) Eurojust Decision.

82 Article 15 Eurojust Decision lists: name(s), date and place of birth, nationality, sex, place of residence, profession and whereabouts of the person concerned, social security number, driving licenses, information concerning legal persons if it includes information

connections, have been added in Article 15 of the Eurojust Decision embracing now up to 30 data elements.[83] Noticeably, after criticism from the EDPS, the proposition to introduce an open list not even specifying the data elements to be stored, provided for in the draft Eurojust Decision, was abandoned. The processing of personal data of witnesses and victims, however, is restricted to a smaller number of components. Only in exceptional cases may Eurojust also process more than the 11 listed data elements. Such a decision shall be taken jointly by at least two national members, and the data protection officer has to be informed.[84] To introduce witness or victim data in the CMS, the College, comprising of judges, prosecutors or other judicial professionals of equivalent competence representing EU Member States (with the exception of Denmark, which by virtue of Protocol No 22 is not bound by the Eurojust Regulation as of 12 December 2019) remedied while exercising its management functions, by a representative of the European Commission, must decide about the inclusion.[85] Similar to Europol, data at Eurojust shall generally be stored for only "as long as it is necessary for the achievement of its objectives".[86] Data may not be stored beyond the date: a) on which the persons were acquitted and the decision became definite; b) 3 years after the date on which the judicial decision of the last Member State concerned by the investigation or prosecution became definite or the date on which Eurojust and the Member States concerned agreed or established that it was no longer necessary for Eurojust to coordinate investigations and prosecutions (unless there is an obligation to provide Eurojust with this information);[87] c) and finally, 3 years after the transmission from the Member States.[88] However, when the above mentioned deadlines expire, Eurojust has to carry out a review examining whether the storage period should be extended in order to enable it "to achieve its objectives".[89] Such reviews shall be carried out on a 3-year basis.[90] Regrettably, as a maximum time limit for storage is not given, persons concerned

relating to the individual who is subject of the investigation or prosecution, bank accounts and accounts of other financial institutions and the description, the nature and the date of the offences involving them as well as the facts pointing to an international extension of the case and details relating to alleged membership of a criminal organization.

83 Compare Article 15 of the Eurojust Decision 2002 with Article 15 of the Eurojust Decision of 2009.

84 Article 15 (3) Eurojust Decision.

85 Article 17 (2) rules of procedure on the processing and the protection of personal data at Eurojust, OJ 2005, C-68/1.

86 Article 21 (1) Eurojust Decision (not amended).

87 Compare Article 21 (2) Eurojust Decision.

88 Ibid, Article 21 (2) (d).

89 Ibid, Article 21 (3) (b).

90 Ibid, Article 21 (3).

are not able to foresee the length of the retention period. To conclude, the policy agenda in the field of freedom, security and justice has been ever since structured around adoption of multi-annual programs set up to be achieved during five-year-periods; as a result, Tampere has been so far followed by the Hague and Stockholm Programmes.

It was expected that the announced in 2004, under the Dutch Presidency, the Hague Programme (2005–2010) would meet the challenges of after match of the events of 9/11 2001 in the USA and 11 March 2004 in Spain. Hence, unlikely to the Tampere Programme that emphasized commitment to freedom, human rights and rule of law, the Hague Programme focused on the urgent need to ensure security of the European Union and its Member States. Consequently, priorities of The Hague Programme consisted of development of a visa-information system, common asylum procedure (Regulation (EC) No 767/2008) as well as equipping identity as well as travel documents with biometric identifiers. In absence of a unified approach to data protection in judicial and criminal matters[91] and without being limited by the former pillar constraints, legally and structurally different bodies equipped with different tasks, exchanged and transferred personal data within and outside the EU. The result was that data collected for one specific purpose may have been transferred and used for other purposes completely unrelated to the original data gathering. In these circumstances, it is crucial to ask whether the EU internal data exchange complies with its own data protection standards[92]. These questions seems to gain in importance due to the establishment by the Council Regulation on the basis of the Hague Programme the European Border and Coast Guard Agency-Frontex- responsible for management of external borders of the European Union.[93] It focuses on the

91 Council Framework Decision 2008/977/JHA on the protection of personal data processed in the framework of police and judicial cooperation in criminal matters, OJ 2008, L-350/60, in the following: FDPJ, OJ 2008, L-350/60, represents a first step towards a comprehensive framework in this area; the FDPJ is however very restricted in scope as it is for instance not applicable to the data processing of most of the AFSJ law enforcement agencies, such as Europol and Eurojust, as well as other AFSJ exchange systems, i.e. the SIS or the CIS; in addition, excluded from the scope is also the internal processing of the Member States in police and criminal matters.

92 F. Boehm, *Information Sharing and Data Protection in the Area of Freedom, Security and Justice,* Springer Berlin-Hildeberg 2012, p. 2.

93 Frontex was established by the Council Regulation (EC) No. 2007/2004 of 26 October 2004 establishing a European Agency for the Management of Operational Cooperation at the External Borders of the Member States of the European Union, OJ 2004, L-349/1; The regulation has already been modified in 2007, 2011, 2013 and 2014. The current consolidated version can be found here: http://eur-lex.europa.eu/legal-content/EN/TXT/?uri=celex:02004R2007-20140717, (Accessed: July 2018).

coordination of operational cooperation between the Member States in the field of external border management[94] by performing the following main tasks: 1) Assisting Member States in training of national border guards, including the establishment of common training standards; 2) Carrying out risk analyses; 3) Following up on the development of research relevant for the control and surveillance of external borders; 4) Assisting Member States (MS) in circumstances requiring increased technical and operational assistance at external borders; 5) Providing MS with the necessary support in organizing joint return operations, e.g. an alien's deportation to its home country. As far as the data processing is concerned, theoretically, Frontex's current legal framework excludes personal data processing. However, in the course of the adoption of Regulation (EC) No. 863/2007 in 2007 Frontex obtained executive competences permitting the creation of so called "Rapid Border Interventions Teams" (RABITs) which could be established by Frontex recruiting staff from the Member States to exercise border checks and surveillance tasks for a limited period of time.[95] The introduction of the RABITs has raised criticism,[96] principally concerning their comprehensive responsibilities, but also as it regards their possibilities to use national as well as European databases. During their operations, members of the RABITs, which are seconded from the Member States, can be authorized by the host Member State to consult national as well as European databases for border checks and surveillance. When doing so they shall consult those data "which are required for performing their tasks and exercising their powers".[97] Frontex shall be informed about the consultation.

94 Article 1 (2) Regulation 2007/2004.

95 Regulation (EC) No. 863/2007 of the European Parliament and of the Council of 11 July 2007 establishing a mechanism for the creation of Rapid Border Intervention Teams and amending Council Regulation (EC) No. 2007/2004 as regards that mechanism and regulating the tasks and powers of guest officers, OJ 2007, L-199/30.

96 Marischka C., Frontex: Im Netz des EU-Sicherheitssektors, in: Komitee für Grundrechte und Demokratie (Hrsg.): Jenseits der Menschenrechte. Die europäische Flüchtlings- und Migrationspolitik, Münster 2009, Jahrbuch 2009, S. 39–52.; Lőhr T., *Frontex-europäischer Grenzschutz im rechtsfreien Raum?* In: Grundrechte-Report 2008 zur Lage der Bürger- und Menschenrechte in Deutschland, Fischer Taschenbuchverlag,Frankfurt, pp. 179–183; Tohidipur T, Fischer-Lescano A (2008–2009) "Europäisches Grenzmanagment: Handlungsrahmender Grenzschutzagentur Fontex", Jahrbuchőffentliche Sicherheit. Verlag für Polizeiwissenschaft, Frankfurt, pp. 505–516

97 Regulation (EC) No. 863/2007 of the European Parliament and of the Council of 11 July 2007 establishing a mechanism for the creation of Rapid Border Intervention Teams and amending Council Regulation (EC) No. 2007/2004 as regards that mechanism and regulating the tasks and powers of guest officers, OJ 2007, L-199/30, Article 6 (8); see also Regulation (EC) No 562/2006 the European Parliament and of the Council of 15 March 2006 establishing a Community Code on the rules governing the movement of persons across borders (Schengen Borders Code), OJ 2006, L-105/1, Article 7 (2).

This nonetheless leads to a schizophrenic situation: on the one hand, Frontex itself, unlike Europol and Eurojust, has a "limited mandate", which does not allow gathering or analysis of personal data from people that have been arrested. On the other hand, members of Frontex's RABITs consult databases and use the relevant data for the performance of their tasks based on the national law of the host Member State. All in all, apart from the RABIT's activities, Frontex has no competence to gather or process personal data. Nonetheless, a House of Lords report revealed that Europol has worked "informally" with Frontex since 2006.[98] An external report evaluating Frontex's work and published on Frontex's webpage casts light on this issue and unveiled further problems. According to the report, Frontex collected data in the framework of joint operations in order to send them to other agencies, such as Europol for threat analysis.[99] Joint operations are described as a "good example of integrated analyses by Europol and Frontex" and are regarded as a working practice in which intelligence and operations are brought together as closely as possible".[100] Pursuant to the report, 10 % percent of the detained persons during a joint operation were interviewed by Frontex staff,[101] which means in the end that in addition to the RABITs, Frontex itself also collects personal data notwithstanding its restrictive legal framework. Consequently, Frontex acted in absence of a legal basis allowing for the collection and processing as well as the transfer of personal data. This sort of legal limbo has been reversed in 2016 by the Regulation 2016/1624 on the European Border and Coast Guard which is the latest (and quite likely not the last) of a chain of legal texts by which the EU has tried in the recent years to legally frame the issue of human mobility and human security in the post-Lisbon legal framework. It is to be acknowledged that this legal step was undoubtedly influenced by the entry into force of the Amsterdam Treaty (1999), and notably of the Lisbon Treaty (2009) which proclaimed fundamental rights protection as a founding element of the European Union and an essential component of the development of the supranational European Area of Freedom, Security and Justice. As a result, the European Border and Coast Guard Agency, to be commonly referred to as Frontex, whose extended tasks and competence should be balanced with

98 House of Lords Europol report, European Union Committee, 29th report of session 2007–2008, "Europol: coordinating the fight against serious and organized crime", published 12 November 2008, p. 80.

99 Final report of COWI (European consulting group) of January 2009 preparing an external evaluation of Frontex provided for in Article 33 of the Council Regulation (EC) No 2007/2004 of 26 October 2004 establishing Frontex, p. 48, available at: http://www.statewatch.org/news/2009/may/frontex-eval-report-2009.pdf (Accessed: July 2018).

100 Final report of COWI (European consulting group) of January 2009 preparing an external evaluation of Frontex ..., p. 48.

101 Ibid.

strengthened fundamental rights safeguards and increased accountability, is obliged to "*develop and operate information systems facilitating an exchange* (with Member States) *in accordance with Union data protection legislation*"[102].

Awareness of the EU Member States' leaders and the Commission about the new phase that the EU's AFSJ was going to enter after entry into force of the Treaty of Lisbon and its nexus with the adoption of the political agenda for the period of 2010–2014, led to endorsement by the European Council in December 2009 of the Stockholm Programme (2010–2015) - An Open and Secure Europe serving and protecting the Citizen. Undoubtedly, the agenda of the Stockholm Programme was influenced by the goals that had been defined by the French Presidency (July-December 2008) in the European Pact on Migration. In this document, immigration was mentioned as one of the key priorities of the French six-month presidency of the Union. Specifically, the Pact paid attention to - on the one hand - Europe's reception capacity in terms of its labor market, housing and health, education and social services and, - on the other - protection of migrants against possible exploitation by criminal networks. This approach to immigration was mirrored in the Stockholm Programme that promoted border controls as means of countering illegal immigration and cross-border crime (The second generation Schengen Information System (SIS II) and the Visa Information System (VIS)), emphasizing at the same time the need to safeguard access to the EU of those in need of the protection (Common Asylum System).

To conclude, although this new political architecture of the European Union provided greater powers for the EU over national border controls, immigration, and asylum policies, and a new role for the European Commission in developing EU legislation, cooperation on migration, borders and asylum has been to date influenced by a strong intergovernmentalism; transferring Member States' own national priorities and policies into EU level proposals and legislations. The above mentioned developments lead us to the current under the Lisbon Treaty (2009) interplay of, on the one hand, community institutions and, on the other hand, member states. In addition, it was the latter that set an ambitious agenda with calls for an EU border police and a "global approach to migration" – the former premised on the need to police the Mediterranean to prevent the arrival of irregular migrants and refugees, the latter focused on the externalization and imposition

102 See: articles: 42, 49, 50, 57, 58 of the Regulation (EU) 2016/1624 of the European Parliament and of the Council of 14 September 2016 on the European Border and Coast Guard and amending Regulation (EU) 2016/399 of the European Parliament and of the Council and repealing Regulation (EC) No 863/2007 of the European Parliament and of the Council, Council Regulation (EC) No 2007/2004 and Council Decision 2005/267/EC.

of EU controls in states of origin and transit. The Regulation on European Border Surveillance System (EUROSUR) adopted by the Council on 22 October 2013 is essentially the product of this twin-track approach. However, apart from these considerations it is essential to emphasize that it is not without consequences that the Lisbon Treaty in its Article 16 provides for comprehensive data protection in all policy areas, regardless of whether it relates to the internal market, law enforcement, or almost any other part of public sector. Not to mention about the separate right to the protection of personal data laid down in the Article 8 of the Charter of Fundamental Rights that became legally binding on the EU institutions and national governments with the entry into force of the Treaty of Lisbon[103].

2 Power of migration technology

In order to ascertain the impact of the large scale data systems on individual rights and freedoms described in the next chapter, it is necessary to understand their initial objectives and technical specification; hence, the first part of this section elaborates on the so-called migration technology, such as biometrics. The second describes the most important data basis within the field of EU border and immigration control such as: a) Schengen Information System (SIS (1995), SIS1+ (2001), SISone4all (2007)/SIS II (2013)); b) Eurodac (2000); c) Visa Information System (VIS) (2008), Smart border package: d) An Entry/Exit System (EES) (2013); e) A Registered Traveller Programme (RTP); f) Automated Border Crossings (ABC); g) EU-LISA - the European Agency for the operational management of large-scale IT systems in the area of freedom, security and justice (Regulation (EU) No 1077/2011); h) European Border Surveillance System (EUROSUR) became operational on the 2 December 2013; I) ETIAS-European Travel Information and Authorization System.

Just a few decades ago, border control in Europe was generally associated with the circumstances in which an officer would check a passport and look in the eyes of an individual with a stern face to find out if there is something suspicious. However, nowadays the border is no longer a line delineating territory, but rather shifts in place, meaning and way in which it is experienced[104]. Nowadays,

---

103 S. Gutwirth–R. Leenes– P. de Hert, *Reforming European Data Protection Law*, Springer 2015, pp. 1–14.

104 E. Balibar, *Politics and the Other Scene*, London 2002, p. 77; See also: E. Guild, Moving the Borders of Europe, inaugural lecture delivered at the official ceremony of the assumption of the professorship of the CPO Wisselleerstoel at the University of Nijmegen 2001; A. G. Kesby, *The Shifting and Multiple Border and International Law*, 27 OJLS 101, 2007, pp. 101–119.

by means of biometrics, an information technology that allows for translation of such data as DNA, fingerprints, eye retinas and irises, voice patterns, facial patterns and hand measurements into digitally processable data, human body becomes "machine-readable"[105]. All these technical arrangements are metaphorically described in the surveillance literature as panopticon-originally designed to discipline prisoners who while being constantly supervised, lose the opportunity, capacity and will to deviate. However, the *panopticon Europe* that is being built to control irregular immigration differs from the prison and correction system that inspired its name. First, the *panopticon Europe*, unlike most of the surveillance systems the state has created, is not primarily aimed at citizens or even subjects of the state. The system of immigration databases under construction is meant to gain knowledge on the actions and movements of non-citizens. Moreover, they are not watched with the ultimate aim of structuring their behavior in line with socially accepted standards (as defined by the state). *Panopticon Europe* is not a "factory of correction". Its aim is not disciplining and correcting undesirable migrants. *Panopticon Europe* is designed as a factory of exclusion and of people habituated to their status of the excluded'[106]. In other words, the state gathers information on the doings and whereabouts of irregular migrants with the explicit aim to exclude them from both its territorial and membership associations. This activity is in line with the traditional role of a state as the one of the oldest and largest collectors of information about citizens and non-citizens. Since *knowledge* has always been *power*, it is the state that is one of the foremost drivers and funders of technological developments and applications for use in its own policies. In this context, it is worth to mention M. Foucault's positive concept of power that produces reality understood as domains of objects and rituals of truth. The individual and the knowledge that may be gained of him belong to this production process[107]. What is more, in Foucault's view *power* is also a major source of social discipline and conformity. Fascinated by the mechanisms of prison surveillance, school discipline, systems

---

105 I.van der Ploeg, *Biometrics and the Body as Information: Normative Issues in the Socio-technical Coding of the Body*, (in): D. Lyon (ed.), *Surveillance as Social Sorting: Privacy, Risk, and Automated Discrimination*, Routledge New York 2002, pp. 57–73;

106 G. Engbersen, *The Unanticipated Consequences of Panopticon Europe. Residence Strategies of Illegal Immigrants*, in: V. Guiraudon and C. Joppke (eds) *Controlling a New Migration World*, pp. 242. Routledge London 2001.

107 M. Foucault, (1991). Discipline and Punish: the birth of a prison. London, Penguin, p. 194.

for the administration and control of populations, not to mention about promotion of norms about bodily conduct, including sex, he studied psychology, medicine and criminology and their roles as bodies of knowledge that define norms of behavior and deviance. Physical bodies are subjugated and made to behave in certain ways, as a microcosm of social control of the wider population, through what he called 'bio-power'. Disciplinary and bio-power create a 'discursive practice' or a body of knowledge and behavior that defines what is normal, acceptable, deviant, etc. – but it is a discursive practice that is nonetheless in constant flux[108]. To conclude, in shifting attention away from the 'sovereign' and 'episodic' exercise of power, traditionally centered in feudal states to coerce their subjects, Foucault pointed to a new kind of 'disciplinary power' that could be observed in the administrative systems and social services created in 18th century Europe, such as prisons, schools and mental hospitals. Their systems of surveillance and assessment no longer required force or violence, as people learned to discipline themselves and behave in expected ways. Furthermore, the development of a modern state was closely interwoven with the development of the bureaucratic state that has become increasingly capable of tracking, cataloguing and controlling its population. Scott described the emergence of the modern national state as a process in which these states made their populations 'legible' by collecting and recording information about citizens in a variety of roles and functions[109]. Caplan and Torpey emphasized the role of 'individual identity'[110] in the development of a modern state where population is sorted into categories that document individuals in their roles as taxpayers, employees, soldiers, travelers, criminals, etc. According to Giddens, the rise of surveillance in the modern state is in fact one of the building blocks of modernity[111]. Documentation and registration as instruments of *power* enabled the state to gain knowledge about its territory and population and as a result control the latter more efficiently. This advantage of bureaucracy may, however, in particular circumstances become a tool of

108 Ibid.

109 J. Scott, Seeing like a State: How Certain Schemes to Improve the Human Condition Have Failed, New Heaven: Yale University Press 1998.

110 J. Caplan (ed), Written on the Body: The Tatto in European and American History, London: Reaktion Books 2000; J. Torpey, *The Invention of the Passport: Surveillance, Citizenship and the State,* Cambridge University Press, 2000; Z. Mach, *Symbols, Conflict and Identity, Essays in Political Anthropology,* State University of New York Press 1993.

111 A. Giddens, *The Nation-State and Violence*, Cambridge: Polity Press 1985.

authoritarian regimes; both fiction - Orwell's all-seeing Big Brother - and history - the highly organized bureaucratic power of the German Third Reich – exemplify vivid images of unrestrained power of surveillance.

In the 21 century, especially in the wake of the attacks of 11 September 2001, as numerous academic studies documented, the state surveillance led by the example of the United States of America has been applying new technological endeavors in the field of migration policy such as databases, high-tech passports and visas; inclusion of biometric data in documents and computer records has been on the rise. It was, however, already in the late 1980s when the concept of dataveillance was coined to refer to the "systematic monitoring of people's actions or communications through the application of information technology". While in a traditional sense, surveillance means close and exceptional observation of a person or group; dataveillance, says Clarke, is put in practice by organizations in both a personal and collective manner, meaning they refer to specific individuals and groups but also to indiscriminate mass data collection. A shift from an individual to the individual and collective is also the shift from exceptional surveillance to the generalized one. While within the techniques of personal surveillance the rationale was to check transactions that appeared to be unusual; in mass surveillance the principle is to involve all transactions, whether or not they appear to be unusual; hence, investigation becomes a matter of mass or class investigation rather than of keeping an eye on specific individuals. What is more, facilitative mechanisms such as cross-referencing of data brought dataveillance to higher levels; the first large program to use this kind of facilitative mechanism was Project Match, undertaken by the US Department of Health. Based on a generalized suspicion of fraud in welfare funding, the system made matching among the data available, correlating as much of the available data as possible. What dataveillance announced – the turning point of surveillance from the individual to the collective, from specific to indiscriminate data collection – the "new surveillance" confirms: a world where everything is collected, registered and processed. Marx emphasizes four points that distinguish new from old surveillance and are worth noting here. *First*, the traditional definition of surveillance presupposes there is someone to be especially placed under surveillance, be it a person or a group of persons. In the new surveillance, there is no need to focus especially on an individual: building access logs and credit card records, to mention just two examples, imply indiscriminate data processing. An individual does not have to be a suspect to have his or her name, photos and financial information collected and registered. *Second*, while in the traditional notion of surveillance there is a clear distinction between an organization conducting the surveillance and the object (person or group), in the new surveillance paradigm, this is not always the case – for example, when civilians photograph government officials in situations of abuse of power. *Third*, observation in the new surveillance is not necessarily close, as it is carried from remote places. *Fourth*, surveillance is executed not only through visualization, i.e., observation, but also through any means of data collection, for instance movement, sound and temperature detection. In addition, the "new surveillance" exploits not only hard data – meaning data as collected and structured by administrations and related entities – but also soft data – collected and processed in an unstructured form from multiple sources such as social networks and localization systems. Finally, the "new surveillance" enabled by the technological endeavors is no longer just a means to detect potential threats but also potential opportunities such as in market analysis, human resources management and many other aspects of human beings' existence.

Surveillance technologies, however, represent only one aspect of the emerging phenomenon of artificial intelligence-that can be divided into two broad categories: efforts focused on interpreting sophisticated input (such as speech, emotions, or coordinated movements) and those aiming to recreate higher-level cognitive capabilities like learning and decision-making. Already, Artificial Intelligence-powered systems from antilock brakes to Siri have come to surround us in everyday life, and recently these examples have grown in ambition and scale to include drones, self-driving cars, and humanoid robots.[112] This process is stimulated by rapid advancements in computing power and falling hardware costs resulting in AI-related computations cheaper to perform. Not without an influence is the advent of Big Data, which has enabled deep-learning algorithms, in which the systems themselves learn bottom-up from a vast, fast-expanding universe of digital information. In addition, tech gurus speculate that the marriage of Big Data, the Internet of Things, and Artificial Intelligence will eventually result in "ambient intelligence"—an ever-present digital fog in tune with our behavior and physiological state. Affectiva's founder, Rana el Kaliouby, predicts that before long, devices will have an "emotion chip" that functions unseen in the background the way that geolocation does in phones.[113] Verizon has drafted plans for a sensor-laden media console that could scan a room and

112 N. Howe, Artificial Intelligence Paves The Way For Ambient Intelligence, in: "Forbes magazine" May 14, 2015, at: https://www.forbes.com/sites/neilhowe/2015/05/14/artificial-intelligence-paves-the-way-for-ambient-intelligence/#5ed8f28d776f (Accessed: June 2018).

113 Rana el Kaliouby, *We know how You feel,* in: "The New Yorker", January 2015, at: https://www.newyorker.com/magazine/2015/01/19/know-feel, (Accessed: January 2018).

determine a driver's license worth of information about its occupants. All these data would then determine the console's selection of TV advertising: Signs of stress might prompt a commercial for a vacation, while cheery humming could result in more ads with upbeat messages.[114]

More and more often artificial intelligence is exposed in reality of so called "Smart city" defined in a language of the European Commission as a place where traditional networks and services are made more efficient with the use of digital and telecommunication technologies for the benefit of its inhabitants and business. It is to be emphasized that the smart city goes beyond the use of information and communication technologies (ICT) for better resource use and less emissions. It means smarter urban transport networks, upgraded water supply, waste disposal facilities and more efficient ways to light and heat buildings. It also guarantees a more interactive and responsive city administration, safer public spaces meeting the needs of an ageing population.[115] Songdo (vision of "the city of the future" as outlined by Cisco, a multinational company being part of the consortium that was building Songdo) is one, among others such as Masdar[116] in the United Arab Emirates, PlanIT[117] in Portugal or Santander in Spain[118], example of a "*smart city*", projected to offer "high quality eco-friendly living" in a world of population overload. The city is part of one of the South Korea's free economic zones, a project led by the government to offer optimum business conditions for foreign executives and staff. Built from scratch, Songdo is meant to be a model for future cities in South Korea. Its infrastructure is said to establish a standard for the planning and building of all future cities. Houses are embedded with ICT's. If certain objects are touched, an array of services will be displayed. This means there will be many of the communicating objects that home automation offers, like the mirror in the bathroom that is also an interface to access the internet or the fridge that informs you about the stock of

---

114 N. Howe, Artificial ..., Ibidem.

115 European Commission: smart cities, at:https://ec.europa.eu/info/eu-regional-and-urban-development/topics/cities-and-urban-development/city-initiatives/smart-cities_en (Accessed: September 2018).

116 Reality of Masdar smart city: https://www.archdaily.com/tag/masdar-city/, (Accessed: June 2018).

117 PlanIT in Portugal: https://www.urenio.org/2015/01/26/smart-city-strategy-planlt-valley-portugal/, (Accessed: June 2018).

118 SmartSantander proposes a unique in the world city-scale experimental research facility in support of typical applications and services for a smart city, at: http://www.smartsantander.eu/ (Accessed: June 2018).

basic foods inside and automatically passes a command to your preferred online grocery shop. Home security and automation systems integrate multiple devices in the house such as: cameras, windows and door sensors, smoke, motion and glass break sensors and thermostatic lighting controls. As a result, consumers are able to manage their home "from virtually anywhere", with the possibility of viewing live video inside and outside the home, controlling the alarm system, heating, ventilation and air conditioning, or locking and unlocking doors (Cisco Systems, Inc. 2013). There is no need to put the garbage out since all household waste is sucked directly from the kitchen to an underground network of tunnels and to waste processing centers, where it is automatically sorted, deodorized and treated. Office buildings are managed in a more efficient way: applications turn on and off based on usage, facilities are notified of peaking energy use and security alerts are sent when unidentified people enter the building or when unknown materials are found. Also, "Telepresence", connects every home, office and school through video, eliminating people's need to move from place to place. Worries about traffic jams and reaching work meetings on time are removed since every building is connected and there is no need to physically attend the gathering, while being "always there". Public transportation in the smart city is more "intelligent" and "flexible"; by taking advantage of GPS and wireless technologies, it is possible to charge "intelligent fees for road use" and communicate transport-related information in real time. Retail innovations include customer tracking and analysis, use of "smart" walls to select clothing or other goods and personalized advertising through screens that switch context according to the profile of the viewers.

In Europe, on the other hand, the city of Santander in Spain had turned itself, as a part of the Future Internet Research and Experimentation initiative of the European Commission, into a huge experimental research facility, Smart Santander.[119] In its urban reality intelligent acoustic technology is designed to provide "situational awareness" by using audio monitoring in combination with Internet of Things (IoT) technologies. This was achieved via a deployment of Audio Processing Units (APUs) in the targeted in-door and out-door environments as complementary to intelligent sensors already available in two test-beds (HOBNET, ID 257466; Santander, ID 257992). The APU consisted of a microphone and an embedded processing platform that continuously "listened" to its environment and analyzed the sound locally. As a result, by means of this technology implemented and tested outdoor in a city context and indoor in

119 Smart city Santander: http://www.smartsantander.eu/ (Accessed: September 2018).

public buildings such as a university and an office, it was possible to detect events such as sirens, recognize speech commands and detect presence in public buildings. Since audio monitoring is a relatively new and under research phenomena, it caused privacy concerns to be raised by some academic circles. Academics conducted also research in this respect; a survey on information privacy concerns related to appliance of the above-mentioned intelligent acoustic technology, carried out with 1000 respondents around Europe, evidenced their information privacy concerns related to this type of solution on a general level. However, when being more thoroughly introduced to the solution and its usage area, the citizens became more positive towards this technology.[120]

It has to be, however, acknowledged that the smart city vision comes with an Achilles' heel-cyber vulnerability exemplified by the EnergyLab smart city project that covers about 1,400 households in Copenhagen's Nordhavn district, an up-and coming neighborhood boasting futuristic architecture that used to be an industrial port area.[121] The project, which brings together utilities, operators, the municipality, a university and key technology providers, is testing how automated technology can integrate electricity and heating with energy sufficient buildings and electric transport to create a more sustainable energy system. As a result, the smart city project involves sharing large amounts of data, e.g. information about energy consumption, across the various infrastructures to make sure the system runs properly. Furthermore, each apartment has a router and data is transferred through a VPN connection to a protected server room at the Technical University of Denmark. The goal is to design smart energy solutions that minimize the amount of personal identifiable information that needs to be collected. In this context, it is worth to emphasize that Danish law has at its disposal particular safeguards; for example, the energy data cannot be used to investigate whether a person is breaking the rules by having too many people living in a house. In other words, it is unlawful to use the same data to detect social fraud. But, as it occurs, there are more risks than just keeping the information private. According to the Danish Center for Cyber Security the threats

120 Ståhlbröst A. Padyab A. Sällström A. Hollosi D., *Design of smart city systems from a privacy perspective,* IADIS International Journal on WWW/Internet Vol. 13, No. 1, pp. 1–16 .

121 Gurzu A., Cyberthreats could turn smart cities into dumb ones, in: „Politico", 8/27/19 at: https://www.politico.edu/article/cyber-threats-could-turn-smart-cities-into-sumb-ones-copenhagen/, (Accessed: September 2019)

of cyber espionage and cybercrime against the Danish energy sector are both „very high".[122]

To conclude, connecting buildings and facilities through Information& Communication Technology(ICT) is a crucial aspect of smart cities.[123] The network developed in Songdo is intended to connect all of its components: "residences, offices, schools everywhere, all of the"[124]. While life as projected in Songdo-an Ambient Intelligence City-sounds like a synonym for convenience, purchasing power and comfort – something certainly arguable from an urbanistic and environmental point of view– the name "Automated Target System", betrays itself, evoking traditional representations of the power of governments/corporations of the Leviathan or Big Brother style. In this context, it is worth to mention that the "*Automated Target System*" was applied by the US Department of Homeland Security (DHS) as a means of border control. According to the Privacy Impact Assessment (PIA) produced by the DHS:[t]he project involved conducting research to select the specific sensors that would capture video images, audio recordings, cardiovascular signals, pheromones, electrodermal activity, and respiratory measurements. For example, one potential measurement was heart rate. There was a number of technologies that a sensor could use to capture heart rate. One aspect of the research was to determine which specific sensor technology most accurately captures the desired measurement. Another aspect was reviewing the research records to determine if the measurement being captured is actually an indicator of the behavior being evaluated (i.e., did increased heart rate actually occur when the subject was intending to cause a disturbance) [...].[125] Furthermore, another evidence of "smart" environments might be provided by appliance of technologies to track customers' movements inside bricks- and mortar retailers in the USA. In this way, data about shoppers' behavior and

---

122 *The cyber threat against the Danish energy sector*, Threat Assessment by the Center for Cyber Security, September 2018, at: fe-ddis.dk, (Accessed: September 2019)

123 Stockholm is experimenting with smart trash bins and smart traffic control; Vienna is adopting electric-powered waste collection vehicles and testing the use of plants to green building facades in order to boost climate adaptation.

124 Tanaka, W. 2012. *'Cities of the Future: Songdo, South Korea – A New Approach – The Network: Cisco's Technology News Site'. Cisco's The Network*, at: http://newsroom.cisco.com/feature-content?type=webcontent&articleId=630153, (Accessed: September 2018).

125 *'Privacy Impact Assessment for the Future Attribute Screening Technology (FAST) Project'*. United States Department of Homeland Security 2008.

moods are gathered, using video surveillance and signals from their cellphones and apps to glean information such as sex, how many minutes people spend in a specific aisle and how long they look at merchandise before buying it. Several systems are capable not only of collecting data but also of providing outputs that influence action, such as the earlier example of the use of facial recognition to offer a bottle of whiskey to the angry man in his 30s. In this context, it is worth to mention about a global race to automate stores, that is already going on among several of the world's top retailers and small tech start-ups, which are motivated to shave labor costs and minimize shoppers' frustrations, like waiting for cashiers. In addition, companies are testing robots that help keep shelves stocked, as well as apps that let shoppers ring up items with a smartphone.[126]

Already inside the world's top artificial intelligence labs, researchers are getting closer to creating robotic hands that can mimic the real thing and as a result perform more complex tasks on their own. Inside OpenAI, the San Francisco artificial intelligence lab founded by Elon Musk and several other big Silicon Valley names, you will find a robotic hand called Dactyl- mechanical prosthetic in the latest Star Wars film: mechanical digits that bend and straighten like a human hand. If you give Dactyl an alphabet block and ask it to show you particular letters — let's say the red O, the orange P and the blue I — it will show them to you and spin, twist and flip the toy in nimble ways. Although for a human hand, that is a simple task; for an autonomous machine, it is a notable achievement: Dactyl was trained by researchers in simulation—a digital recreation of the real world. As a result, the process of learning to spin the alphabet block through what would have been 100 years of trial and error, is shortened by means of digital simulation, running across thousands of computer chips, to two days; the robotic hand learns these tasks by repeated trial and error. Once it learns what works in the simulation, it can apply this knowledge to the real world. Furthermore, mathematical methods that allowed Dactyl to learn are believed by researchers to be useful in training robotic hands and other machines to perform far more complex tasks. In this vain, other Autolab researchers have managed to build over the last few years a robot that can pick up anything, even stuff it has never seen before. This system still uses simple hardware: a gripper and a suction cup. But it can pick up all sorts of random items, from a pair of scissors to a plastic toy dinosaur. The Berkeley researchers

126 *Retailers race against Amazon to automate stores* by Nick Wingfield, Paul Mozur and Michael Corkery, in: "International New York Times", April 1, 2018:https://www.nytimes.com/2018/04/01/technology/retailer-stores-automation-amazon.html (Accessed: September 2018).

benefiting from dramatic advances in machine learning, modeled the physics of more than 10,000 objects, identifying the best way to pick up each one. Then, using an algorithm called a neural network, the system analyzed all this data, learning to recognize the best way to pick up any item. While in the past, researchers had to program a robot to perform each task, in the above-described circumstances, it can learn these tasks on its own. Such robots are thought to provide services in shops of the future to be exemplified here by the Amazon's convenience store opened in Seattle (2018); its uniqueness is to be felt right at the front door. An individual consumer might feel as if he/she was entering a subway station. Rows of gates guard the entrance to the store, known as Amazon Go, allowing in only people with the store's smartphone app. The shopping experience like no other relies, however, not in a range of products to be offered there – inside a 1,800-square foot mini-market shelves are packed with food that can be found in a lot of other convenience stores – but on technology mostly tucked away out of sight. There are no cashiers or registers anywhere. Every time customers grab an item off a shelf, the product is automatically put into the shopping cart of their online account. If the item is put back on the shelf, Amazon removes it from their virtual basket. In the end, shoppers leave the store through the same gates, without pausing to pull out a credit card. Their Amazon account automatically gets charged for what they take out the door. Technology that makes this possible floats above the store shelves – arrays of small cameras, hundreds of them throughout the store. What is more, companies are testing robots that help keep shelves stocked, as well as apps that let shoppers ring up items with a smart phone. Walmart, the world's largest retailer, is testing out the Bossa Nova robots in dozens of its locations to reduce some tedious tasks that can eat up a worker's time. The robots, which look like giant wheeled luggage bags, roll up and down the aisles looking for shelves where cereal boxes are out of stock and items like toys are mislabeled. The machines then report to workers, who restock the shelves and apply new labels. At 120 of Walmart's 4,700 American stores, shoppers can also scan items, including fruits and vegetables, using the camera on their smart phones and pay for them using the devices. When customers walk out, an employee checks their receipts and does a "spot check" of the items they bought. Kroger, one of the country's largest grocery chains, has also been testing a mobile scanning service in its supermarkets, recently announcing that it would expand it to 400 of its more 2,700 stores. Amazon's competitors like AiFi, concentrate their efforts on cashierless checkout technology that will be flexible and affordable for modest as well as bigger retailers. This is illustrated by the expenditure of $ 100 million (up from about $64 million in 2015) put in the United States by venture capitalists, according to Pitchbook, a financial data firm, into retail automation start-ups in each of the past two years.

It is to be acknowledged however, that nowhere are retailers experimenting more avidly with automating store shopping than in China. One effort is a chain of more than 100 unmanned convenience shops from a start-up called Bingo Box headquartered in a Shanghai's business park. Shoppers scan a code on their phones to enter and, once inside, scan the items they want to buy. The store unlocks the exit door after they have paid through their phones. Another example is provided by Alibaba, one of China's largest internet companies, that has opened 35 of its Hema automated grocery stores, which blend online ordering with automated checkout. Customers scan their groceries at checkout kiosks, using facial recognition to pay electronically, while bags of groceries ordered by customers online float overhead on aerial conveyors, headed to a loading dock for delivery to shoppers. JD, another big internet retailer in China, at its huge campus south of Beijing, is testing a new store that relies on computer vision and sensors on the shelves to know when items have been taken. The system tracks shopping without tagging products with chips. Payment, which for now still happens at a kiosk, is done with facial recognition.[127] One more Chinese artificial intelligence company-iFlyTek, uses sophisticated A.I. to power image and voice recognition systems that can help doctors with their diagnoses, aid teachers in grading tests and let drivers control their cars with their voices. Occasionally, during President Trump's visit to Beijing, he appeared on screen for a special address at a tech conference; first he spoke in English. Then he switched to Mandarin Chinese. Mr. Trump does not speak Chinese. The video was a publicity stunt, designed to show off the voice capabilities of iFlyTek[128]. At the same time, however, iFlyTek hosts a laboratory to develop voice surveillance capabilities for China's domestic security forces. With a long history of unchecked surveillance and retaliation against critics the Chinese government has been collecting by means of artificial intelligence called Automatic Speaker Recognition forensics the voice patterns of tens of thousands of people with little transparency about the program or laws regulating who can be targeted or how that information is going to be used. To illustrate, in 2012, the Ministry of Public Security started the construction of a national voice pattern database and designated Anhui as one of the pilot provinces. As a result, in its home province

127 *Retailers race …*, Ibidem.

128 *China's A.I. Advances Help Its Tech Industry, and State Security* by Paul Mozur and Keith Bradsher, in: "International New York Times" Dec. 3 2017, at: https://www.nytimes.com/2017/12/03/business/china-artificial-intelligence.html (Accessed: September 2019).

of Anhui, iFlyTek has assembled a database of 70,000 voice patterns, according to the report, which also said that the police had begun collecting records of voice patterns as they would fingerprints. According to Human Rights Watch, similar purchases for voice pattern collection systems were also made in 2016 by the police bureaus in Xinjiang, a repressive region with 11 million ethnic minority Uyghurs, following the "Notice to Fully Carry Out the Construction of Three-Dimensional Portraits, Voice Pattern, and DNA Fingerprint Biometrics Collection System". The practice of collecting voice patterns of ordinary citizens such as migrant workers in Xuancheng city, Anhui province (April 27, 2017), Bole city, Xinjiang Autonomous Region, Zhengzhou city, Henan province (April-May 2017) are also well documented.[129] In addition, according to Human Rights Watch the company was helping the authorities compile a biometric voice database of Chinese citizens that could be used to track activists and others. The tight ties with the government could give iFlyTek and other Chinese companies an edge in an emerging new field. Not without influence remains China's state apparatus financial support and its loosely enforced and untested privacy laws that give Chinese companies access to voices, faces and other biometric data in vast quantities, that are used in a process of technological exploration. While Chinese law appears to limit police collection of biometric samples to people connected to the investigation of a specific criminal case[130], there are no legal guidelines or limitations on how long biometric samples can be stored, shared, or used, or how their collection or use can be challenged. Chinese law also does not authorize the police to collect individuals' biometric data in cases of administrative offences; in early 2017, however, the Chinese government issued new draft amendments to its Public Security Administrative Punishments Law, in which a new provision, article 112, authorizes police to collect biometrics to identify victims and offenders in minor administrative cases.[131] It is assumed that disproportionate,

129 *China: Voice Biometric Collection Threatens Privacy Police, AI Giant Collaboration in Legal Gray Area*, October 22, 2017, at: https://www.hrw.org/news/2017/10/22/ china-voice-biometric-collection-threatens-privacy (Accessed: September 2018).

130 Article 130 of the Criminal Procedure Law (CPL) states that in the course of criminal investigations, to "ascertain certain features, conditions of injuries, or physical conditions of a victim or a criminal suspect, a physical examination may be conducted, and fingerprints, blood, urine and other biological samples may be collected. If a criminal suspect refuses to be examined, the investigators, when they deem it necessary, may conduct a compulsory examination."

131 As far as the Criminal Procedure Law is considered Article 148 allows criminal investigators to wiretap criminal suspects as well as anyone connected to the crime

while being compared with the Western countries, investment in the development of AI technologies accompanied by modest privacy laws and social complicity of the state's policy, have significantly contributed to reinforcement of China's companies on a global market; IFlyTek has won major competitions for speech recognition and translation. Two years before Microsoft did, Baidu, the Chinese internet search company, created software capable of matching human skills at understanding speech. In 2017, the Shanghai-based start-up Yitu took first place in a major facial recognition contest run by the United States government, overtaking the Russia company Vocord, a long-established international security brand that beat Google in various facial recognition benchmarks for years, and Morpho, a well-known French biometrics company.[132]

Paradoxically, due to the 2020 outbreak of pandemic countries around the world employed Coronavirus digital surveillance tools as a means to exert social control, even turning security agency technologies on their own civilians. In South Korea, government agencies were harnessing surveillance-camera footage, smart- phone location data and credit card purchase records to help trace the recent movements of coronavirus patients and establish virus transmission chains. In addition, South Korean authorities began posting detailed location histories on each person who tested positive for the coronavirus. The site has included a wealth of information—such as details about when people left for work, whether they wore masks in the subway, the name of the stations where they changed trains, the massage parlors and karaoke bars they frequented and the names of the clinics where they were tested for the virus. In Lombardy, Italy, the authorities analyzed loca- tion data transmitted by citizens' mobile phones to determine how many people were obeying a government lockdown order and the typical distances they move every day. In Israel, the country's internal security agency was poised to start using a cache of mobile phone location data—originally intended for counterterrorism operations—to try to pinpoint citizens who may have been exposed to the virus. Yet ratcheting up surveillance to combat the pandemic could permanently open the doors to

---

for serious crimes, including endangering state security, terrorism, organized crime, drug-related crimes, and corruption. Such wiretapping does not require a court warrant – approval from supervisors in the relevant criminal investigation units is adequate under the law. Compare: *China: Voice Biometric Collection ..., Op. Cit.*

132 Yitu Technology won first place in prestigious global facial recognition benchmark test, at: https://www.prnewswire.com/news-releases/yitu-technology-won-first-place-in-prestigious-global-facial-recognition-benchmark-test-300513646.html, (Accessed: September 2018).

more invasive forms of snooping later. It is a lesson Americans learned after the terrorist attacks of Sept. 11, 2001. In 2020 due to the Coronavirus pandemic experienced in the United States, the White House officials spoke with Google, Facebook and other tech companies about potentially using aggregated location data captured from Americans' mobile phones for public health surveillance of the virus. It is to be acknowledged at the same time that nearly two decades later, law enforcement agencies have access to higher-powered surveillance systems, like fine-grained location tracking and facial recognition—technologies that may be repurposed to further political agendas like anti-immigration policies. What is more, according to Civil liberties experts the public has little recourse to challenge these digital exercises of state power. On the other hand, however, in emergencies like pandemics, privacy must be weighed against other considerations, like saving lives. While companies and public authorities cooperate to enable proper response for the public good, governments as well as commercial business should limit the collection and use of data to only what is needed. This could be exemplified by unusual reaction of the South Korean authorities who announced that in order to balance the value of protecting individual human rights and privacy and the value of upholding public interest in preventing mass infections, data-sharing guidelines were due to be refined to minimize patient risk.[133]

To conclude, a common trait of the above-described smart cities and other environments is the way in which powerful institutions define the technological infrastructures that shape our societies opaquely and with unsuspected power.[134] Coupled with this "power in designing" the technological infrastructure, are the asymmetries between people and those who determine individual experience.[135] These asymmetries tend to be amplified in Ambient Intelligence (AmI), a world where objects are "smart", environments are "sensible" and technology anticipates and satisfies our needs and desires; a world where "[t]echnology becomes invisible, embedded in our natural surroundings, present whenever we need it, enabled by simple and effortless interactions, attuned to all our senses, adaptive to users and context and autonomously acting".[136] Rising with

133 *As Coronavirus Surveillance Escalates, Personal Privacy Plummets* by Natasha Singer and Choe Sang-Hun, "International New York Times" March 23, 2020.

134 L. Costa, *Virtuality and Capabilities in a World of Ambient Intelligence New Challenges to Privacy and Data Protection, Springer 2016.*

135 Cohen, J. E. 2012. *Configuring the Networked Self.* New Haven: Yale University Press.

136 Lindwer, M., D. Marculescu, T. Basten, R. Zimmermann, R. Marculescu, S. Jung, and E. Cantatore. 2003. 'Ambient Intelligence Visions and Achievements: Linking Abstract

the assemblage of already existing and developing multiple terminals, infrastructure and services, AmI tends to dismiss the very need to act intentionally; after all, it is about technologies that are precisely conceived to avoid awareness (systems are non-noticeable) and conscious actions to trigger systems. It cannot be denied at the same time, that AmI systems can contribute to human development and enhancement– for instance, liberating us from repetitive tasks or opening new possibilities for action – the promise of convenience, better life and a terrorist-free world will nevertheless be received with a fair dose of skepticism. If freedoms matter – we may think about freedom of choice or freedom of action – one may reasonably be concerned about "environments" whose structures are determined by private and public institutions and that have a high potential to determine individual "experience". As expressed by M. Foucault power is less a confrontation between two adversaries or their mutual engagement than a question of "government". In addition, this word must be allowed the very broad meaning it had in the sixteenth century. "Government" did not refer only to political structures or to the management of states; rather, it designated the way in which the conduct of individuals or of groups might be directed – the government of children, of souls, of communities, of families, of the sick. It covered not only the legitimately constituted forms of political or economic subjection but also modes of action, more or less considered and calculated, that were destined to act upon the possibilities of action of other people. To govern, in this sense, is to structure the possible field of action of others.[137]

While enhancement is beneficial, dependency may be a problem both at the social and individual level. "If some day we build machine brains that surpass human brains in general intelligence, then this new superintelligence could become very powerful. And, as the fate of the gorillas now depends more on us humans than on the gorillas themselves, so the fate of our species would depend on the actions of the machine superintelligence"[138]– predicts Oxford philosopher Nick Bostrom. Sharing this awareness cosmologist Stephen Hawking and Tesla Chief executive officer-Elon Musk endorsed the 23 principles designed to ensure that Ambient Intelligence (AI) remains a force for good- known as Asilomar AI Principles because they were developed at the Asilomar conference venue in

Ideas to Real-World Concepts'. In *Design, Automation & Test in Europe Conference & Exhibition*. Vol. 1. Los Alamitos, California: IEEE Computer Society.

137 Foucault, M. 1997. 'The Subject and Power'. In *Essential Works of Foucault: 1954–1984*, edited by P. Rabinow. New York: The New Press, p. 340.

138 Bolstrom N., *Superintelligence: Paths, Dangers, Strategies,* Oxford University Press 2014.

California. The principles were broken down into three categories: 1) Research issues; 2) Ethics and values; 3) Longer-term issues[139]. Among those, rules that refer to AI-powered autonomous weapons and self-replicating AIs, were created by the Future of Life Institute- an entity, founded by Massachusetts Institute of Technology (MIT) cosmologist Max Tegmark and Skype cofounder Jaan Tallinn, and DeepMind research scientist Viktoriya Krakovna in March 2014[140], working to ensure that tomorrow's most powerful technologies are beneficial for humanity.[141]

Such initiatives are to be appreciated, especially in a world of omnipresent surveillance and others technologies, that are considered as instruments to make people's behavior conform to social standards.[142] For instance, building on a model idealized by Marx[143], Greenfield points out that ubiquitous technologies have the potential to reinforce strategies of social control through: (a) target or facility removal, meaning that something that is not there cannot be taken or used; for instance, as with credit and debit cards, RFID equipped transport cards remove money from sight; (b) target devaluation, meaning that the value of a potential target is reduced or eliminated, in other words, smart phones and vehicles that can be remotely traced; (c) target insulation, isolating a target as a means to protect it, such as within the use of networked sensors or biometrics to control access to buildings; (d) offender weakening or incapacitation, which renders potential offenders harmless, such as wireless muzzling devices which prevent the use of cell phones while driving; (e) exclusion such as keeping someone away from targets, say with the use

---

139 AI Principles, at: https://futureoflife.org/ai-principles/ (Accessed: September 2018).

140 Hawking and Musk are on the board of advisors.

141 "Artificial intelligence has already provided beneficial tools that are used everyday by people around the world," wrote the Future of Life on its website. "Its continued development, guided by the following principles, will offer amazing opportunities to help and empower people in the decades and centuries ahead.", in: Shead S., *Stephen Hawking and Elon Musk backed 23 principles to ensure humanity benefits from AI, "Business Insider"*, Feb. 1, 2017, at: https://www.businessinsider.com/stephen-hawking-elon-musk-backed-asimolar-ai-principles-for-artificial-intelligence-2017-2?IR=T (Accessed: September 2018).

142 *Embedded, Everywhere a Research Agenda for Networked Systems of Embedded Computers,* United States National Research Council. 2001, Washington, D.C.: National Academy Press, p. 181.

143 Marx, G. T. 2013. 'Technology and Social Control – The Search for the Illusive Silver Bullet Continues', Encyclopedia of the Social & Behavioral Sciences, 2nd edition, at: http://web.mit.edu/gtmarx/www/techsoccon.html, (Accessed: September 2018).

of GPS monitoring bracelets and (f) identification of potential offenders, for example within crime mapping systems that aggregate data such as location and communications.[144] What is more, in a world of AmI, technologies are pervasive and ever present to the point of making surveillance a regular part of people's lives, as illustrated by Gilliom: a typical worker, for example, would face the ongoing surveillance related to policing, taxation, and consumerism, but also such things as workplace drug testing, performance monitoring and evaluation, and other forms of observation, measurement and analysis. A typical student would also face the background surveillance of policing, taxation, and consumerism, but may also experience academic testing, dormitory searches, athletic drug testing, and the general scrutiny of university life. A credit card user or World Wide Web traveler undergoes constant assessment and analysis as often-unseen systems record and apply information about their habits.[145] In addition, the size of the shift from personalized supervision to technological surveillance can be illustrated in the context of Aid to Families with Dependent Children. Visits from caseworkers gave place to the use of highly performing systems, capable of interconnecting large amounts of information. For instance, a welfare information system in the state of Ohio gathers data on costs of telephone, sewerage, garbage removal, electricity, gas, number of work hours, and expected changes in the household income. The system may also have access to saving accounts, unknown to the interested person.[146] This type of bold surveillance scheme, grounded in the promotion of the efficiency of the welfare system and the avoidance of fraud, is extreme in determining and normalizing people's lives through surveillance. Where social norms would leave space for human perception – for instance a norm that one should have compassion for single, working mothers – data mining and automated profiling may reduce those who depend on social services to nothing more than potential fraudsters.[147] Surveillance accounts of technology are particularly seductive as they focus on problems of observation and power. But equating power to social control, these accounts give oversimplified answers to problems that are not just about social control. With automated profiling control has never been less "social". Profiles are being built not

144 Greenfield, A. 2006. *Everywhere – The Dawning Age of Ubiquitous Computing.* Berkeley: New Riders, pp. 109–110.

145 Gilliom, J. 2001. *Overseers of the Poor: Surveillance, Resistance, and the Limits of Privacy.* Chicago: University of Chicago Press, p. 42.

146 Ibid.

147 L. Costa, *Virtuality and Capabilities ...*, Op. Cit., p. 51.

in accordance with social norms but rather according to algorithmic induction; threats and opportunities are detected at the infra- (i.e., profile relies on the building of data traces rather than considering the individual as such) and supra-individual level (profiles are types; general rather than individual). If the power within AmI is not necessarily social, a further investigation of the technique within AmI – particularly with regard to the role of algorithms – seems to be necessary.

Smart metering systems refer to the ensemble of technologies able to measure energy consumption and build knowledge about it.[148] In Europe, its spread was particularly related to an energy policy faced with the challenges of "energy imports and scarce energy resources, and the need to limit climate change and overcome the economic crisis" (recital 1 of the Energy Efficiency Directive). A response to these challenges was given through the adoption of a Directive promoting energy efficiency – i.e., "the ratio of output of performance, service, goods or energy, to input of energy" (article 2.4 1 of the Energy Efficiency Directive) – the adoption of smart metering systems being one of the improvement measures. It is expected that 80 % of consumers will have been equipped with smart metering systems by 2020. From a consumer point-of-view, the Directive considers smart metering to be self-controlling of energy costs, since consumers must be enabled to regulate their own energy consumption. In the Netherlands, however, the adoption of legislation on smart metering was the subject of lively debate. Cuijpers and Koops[149] have extensively exploited the Dutch Case vis-à-vis impacts on privacy from the perspective of Article 8 of the European Convention of Human Rights

---

148 Knyrim, R., and G. Trieb, 'Smart Metering under EU Data Protection Law', in: "*International Data Privacy Law*", March 2011, Vol. 1, No 2, pp. 121–128. Knyrim and Trieb define and describe smart meters as: "[…] a new generation of advanced and intelligent metering devices which have the ability to record the energy consumption of a particular measuring point in intervals of fifteen minutes or even less. These so called 'smart meters' can also communicate and transfer the information recorded in real time or at least on a daily basis by means of any communications network to the utility company for purposes such as monitoring of the system load as well as for billing purposes ('tele-metering')". Article 2, 28 of Directive 2012/27/EU (hereafter "Energy Efficiency Directive") defines smart metering system or intelligent metering system as "an electronic system that can measure energy consumption, providing more information than a conventional meter, and can transmit and receive data using a form of electronic communication".

149 Cuijpers, C., and B.-J. Koops, 'Smart Metering and Privacy in Europe'. In: *European Data Protection Coming of Age*, Gutwirth, S., Leenes, R., de Hert, P., Poullet, Y. (Eds.), Dordrecht; New York 2013: Springer. Similarly, McStay explores an example in the

(ECHR). I their analysis scientists highlighted the very specific knowledge smart metering systems were able to create. As it was emphasized: [...] smart meter data, when measured in intervals of 4 h, exactly reveal when a person is at home, when he/she is sleeping or preparing meals. When using shorter intervals, of minutes or seconds, electric devices can be identified on the basis of use profiles, such as a fridge, coffee machine, washing machine, toaster, microwave, and TV.[150] These data could reveal if someone eats a cold or a hot breakfast, when laundry is done, or whether the kids are alone at home. It is even possible to determine which channel a TV is tuned to, through an analysis of the broadcast programs, particularly if the TV is tuned to a longer program such as a movie. The interfering noise in the meter data of other energy-consuming devices can most likely be filtered out in case movies are watched of 90 min or longer.[151] Therefore, smart meter systems were able to "know" what was going on inside a house with a quite high level of granularity. The second point raised by Cuijpers and Koops concerned the rigorous enforcement regime initially envisaged by the Dutch government in order to "enable customers to regulate their own energy consumption". Namely, not accepting the installation of a smart meter was made punishable as an economic offense, sanctioned with a fine of up to 17,000 euro or imprisonment for a maximum of 6 months. The smart meter would record and forward to the network operators (also called grid managers) data about consumers' energy consumption at detailed interval periods, namely hourly measurements for gas and quarter-hourly measurements for electricity. These data being forwarded to the energy suppliers would then be used to provide consumers with detailed information about their energy consumption, so that the consumers could adapt their energy-consuming behavior accordingly.[152] Such techniques as the above-described smart metering system have an important role in our information societies, particularly vis-à-vis the knowledge they produce. Furthermore, according to Rouvroy, within the ritual of "knowledge production" data behaviorism, in the first place, is *immanent*, in the sense that it

---

US, where the company Verizon submitted an application in order to obtain patent protection for a media system capable of "triggering tailored advertisements based on whether viewers are eating, playing, cuddling, laughing, singing, fighting, talking or gesturing in from of their sets", in: McStay, A. 2014. *Privacy and Philosophy: New Media and Affective Protocol.*

150 L. Costa, „Virtual Capabilities in a World of Ambient Intelligence", Springer International Publishing 2016, p. 53.

151 Ibid., pp. 284–285.

152 Ibid, pp. 278–279.

leaves the field of uncertainty and speculation to become an operation supposed to "reveal" the world through the use of data processing.[153] Contrary to the artificiality of technology, the knowledge of data behaviorism does not appear as a 'production of the mind', with all the artificiality and cognitive and emotional biases unavoidably connoting mental productions, but as always already 'given', immanent to the (digitally recorded) world, in which it is merely automatically 'discovered' or from which it literally flourishes thanks to algorithmic operations rendering invisible correlations operational.[154] *Secondly*, this knowledge is *atopical* in the sense that it is not anchored to temporal or spatial landmarks, but rather to actuality, to real time according to which it refines itself, "building and rebuilding itself from within the huge 'numerical memories' ".[155] With the absence of landmarks, as Rouvroy underlines, comes the absence of traditional criteria to evaluate knowledge such as "authenticity, historical coherence, or critical apperception"; what matters is "immediate operationality, plasticity, flexible adaptation to changing circumstances, and immediate availability".[156] This point may be illustrated by the Tucker's description of the operations of a multinational data brokerage company: [...] they are also selling your future decisions [...] For instance, let's say you have a discounted insurance product and you want to reach only those potential customers who would be extremely unlikely to buy that product at full price [...] In a matter of minutes the Acxiom system crunched 700 million rows of data and outputted a number. Mui [the company CEO] revealed to the audience that if they were looking for someone with that propensity, "there are 275,012 people that you can reach out to". Mui was careful to point out, 'This is live. You can buy this audience *today*'. There are three thousand such propensities Acxiom can model.[157] Thirdly, and despite dealing with

153 Rouvroy, A. 2014. 'Des données sans personne: le fétichisme de la donnée à caractère personnel à l'épreuve de l'idéologie des Big data'. Conseil d'État.

154 Rouvroy, A. 2013. 'The End(s) of Critique: Data Behaviourism versus Due Process'. In *Privacy, Due Process and the Computational Turn: The Philosophy of Law Meets the Philosophy of Technology*, Hildebrandt M. and Katia de Vries, Routledge 2013, pp. 143–68. See also: L. Costa, *Virtuality and Capabilities in a World of Ambient Intelligence New Challenges to Privacy and Data Protection,* Springer 2016, pp. 15–42.

155 Rouvroy, A. 2013, p. 148.

156 Ibid.

157 Tucker, P. 2014. *The Naked Future: What Happens in a World That Anticipates Your Every Move*. United States General Accounting Office. 2004. 'Report to the Ranking Minority Member, Subcommittee on Financial Management, the Budget, and International Security, Committee on Governmental Affairs, U.S. Senate'. United States General Accounting Office, p. 120.

data, data behaviorism is *not synonymous with statistics,* as it does not presuppose per se a relationship between data and hypotheses.[158] While techniques such as data mining may play a significant role in the understanding of the phenomena about which they collect data – for instance in confirming or denying the validity of a scientific hypothesis – they should not be taken as an explanation themselves.[159] Even when algorithms are used to test hypotheses, they are not exempt from the problems of statistics; besides, they pose problems of comprehensibility in human understandability terms and the feedback loop. Different from statistical, scientific knowledge, data behaviorism engages a system where raw data is taken for objective knowledge.[160] Fourthly, data behaviorism's attachment to correlation diminishes the place or the rates of causality and intentionality, meaning that we become less able to use such categories "to predict, regulate and give account of phenomena". Data behaviorism's operationality, immediacy and objectivity – as pointed out by Rouvroy – divert attention from previous perspectives on causality and intentionality such as testimony and expertise. Where the spread of techniques such as data mining creates the impression that "data is enough", one can expect a devaluation of alternative approaches to explain phenomena. This connects to what Stiegler named the "performativity of algorithms", building on the concept of performativity as conceived by Austin. It is as if algorithms emoted utterances that constitute the very acts on which they will impact. Within such logic, there is no need to inquire about agency and causality – for instance the intimate reasons for which someone acted – since algorithms are able to analyze behavior in real time and constantly respond in order to direct them. The knowledge we deal with here is built on the availability

158 "Statistics investigates and develops specific methods for evaluating hypotheses in the light of empirical facts. A method is called statistical, and thus the subject of study in statistics, if it relates facts and hypotheses of a particular kind: the empirical facts must be codified and structured into data sets, and the hypotheses must be formulated in terms of probability distributions over possible data sets". See: Romeijn, J.-W. 2014. 'Philosophy of Statistics'. In *The Stanford Encyclopedia of Philosophy* edited by E. N. Zalta, Fall 2014, at: http://plato.stanford.edu/archives/fall2014/entries/statistics/, (Accessed: September 2018)

159 For a critique of "data as knowledge" in Big Data see Boyd D. and Kate Crawford, *'Critical Questions for Big Data'*. "Information, Communication & Society" 15 (5):2012, pp. 662–79; Anderson, Chris. 2008. *'The End of Theory: The Data Deluge Makes the Scientific Method Obsolete'*. "Wired" May 23rd. http://archive.wired.com/science/—discoveries/magazine/16-07/pb_theory, (Accessed: September 2018).

160 Rouvroy, A. 2013, pp. 148–152.

of huge amounts of data and data processing operations and it clearly plays a fundamental role in our information societies. Such knowledge creates a new "truth regime", that Rouvroy calls data behaviorism.

Since the world of Ambient Intelligence is about "knowing", one may refer to the so-called algorithmic governmentality defined as a form of power grounded in profiling algorithms and the structuring of the possible fields where individuals may act. Knowledge built through observation and quantification is operationalized through prediction and preemption, the last two performing what the first two created. Algorithmic governmentality is precisely placed on the indistinctiveness or fusion between "knowledge of algorithms" and power, between «savoirs et pouvoirs». Foucauldian power/knowledge could not be better transposed here: data behaviorism ("knowing"), the prediction and preemption of behaviors ("acting") are one and the same thing. Furthermore, two elements of algorithmic governmentality related to the operation of such power/knowledge are to be acknowledged here: dividualism and the focus on potentiality. As far as the former is concerned, algorithmic governmentality sees the individual not as "the actual, experiential, present and sentient subject"[161]; but rather apprehends persons dividually, i.e., as fragmented, atomized in large amounts of disjointed personal data. At odds with the idea of AmI personalization algorithmic governmentality dismisses the very idea of subjects as moral agents, rather confronting persons through the predictions made on the basis of their digital bodies, i.e., an ensemble of "infra-individual digital traces of impersonal, disparate, heterogeneous and 'dividualised' facets of daily life and interactions"[162] In the example of "smart" metering in the Netherlands, rather than a narrative of invasion, what algorithmic governmentality makes evident, is the inevitability and inscrutability of knowledge built on data crunching and indifference vis-à-vis the individual. While power is exercised over "dividuals", the question is then "who is benefitting from the power/knowledge of algorithms?" Or "from whose point-of-view does algorithmic governmentality reduce the social effects of uncertainty?" The very examples of existent AmI applications give some good clues: for example, mining signs of affect in faces to sell merchandise, exploiting border control systems, search engines selling data to companies that further fix product prices according to consumer profiles and energy consumption management. The multiple concrete examples pointing essentially to the convenience of governments and companies are not balanced by even a minimal number of

161 Rouvroy, Op. Cit., p. 153.
162 Rouvroy, Op. Cit., p. 157.

examples where individuals profit directly from algorithms as a tool of effective empowerment.[163] Information systems are not supposed to see human beings in all their complexity, but to sort individuals in a variety of heterogeneous categories for the purpose of predicting their willingness or need to buy specific commodities, their risks to fill claims with health and disability insurances, the danger they represent for themselves or for others, or other propensities that marketers, insurers, law enforcement officials and many others may find useful to have.[164]

Summarizing, the power/knowledge of algorithms lies in prediction and especially the preemption of behavior, by applying profiling algorithms to massive amounts of data (emitted by the human body), and structuring (physical, architectural, informational, contextual) of the possible range of actions of individuals. What is more, it focuses on the prediction no longer to control the actual but to eradicate the 'virtual', to control the range of actions of bodies, at a preconscious stage if possible.[165] "Such focus on the "potential" seems to harbor one major risk engaged by algorithmic governmentality vis-à-vis our freedoms.[166]

First, freedoms are at play in AmI when our autonomy-understood as a right to self-determination which is guaranteed to human subjects insofar as they can be obstructed in their individual decision making by either physical or psychical influences"[167] -is affected by a certain mode of action. For instance, in the name of security and grounded in risk management strategies whose bases and effectiveness are far from clear, governments drastically implement new surveillance systems and integrate them with existing ones. The use of smart border information systems is a meaningful example of how democracies engage in promoting high levels of control on people's lives in the name of a more secure, better world. Governing the mobility of our bodies is at the core of schemes that process data related to health, finances, travel records, biometrics, flight lists, banking, education, and so on.[168] Such governance is improved not only by the quantity and quality of data processed but also by the ever-increasing categorization through automated

163 Tucker P., *The Naked Future: What Happens in a World That Anticipates Your Every Move*, Penguin Publishing, New York 2014.

164 Rouvroy 2011, p. 188.

165 Rouvroy 2010, p. 13.

166 L. Costa, „*Virtual Capabilities in a World of Ambient Intelligence*", Springer International Publishing 2016, p. 58.

167 Honneth 1995, p. 265.

168 Amoore L., *Biometric Borders: Governing Mobilities in the War on Terror*, in: „Political Geography" 25(3), 2006, pp. 336–51.

profiling. Here people are categorized – potential car buyers, potential fraudsters, people discontented with their bodies and willing to pay for related products and services, rich people aiming to waste money on frivolities, someone willing to buy a house and ready to pay high interest rates, poor people depending on welfare or terrorists – through procedures whose logic is unattainable. Unawareness of the rationale of such information systems and as a result categorization that impacts on potential actions of individuals, one may reasonably doubt whether and to what extent people's actions are free or autonomous. Second, freedoms are also at play in AmI when people are affected by relations they value, of which trust is an example. Recent research draws attention to the high incidence of responses on the negative impact of Location Based Social Networking (LBSN) on trust.[169] Parents, while recognizing their responsibility to provide care for their children, also acknowledge how difficult it is to build a relationship based on trust bearing in mind that they are tracking their children all the time; it goes without saying that there is a lack of trust also on the part of children, who are under surveillance. Friends and companions report similar concerns, related to the decision to disclose their location or not, as well as feelings of suspicion when they see that their loved one spent large periods of time at specific locations[170] The example illustrates how technological design informed by a rationale of control clearly affects trust relations between people and their companions, friends and relatives. The third example connected to freedoms is related to how AmI technologies may affect well-being, both individual and collective. Disengaging from the view according to which the "rational subject" is the one that promotes self-interest, it is plausible to assume that the freedoms of others are also important. Consider what is called the "privacy divide"– i.e., the inequality in the protection of privacy and personal data for reasons other than a person's will meaning that people enjoy different levels of privacy according to factors such as technological literacy, financial status, technology and personal abilities.[171] For instance, welfare and asylum seekers are subjected to a wide range

---

169 LBSN applications allow users to view the location of their friends or other unknown users in proximity.

170 S. J. Fusco, R. Abbas, K. Michael, A. Aloudat, Location-Based Social Networking and Its Impact on Trust in Relationships, in: „IEEE Technology and Society Magazine" 31 (2), 2012, pp. 1–10.

171 Privacy Implications of Emerging & Future Technologies / Birnhack & Ahituv, PRACTIS, Dec. 2013, at:https://poseidon01.ssrn.com/delivery.php?ID=431123081119072010 116006024102104069016017050081065039090094002091122114086004108022107096017002029 1270370660060031240900201180600090440290351050870180

of prying into their lives in order to obtain a benefit. In a much less sensitive situation than welfare and asylum seeking, consumers who cannot pay for privacy protection may be considered underprivileged in relation to other users. Implants for human enhancement provide another example. Though still largely used for restorative purposes[172], research predicts that implant technologies – some of them Information & Communication Technologies (ICTs) – will be used for enhancement purposes in the future, such as brain prosthesis to improve memory and prosthetic cortical implants to amplify senses (European Group on Ethics in Science and New Technologies to the European Commission 2005). The ethical challenges of human enhancement are numerous; more generally, the "future of AmI" is intimately related to the challenge of divides: digital perhaps but, more importantly, also political and economic.

To sum up, AmI technologies significantly translate human lives into more inputs and outputs of data to be processed and embed technology everywhere, that analogously increase human dependency on it. While privacy theory generally presupposes self-governed, independent individuals, capable of mastering their own freedoms and rights; such a model of a human being is on a collision course with the one assumed above: subjected to and affected by more and more complex Information & Communication technologies (ICT), such as automated profiling to be described in the next section.

3 Biometrics

In today's world, an attempt to diminish the production of digital traces, the processing of personal data-from digital abstention to temporary disconnection - the possibility of being „off" vis-a-vis ICTs is rare if not existent due to AmI technologies. Specifically, the use of biometric data is not new, and refers back to the fourteenth century in China;[173] however, biometrics systems close to

---

140941161060290470770031 140000920690661230291200950800020190700240 10014071105022103068027126102088&EXT=pdf (Accessed: September 2018).

172 Gasson, M. 2012. 'Human ICT Implants: From Restorative Application to Human Enhancement', in: *Human ICT Implants: Technical, Legal and Ethical Considerations*, edited by M. Gasson, E. Kosta, and D. M. Bowman, pp. 11–28. Information Technology and Law Series 23. T.M.C Asser Press 2012.; L. Costa, *Virtuality and Capabilities in a World of Ambient Intelligence New Challenges to Privacy and Data Protection, Chapter A World of Ambient Intelligence*, pp. 15–39.

173 Fingerprints were used by Chinese merchants to settle business transactions; fingerprints and footprints were used by parents to differentiate children.

modern – i.e. automated – started to be used in the 1960s, with great increase in 1990s and early 2000s.[174] Precisely biometrics (derived from the Greek words bio (life) and metric (measure of) are referred to "technologies that measure and analyze physical, physiological or behavioral characteristics of a natural person, which allow or confirm the unique identification of that natural person such as facial images or dactyloscopic data".[175] Physical/physiological characteristics are presented by fingerprint, finger vein, finger geometry, or wrinkles, palm print, odor, pores, bite marks, hand geometry, dental geometry, ear, facial geometry, facial thermogram, iris, skin patterns, smile, lips, DNA, etc. As far as the latter is concerned, it is crucial to note that DNA-based technologies do differ from standard biometrics in a number of ways: a) DNA requires an actual physical sample as opposed to an image, photograph or scan; b) DNA matching: a) is not done in a real time and, for the most part, is not automated; b) does not employ templates or feature extraction, but rather represents the comparison of actual samples.[176] Behavior characteristics include dynamic grip recognition, handwriting, tapping, eye movement tracking, keystroke dynamics, gait, mouse dynamics, etc.[177] Despite these many types, the most common used, in terms of identification of individuals and identity verification, are facial, iris or finger recognition. In this context, it is worth to specify that identyfication (one-to-many) means an act of identifying a person, i.e. to establish that a passenger is a particular person. It is typically the process of comparing biometric data of an individual (acquired at the time of the identification) to a number of biometric templates stored in a database. For instance, it can be used where authorities aim to identify criminals or potential offenders among the passengers through comparison against a watch list. This means that biometric data are stored on a database. Identity verification (one-to-one), on the other hand, means that the identity of the person is compared to a claimed identity. It is typically the process of comparing the biometric data of an individual acquired at the time of the verification to a single biometric template stored in a device. Furthermore, the digital biometric data are algorithmically

---

In: N. Yue Liu, *"Bio-privacy. Privacy, Regulations and the Challenge of Biometrics"*, Routledge Taylor&Francis Group, New York 2012, p. 3.

174 Ibid. p. 3.

175 GDPR Art.4(14).

176 *Biometric-based technologies*, in: „OECD Digital Economy Papers" No. 101 (2004), OECD Publishing, Paris, p. 11, at: http://dx.doi.org/10.1787/232075642747 (Accessed: September 2017)

177 Liu (2012) p. 45.

converted into what is called a template. It is defined although in a *very broad way* as the 'reference biometric feature set' and the 'set of stored biometric features comparable directly to probe biometric features'. The extracted reference biometric features (i.e. a template) can take many forms: a table or a (fixed-length) numerical (binary) string (e.g., 101010 representing a feature vector or not), differing in details and length. The templates will also vary for each of the characteristics. For example, for fingerprint, the minutiae features may be represented as an unordered set of tulles consisting of the minutiae's coordinates and local orientation. For hand geometry, the geometrical properties of the hand are represented by a fixed-length ordered vector of the lengths and widths of the fingers and/or palm. Iris is represented as fixed-length binary strings. A biometric sample can also be processed in several successive templates.[178] The main idea, however, is that the template does not contain the full (biometric) information as contained in a sample, but *only represents the particular features selected by the algorithm*(s). Furthermore, these selected features, once extracted, are represented in a chosen specific (sometimes proprietary) format and are stored for later use. This processing is in most cases irreversible, which means that a 'raw' biometric data cannot be retrieved from the template. These templates are usually stored in a database that is contacted as soon as a face, eye, hand, finger or voice is presented to the system in a particular identification or verification procedure. Once this second biometric image has been subjected to the same algorithmic transformation, an identical template is searched for in the database, and, if found, the individual is recognized in the system.[179]

Face, fingerprints, iris, retinas, hand geometry are widely used in biometrics systems biological characteristics. To illustrate, the concept of on-the-fly biometrics suggests that the capture of biometric details (primarily in the form of fingerprints, face or iris recognition, but also vein or gait recognition) is executed automatically while the passenger is walking through the airport. The

---

178 *Privacy and Data Protection Issues of Biometric Applications. A Comparative Legal Study*, p. 44.

179 Another possibility is that the templates are not stored centrally, but on a chip card, in which case the user needs to show both the card and the required part of the body to 'prove' that he/she is the legitimate user of the card. Biometric data stored on a chip card do not need to be kept in a database by the organization concerned, and could be deleted without loss of functionality., in: I. van der Ploeg and I. Sprenkels, *Migration and Machine-Readable Body: Identification and Biometrics, in: Migration and the New Technological Borders of Europe,* H. Dijstelbloem, A. Meijer (eds.), Palgrave Macmillan 2011, p. 75.

idea is that each one of the biometrics solutions should complement the others, so that the same biometric data and token can be used throughout the system. This should facilitate identity verification at several points in the infrastructure, enabling person-tracking capabilities. The expectation is that within the next 10 years, the majority of airports will trial single biometric travel tokens and 54 % airlines plan to evaluate the technology. But today, although it has great potential, this technology is still being developed, with a number of challenges regarding performance (accuracy, speed) and operational requirements. Thus, further research and development is needed.

An image of the face can easily be captured, with or without the cooperation (and knowledge) of an individual, even from a distance. Facial scans are sometimes equipped with infrared illumination. The facial image can be analyzed in various ways. The analysis may focus on for example the geometric distinguishing features of the face, the relative distance between and directions of specific points, but also on skin texture. The distinctiveness of faces is, however, limited. As far as the facial recognition technology is concerned, the main idea is to collect face images of persons by Closed Circuit TV (CCTV) and compare them to existing biometric data stored in the form of high-resolution images, allowing to verify or identify a person. In general, facial recognition implies the use of the unique configuration of a person's facial features for identification and verification. A number of technologies are used, including 2D, 3D, infrared facial scans.[180] The most systems work with two properties of the face: geometry – the configuration and placement of features, and the texture – colors, tones and condition. In Chinese city of Zhengzhou, for instance, a police officer wearing facial recognition glasses spotted a heroin smuggler at a train station. In Qingdao, a city famous for its German colonial heritage, cameras powered by artificial Intelligence helped the police snatch two dozen criminal suspects in the midst of a big annual festival. In Wuhu, a fugitive murder suspect was identified by a camera as he was buying food from a street vendor. Beijing is embracing technologies like facial recognition and AI to identify and track 1.4 bilion people.[181] Consequently, in aviation security, facial recognition was initially developed in order to identify dangerous persons by comparing the live biometric input data – passenger's face image captured on CCTV – with the databases of known criminals or suspects. Such identification is still one of the main purposes of facial recognition technology at the airports.

180 Nancy Yue Liu, *Bio-Privacy: Privacy Regulations and the Challenge of Biometrics*, Routledge New York 2012, pp. 41-46.

181 *Inside China's dystopian dreams: A.I., shame and lots of cameras* by Paul Mozur, „International New York Times" July 8, 2018, at: https://www.nytimes.com/2018/07/08/business/china-surveillance-technology.html (Accessed: March 2020)

Accordingly, many states issue biometric passports, e.g. Russia and EU Member States,[182] allowing comparison of input data with faces in travel documents at border control. Biometric passports have mainly been used in automated border control and/or Trusted Traveller Programs (TTP). In addition, the use of facial recognition for passenger verification grows rapidly. One of the reasons for this is the fact that the International Civil Aviation Organization (ICAO) selected face image as the primary biometric identifier for travel documents, with iris and fingerprints being optional.[183]

Fingertips contain ridges and valleys. The ridge-flows form patterns such as arches, whorls and loops, three basic patterns recognized and used in the classification systems developed by Vucetich and Henry. Other biometric properties based on patterns are so-called cores and deltas.[184] Specific points known as minutiae are used as well. Minutiae are discontinuities in the flow of the ridges and are mainly the ending or the bifurcation of the ridges. Minutiae and patterns are used in biometric fingerprint systems. Fingerprints, which are the prints left by the ridges of a finger due to secretions of sweat or ink use, are considered unique. Images of the fingerprint are collected by sensors. Cooperation of the data subject is in principle needed, but latent fingerprints, such as prints left on the sensor or prints found on objects at a crime scene, can also be used, with or without the knowledge of the data subject. The quality of the image is of high importance. Algorithms, proprietary to the vendor or the system developer(s), are used to reduce the 'noise' of the image and to enhance the ridges. Fingerprint, which has been used in forensic applications for over hundred years, is now widely used in biometric systems in the private sector.

As far as the geometry of the hand is concerned, it was one of the first biometric characteristics used for automated verification against a stored reference. The shape and size of the hand palm, finger length, width and thickness of the fingers are measured, as well as curves and the relative locations of these features. In principle, only the geometric features are used for hand geometry and no surface details are recorded, ignoring fingerprints and ridges of the palm, lines, scars and color. Unlike fingerprint, the uniqueness of a human hand is limited. The individual hand geometry features therefore do not scale well for identification (in large-scale

182 See, e.g. Commission Decision of 28 June 2006 laying down the technical specifications on the standards for security features and biometrics in passports and travel documents issued by Member States, at: https://ec.europa.eu/transparency/regdoc/rep/3/2006/DE/3-2006-2909-DE-F-0.Pdf (Accessed: September 2019).

183 ICAO, Doc 9303, Machine Readable Travel Document, Seventh Edition, 2015.

184 Els J. Kindt, *Privacy and Data Protection Issues of Biometric Applications. A comparative Legal Analysis*, Springer 2013, pp. 20–39.

applications) and limits the use of hand geometry to mainly verification purposes and small-scale identification applications. Furthermore, the biometric method based upon this characteristic is vulnerable to changes of the hand geometry. Such changes may be caused by for example an injury (e.g., loss of one or more fingers or deformation of the hand), diseases (e.g., arthritis) and aging, but also by wearing jewelry. The print of the palm of one's hand is another distinctive biometric characteristic fit for use in biometric systems. A palm of the hand has patterns of ridges and valleys, similar to those of fingerprints, as well as lines and wrinkles. While the use of palm print shall be distinguished from the use of the geometry of one's hand as biometric characteristic as explained above, palm print systems may include hand geometry characteristics in their calculations. Because of their uniqueness, palms can be used for identification purposes.

Behavioral characteristics, such as typing or signature writing characteristics, are also used in biometric systems. They are based on behavior which is deemed to be unique or at least distinctive, universal and (more or less) persistent. Typing characteristics, in particular the way a person types or pushes on a key- board, such as the rhythm and error frequency, is distinctive and may be analyzed by software. The analysis detects the patterns of the typing and produces a digital measurement, which may be compared to previously stored patterns. The dynamic of someone writing a signature is another characteristic used in biometric systems. The way the signature is written with a 'smart pen' including sensors or on a pad is analyzed by software (e.g., the acceleration, pressure, and the direction of the signature strokes). Signatures have in general always been used as a method of verification, for examples in legal or commercial transactions, and the use of the so-called dynamic signature characteristics is therefore considered as being easily accepted.

Such a characteristics as Voice of an individual can be used for comparison in biometric systems as well. The characteristic depends on both one's biological and behavioral traits. Both systems based on text spoken by the individual and stored and those having no advance registration of one's speech are used. Cooperation of the individual is therefore in principle not required. Speaker recognition based upon voice can be used for identification (according to some with smaller databases) and verification. While being used until recently mainly in forensic applications, adoption in the private sector has been slow, but increased use may be expected.

The iris provides rich biometric data in the distinctly colored ring around the pupil. The random, detailed and unique structure is captured via a sensor to which the data subject in principle has to direct his or her eye and which illuminates the iris with near-infrared light. Occluding features such as eyelids, eyelashes, or reflections from glasses, must be detected and excluded from being encoded in the template. Latest technology, however, permits to capture iris information also at a distance and without specific cooperation of the individual.

The analysis of the retina vascular patterns also provides individual traits to be used in automated identification or verification processes. Retinal scanning analyses the layer of the blood vessels located at the back of the eyeball with special lighting. The scan uses infrared or near-infrared illumination and imaging. It has been adopted in various military applications because of good levels of accuracy when other biometric techniques were still developing. However, the retina is rather hard to measure and capturing its image requires a great degree of effort and cooperation of the data subjects. The use of the retina, however, compared with other biometric characteristics declined in popularity. Nowadays, its use is restricted to extremely demanding access control situations, such as in governmental or military settings, for example for access to nuclear weapon or research sites.

Most visible and at the same time most controversial airport security solutions according to both security professionals and civil rights advocates, are body scanners.[185] Traditional measures for detecting hidden objects are metal detectors and hand search. Even if done in private, such searches require additional staff and cause delays for passengers, not to mention about privacy concerns related to prohibition of direct touching of private body areas as part of the search.[186] In terms of relatively easy to hide dangerous items in sensitive body parts the scanner's advantages are quickness and no need of physical contact. The choice between hand search and body scanners is thus a trade-off between security effectiveness and privacy concerns.[187] The first body scanner was created by Dr. Steven W Smith in the USA in 1992. It was an ultra-low-dose Secure 1000 backscatter X-ray scanner. It is believed that the first airport in the world to implement body scanners was the Schiphol in the Netherlands in 2006, but the trials of this technology started much earlier. According to some information, the USA

---

185 It is noteworthy that at present, instead of the term "body scanner" or "whole-body scanner", more neutral and technical terms are used, like "security scanner" in the EU, "advanced imaging technology" (AIT) in the USA, "radio scan portal" in Russia. Clearly, this is done in order to present, via language, the scanning process as automatic, anonymized, universal, neutral, routine, and professional, downplaying the core essence – inspection of the naked body.

186 Mironenko Enerstvedt O., *Aviation Security, Privacy, Data Protection and Other Human Rights: Technologies and Legal Principles,* Springer 2017, p. 213.

187 Neeman, A. Radiation in passenger screening: busting the myths, in: "*Aviation Security International*" 21 (2015), p. 13.

started initial tests not later than in 2002[188], Russia – in the middle of 1990s. But the hour of body scanners came apparently after 25 December 2009, when the so-called "underwear bomber" attempted to detonate plastic explosives hidden in his undergarment. It was the moment when many other states became committed to have such devices at the disposal as well. The UK, for example, installed the machines immediately; Schiphol purchased additional units, etc. Detection performance lies in the scanner's ability to discern any prohibited object that the person screened may be carrying on the body or in the clothing. Several technologies are used in order to identify such hidden objects. They include those based on natural thermal radiation (heat from the body), but the most commercially available security scanners use the following technologies: backscatter X-ray[189], active millimeter wave (MMW), and X-ray transmission imaging technology. The early commonly used backscatter and MMW devices produced and showed to a human operator extremely detailed images of the screened persons as if they were naked. Thus, the reaction of the general public, privacy organizations and other interested persons and agencies was appropriate: protests and scandals. As a result, amendments were made to present images visible to operator in more privacy-friendly forms: blurring faces and intimate parts, using mannequin figures, etc.

Profiling, similar to biometrics, is not new and refers back to the Middle Ages, when the inquisitors tried to "profile" heretics.[190] It is believed that the first "profile" for criminal purposes was created by British detectives in 1880s with regard to serial killer Jack the Ripper.[191] In terms of aviation security, in general, profiling is the practice of categorizing people according to particular characteristics, such as passenger's actual or perceived race, ethnicity, religion, nationality, age, gender, behavioral traits, separately or in combination, or

---

188 For example, Post-gazette.com in March 2002 informed that new X-ray scanners were tested in the government technical center in New Jersey and were tested on volunteers at several airports.

189 Backscatter (low X-ray) technology is based on the X-ray Compton scattering effect. It detects the radiation reflected from the object to form a two-dimensional image, revealing details of the surface of the body and a high-resolution image of any external objects. Passengers must stand between two large boxes and raise their arms above their head.

190 Olga Mironenko Enerstvedt, *Aviation Security, Privacy, …, Op. Cit.*, pp. 212–214.

191 Wikipedia, Offender profiling, at:. https://en.wikipedia.org/wiki/Offender_profiling, (Accessed: September 2018).

together with other factors.[192] The core idea is to create profiles or dossiers – a set of definite characteristics, associations, activities, etc. to predict behavior and more, and then search for individuals with a close fit to that set of distinctive features.[193] For instance, the profile of the terrorist can be deduced by cross-indexing information from various databases, the population roll, the use of credit cards, movements detected through use of mobile phones, brand name discount cards, use of medications, etc.

Furthermore, three types of profiling can be noted: manual performed by a human being, automated profiling performed by computers, and semi-manual, combining the first two. For any type of profiling, particular characteristics may serve as indicators of potentially dangerous behavior, assisting in determining whether to stop, search, or question a person. In aviation security, all types of profiling are used extensively and may refer to all the selected measures; with regard to body scanners, profiling can be relevant if passengers are selected to be scanned by security agents (manually) or automatically via a computer pre-screening system. For CCTV, behavior analysis can be conducted manually by a CCTV operator or automatically by algorithms of Video Analytics.[194]

Concluding, the benefits of applying biometric technology, often referred to by expert circles, as big data analytics into the security domain are many; greater operational efficiency and speed, more precise risk analyses and the discovery of unexpected correlations, all of which feed into risk profiles, better targeted inspections and more efficient use of scarce resources[195]. However, it is crucial to note that biometrics - as a technique, as a concept and as a practice - is imprisoned in a number of paradoxes and dualities that make it unavoidably controversial. Biometric data is typically permanent and stays the same throughout lifetime. Not to mention about the fact that appliance of some of biometric data leaves traces (fingerprints, DNA) and thus increases the risk of unauthorized

192 Quinlan, T., *"Discrimination: the questionable effectiveness of screening based on race, religion, national origin or behaviour"*, in: "Aviation Security International" 21 (2015), p. 36.

193 Clarke, Roger. "Profiling: A hidden challenge to the regulation of data surveillance". *JL & Inf. Sci.*4 (1993), p. 403.

194 Olga Mironenko Enerstvedt, *Aviation Security ...*, Op. Cit, pp. 252–257.

195 D. Broeders, E. Schrijvers, B. van der Sloot, R. van Brakel J. de Hoog, E. Hirsch Ballin, *Big Data and security policies: Towards a framework for regulating the phases of analytics and use of Big Data*, in: „Computer Law & Security Review" 33 (2017) Elsevier, pp. 309–323.

repetitive use.[196] In other words, it is a unique identification instrument what may constitute the risk of identity theft. Furthermore, biometrics transforms the physical characteristics of a person into electronic data; in this process the distinction between - on the one hand - the ‚body itself' as a domain of bodily integrity - and - on the other - the information about the body that belongs to the domain of privacy is endangered. In this context, there appear a variety of dilemmas related to withholding respect for the body which constitutes at the same time a piece of digital information meaning that the digital body can be searched remotely-in both time and place. In other words, without the person being present or knowing what is happening. Furthermore, practices such as searching databases, profiling and classifying target certain groups, which means that they are more vulnerable to social categorization, exclusion and automated decisions with all the risk that may be attached. Finally, no biometric system is infallible. All these currently in use have error margins expressed in 'false acceptance rates' (FAR): the system falsely recognizes someone as being the same person and in 'false rejection rates' (FRR): the opposite case in which the system falsely reports that it is not the same person. As has been evidenced by researchers the percentage of the above-mentioned errors increases when the biometric system tested at first in laboratory conditions with relatively homogeneous sample, is exposed to the outside world with all the variable conditions. Facial-recognition systems, in particular, are still scarcely useable because of this problem. Not to mention about the circumstances where fingerprints may be impossible to read, body parts may be missing or damaged. As regards young children, manual laborers and the elderly - their fingerprint ride pattern is either undeveloped or no longer clear enough to be properly registered by the scanners. To conclude, it is to be observed that a large number of physical & technical variables influence the performance of each biometric system that functions within the EU border and immigration data basis.[197]

4 EU border and immigration data bases

a) Schengen Information System (SIS) was the first and foremost centralized European Information system that was established for the purpose of controlling the external borders and facilitating cooperation between police authorities; it was made operable for the purpose of registering data of persons and

196 Belgian Privacy Commission (CBPL), Opinion N°17/2008 biometric data.
197 I. van der Ploeg and I. Sprenkels, *Migration and Machine-Readable Body* ..., Op. Cit, p. 76.

goods that should be refused entry into Schengen area without internal borders or that are searched for by one of the Schengen Member States, with the exception of the United Kingdom and Ireland, Bulgaria and Romania, but including Iceland, Norway and Switzerland. The SIS is the largest operational database related to police, judicial cooperation and external border control in Europe. Participating states provide entries and alerts on wanted and missing persons, lost and stolen property and entry bans. All third country nationals entering the EU, whether under visa obligation or not, are checked systematically in the SIS. Furthermore, according to article 94 (3) of Agreement Implementing the Schengen Convention (CISA) the information on persons stored in the Schengen Information System data base shall be no more than: surname and forenames, any aliases possibly entered separately; any specific objective physical characteristics not subject to change; first letter of second forename; date and place of birth; sex; nationality; whether the persons concerned are armed; whether the persons concerned are violent; reason for the alert; action to be taken. However, apart from its usefulness at that stage, SIS together with rapid development of the information technology as well as the necessity to expand the maximum capacity of the system of 18 member States in order to accommodate the 2004 enlargement, was gradually giving impetus to the digitalization of the EU external borders control. This phenomenon has found its expression in the second version of the Schengen Information System (SIS I) - SIS II. Namely, in 2006 the legislative measures on the establishment, operation and use of the second generation SIS were adopted under first and third pillars that reflected the dual nature of the SIS as a tool for migration control (under the EC Treaty covered by the first pillar) and criminal law enforcement (the former third pillar).[198] However, it was not until 9th April 2013 that SIS II became operational, after years of delays and cost overruns caused by technical obstacles in its development.[199]

SIS II, while compared with the previous one, had the ability to store new types of data, including biometric identifiers, and further integrate with new member states of the Union. This technology was, by means of the SIS II, at the disposal of a greater number of institutions (for example, by legal authorities, Europol[200]

198 Regulation (EC) 1987/2006, OJ 2006 L 381/4 ('SIS II Regulation') and Council Decision 2007/533/JHA, OJ 2007 L 205/63 ('SIS II Decision').

199 E. Brouwer, *Digital Borders and Real Rights*, Leiden Boston 2008, chapter 4: pp. 104–116.

200 Europol is established on the basis of Council Decision 2009/371/JHA, OJ 2009 L 121/37.

and the security services). In addition, all existing databases allowed for access by national law enforcement agencies for the prevention, detection, or investigation of terrorism or serious crimes. Specifically, new functionalities of the SIS II have transformed the database from a hit/no hit system into a ‚general search and intelligence tool'[201] system that consisted of: a) enhanced alerts on persons and objects; b) new categories of alerts: stolen aircrafts, boats, industrial equipment, securities, etc.; c) direct queries in the central system; d) linking of alerts on persons, objects & vehicles; e) European Arrest Warrant attached directly to alert for persons wanted for arrest, surrender or extradition; f) Information on misused identity preventing the misidentification. As far as the access to the SIS II database is concerned, it depends on the nature of the alert (criminal/non-criminal). Furthermore, Article 27 Reg. 1987/2006 grants access to the authorities responsible for identification of Third Country Nationals (TCN) for the purpose of: a) Border controls; b) Other Police and Custom checks. However, the right to access data entered in SIS II and the right to search such data directly may also be exercised by national judicial authorities, including those responsible for the initiation of public prosecutions in criminal proceedings and for judicial inquiries prior to charge, in the performance of their tasks, as provided for in national legislation, and by their coordinating authorities. In addition, the Counter-terrorism legislation (2004) provided for access to Europol and Eurojust, national judicial authorities, Visa and immigration authorities to information on stolen identity documents.

In December 2016 the European Commission presented a legislative package to improve the SIS from a technical point of view and to respond to the development of certain forms of serious crime, including terrorism. It consisted of three regulations concerning: a) establishment, operation and use the Schengen Information System in the field of police cooperation and judicial cooperation in criminal matters;[202] b) border checks[203] c) last but not least, Regulation on the use of the Schengen Information System for the return of the illegally staying

201 Regulation (EC)2424/2001, Recs 2 and 3. E Brouwer, ibidem, p. 106.

202 Regulation (EU) 2018/1862 of the European Parliament and of the Council of 28 November 2018 on the establishment, operation and use of the Schengen Information System (SIS) in the field of police cooperation and judicial cooperation in criminal matters, amending and repealing Council Decision 2007/533/JHA, and repealing Regulation (EC) No 1986/2006 of the European Parliament and of the Council and Commission Decision 2010/261/EU, at: https://data.consilium.europa.eu/doc/document/PE-36-2018-INIT/en/pdf (Accessed: March 2020)

203 Regulation on the establishment, operation and use of the Schengen Information System in the field of border checks, at: https://data.consilium.europa.eu/doc/document/PE-35-2018-INIT/en/pdf (Accessed: March 2020).

third-country nationals.[204] The new rules governing the Schengen Information System adopted by the Council on 19 November 2018 introduced additional alerts to the System: alerts issued for the purpose of inquiry checks, an intermediary step between discreet checks and specific checks, which allow for individuals to be interviewed; alerts on unknown suspects or wanted persons, which provide for the introduction into the SIS of fingerprints or palm prints discovered at the scenes of serious crimes or terrorist incidents and which are considered to belong to a perpetrator; preventive alerts for children at risk of parental abduction, as well as children and vulnerable persons who need to be prevented from travelling for their own protection (for example, where travel might lead to the risk of forced marriage, female genital mutilation, trafficking of human beings); alerts for the purpose of return, an alert in relation to return decisions issued to illegally staying third-country nationals, thereby improving the exchange of information in relation to return decisions. They also expand the list of objects for which alerts can be issued, including false documents and high-value identifiable objects , as well as IT equipment. In addition, the introduction of alerts in the SIS as regards entry bans for third-country nationals became compulsory. As far as the types of data to be processed within Schengen Information System are concerned, the regulations introduced the possibility of using facial images for identification purposes, in particular to ensure consistency in border control procedures. It was also allowed for the inclusion of a DNA profile to facilitate the identification of missing persons in cases where fingerprint data, photographs or facial images were not available or not suitable for identification. As regards access to data, Europol is due to be able to access all categories of data in the SIS and to exchange supplementary information with Member States SIRENE Bureaux. In addition, member states must inform Europol of any hits when a person is sought in relation to a terrorist offence. This would allow Europol's European Counter Terrorism Centre to check if there is any additional relevant information available in Europol's databases. It is worth to mention in this context that the European Border and Coast Guard Agency (Frontex), for the purposes set out in its mandate, is due to have access to the alert categories in SIS.[205]

204 This legal act is accessible at: https://data.consilium.europa.eu/doc/document/PE-34-2018-INIT/en/pdf (Accessed: March 2020).

205 Schengen Information System: Council adopts new rules to strengthen security in the EU, at: https://www.consilium.europa.eu/en/press/press-releases/2018/11/19/schengen-information-system-council-adopts-new-rules-to-strengthen-security-in-the-eu/ (Accessed: March 2020).

b) EURODAC allows Member States to determine whether a Third Country National (TCN) has previously claimed asylum in another Member State (MS) or has entered Schengen irregularly through another MS. This database is a tool for facilitating the application of the Dublin Regulation on asylum matters, which registers and compares fingerprints of asylum seekers.[206] Member states have agreed to collect fingerprints of each TCN above 14 years of age who applies for asylum in their territory or who is apprehended when irregularly crossing their external border. Where hits reveal that an asylum seeker has already applied for asylum or that she/he entered the territory irregularly in another MS, the individual can, in accordance with the Dublin Regulation, be transferred to the state in question.[207] Member states can also fingerprint aliens found illegally staying in their territory in order to check whether they have applied for asylum. An Automated Fingerprint Identification System (AFIS) receives data and transmits positive and negative replies to the National Access Points (NAPs). In case of a hit, an additional exchange of data takes place through the DubliNet system. The Members States concerned can then exchange further personal data different from the Eurodac data: name, date of birth, nationality and photo, particulars of family members and in certain cases addresses. It is also crucial to note that the revised EURODAC Regulation[208] allowed law enforcement access to the EU database of the fingerprints of asylum seekers under strictly limited circumstances in order to prevent, detect or investigate the most serious crimes, such as murder, and terrorism. To summarize, the EURODAC stored data elong to three categories of applicants: 1) Asylum seekers of at least 14 years of age; 2) Aliens apprehended in connection with the irregular crossing of an external border; and 3) Aliens found illegally present in a Member State.

On 4 May 2016, however, the European Commission presented proposals to reform the Common European Asylum System (CEAS)[209] among them

206 Regulation (EU) 603/2013, OJ 2013 L 180/1.

207 See, for example, COM 2007 299 final.

208 Regulation (EC) 604/2013 L 180/31 (recast, ‚Dublin III Regulation') at: https://eur-lex.europa.eu/legal-content/EN/TXT/PDF/?uri=CELEX:32013R0604&from=EN (Accessed: March 2020).

209 Communication from the European Commission to the European Parliament and the Council Towards a reform of the Common European Asylum System and enhancing legal avenues to Europe, Brussels, 6.4.2016 COM(2016) 197 final, at: https://ec.europa.eu/home-affairs/sites/homeaffairs/files/what-we-do/policies/european-agenda-migration/proposal-implementation-package/docs/20160406/

the review of the Eurodac Regulation for fingerprinting migrants. The proposal is due to extend the scope of the Eurodac Regulation to include the possibility for Member States to store and search data belonging to third-country nationals or stateless persons who are not applicants for international protection and found irregularly staying in the EU, so that they can be identified for return and readmission purposes. It will also allow MS to store more personal data in Eurodac, such as names, dates of birth, nationalities, identity details or travel documents, and facial images of individuals. Increasing the information in the system will allow immigration and asylum authorities to identify an irregular third-country national or asylum applicant easily without having to request the information from another Member State separately, as is currently the case. Law enforcement authorities and Europol will continue to be able to search Eurodac to prevent, detect or investigate a serious crime or terrorist offence. What is more, the new proposal permits Member States to introduce sanctions, in accordance with their national law, for those individuals who refuse to comply with the fingerprinting procedure. It is up to the Member State to decide the form of penalties or sanctions to be introduced, as long as it does not breach the fundamental rights of the individual concerned. It is to be acknowledged, however, that the use of detention or any form of coercion should only be used as a means of last resort. Furthermore, in his 2017 State of the Union Letter of Intent the Commission president Juncker called upon the EUropean Parliament (EP) and the Council to adopt the CEAS proposals by the end of 2018. Ahead of the December 2018 European Council, the Commission repeated its call on Member States and the European Parliament to adopt the outstanding reform proposals, including the Eurodac Regulation, even before an agreement is achieved on the Dublin Regulation. Consequently, the proposal was assigned to the EP Civil Liberties, Justice and Home Affairs Committee which adopted the report on 30 May 2017 by 35 votes to 10 with 8 abstentions and received a mandate for negotiations with the Council. The Committee held that Europol should have direct access to the EURODAC database holding fingerprints of asylum seekers. In addition to fingerprints, also facial images, names and ID-numbers should be stored in EURODAC, if available. In order to improve safety of refugee minors, children from the age of six should be fingerprinted to facilitate tracking and family reunifications.

---

towards_a_reform_of_the_common_european_asylum_system_and_enhancing_legal_avenues_to_europe_-_20160406_en.pdf (Accessed: March 2020).

The date of a vote in the Civil Liberties Committee depends on the final negotiations on the rest of the asylum package.

As a result, trilogues (Parliament, the Council and the Commission, are ongoing since September 2017. While common ground was found on most provisions of the recast Regulation,[210] the Council and the EP continued to have divergent views on the length of the data storage period for asylum seekers. During the term of the Estonian Presidency, it has been agreed that the main database for asylum seekers fingerprints will be updated and law enforcement will be granted access. Certain open issues remain unresolved: data retention periods and information rights of data subjects. The file was then handed over to the Bulgarian Presidency. In a provisional agreement, reached on 19 June 2018, the Parliament and the Council have agreed: to store in addition to fingerprints, the facial images and alphanumeric data of asylum seekers and irregular migrants; to lower the age for obtaining fingerprints and facial images of minors from 14 to 6 years; Europol will be able to enquire the database more efficiently; and persons falling under the Union or national resettlement schemes would also be registered. The Austrian Presidency continued work at a technical level on the resettlement related provisions in the Eurodac Regulation. The European Council assessed the progress achieved at its meeting on 18 October 2018 and called for efforts to conclude the reform of the CEAS as soon as possible. Under the Romanian Presidency, however, in the framework of an informal meeting of justice and home affairs ministers (6-8 February 2019) to discuss migration and asylum, among other issues, the Member States did not give a mandate to the presidency to continue trilogues with the European Parliament due to the 'package approach' on the asylum-related files.

c) The Visa Information System was established on the basis of comprehensive legal framework that consists of: a) Council Decision 2004/512/EC of 8 June 2004 established the VIS as a system for exchanging visa data between Member States; b) Regulation (EC) No 767/2008 of 9 July 2008 laid down the VIS's purpose, functionalities and responsibilities and laid down the conditions and procedures for the exchange of visa data between Member States to facilitate the examination of visa applications and related decisions; and c) Regulation (EC) No 810/2009 of 13 July 2009 (the Visa Code) set out

210 https://www.europarl.europa.eu/legislative-train/theme-towards-a-new-policy-on-migration/file-jd-recast-eurodac-regulation (Accessed: March 2020)

the rules on the registration of biometric identifiers in the VIS. The above described legal architecture provided for an evaluation of the implementation of the VIS Regulation and of the VIS founding Decision, as well as of the use of VIS by law enforcement authorities on the basis of the VIS Law Enforcement Access (LEA) Decision; and the use of biometrics in the visa application procedure on the basis of the Visa Code. This information system collects data of all visa applicants and serves to facilitate the work of Member States' consular services and visa authorities. In other words, its main purpose is, on entry, to verify the authenticity of the visa and the identity of its holder. VIS is a Schengen instrument and is based on a centralized architecture. It consists of a central information system, the Central Visa Information System (CS-VIS), of an interface in each Member State, the National Interfaces (NI-VIS) that provide the connection to the relevant central national authorities of the respective Member States, and of a communication infrastructure between the Central Visa Information System and the National Interfaces. In addition to personal information on third country visa holders, VIS also collects biometric data-facial images and 10 fingerprints-and is estimated to become the world's largest biometric database, potentially holding 70 million records. As a result, the VIS allows competent authorities to access the data in the VIS for the identification of a third country national and to see if they are legally present. The same is allowed for *any person* who may not be legally present.[211] The Commission's proposal for the Entry/Exit System duplicates these provisions in Articles 18 and 19.[212]

To conclude, the three analyzed above databases do contain vast amount of data, mostly on third country nationals. Hence, on December 31 2016 there were in total 70,827,959 alerts in SIS II.[213] Furthermore, statistics published by the European Commission show that 15.2 million applications for short-stay

211 Arts 19 and 20 VIS Regulation.

212 Proposal for the Regulation of the European Parliament and of the Council establishing an Entry/Exit System (EES) to register entry and exit data and refusal of entry data of third country nationals crossing the external borders of the Member States of the European Union and determining the conditions for access to the EES for law enforcement purposes and amending Regulation (EC) No 767/2008 and Regulation (EU) No 1077/2011, at: https://ec.europa.eu/home-affairs/sites/homeaffairs/files/what-we-do/policies/securing-eu-borders/legal-documents/docs/20160406/regulation_proposal_entryexit_system_borders_package_en.pdf (Accessed: January 2020).

213 SIS II - 2016 Statistics, eu-LISA, at:http://www.eulisa.europa.eu/Publications/Reports/SIS%20II%20-%20Statistics%202016.pdf (Accessed: January 2018).

visas were lodged at Schengen States' consulates in 2016, resulting in 14 million issued visas[214]; as far as the Eurodac Information System is concerned, in 2016 it processed: over 1,000,000 fingerprints of applicants for international protection aged 14 or more, more than 370,000 fingerprints of persons aged 14 or older, apprehended when irregularly crossing the external border of a Member State, over 252,000 fingerprints of persons aged 14 or older, apprehended illegally present on the territory of a Member State.[215]

(d) Entry/Exits System: part of the same Border Package (COM 2008 69) as the two systems (Automated Border Crossing; Registered Traveler System) to be announced, in the first place, in the European Commission's (EC) Communication of February 2008; secondly, officially proposed as the ‚Smart Borders Package' in February 2013. Furthermore, on 6 April 2016, the Commission adopted a legislative package which included a Regulation for the establishment of an Entry/Exit System and an essentially consequential amendment to the Schengen Borders Code to integrate the technical changes needed. To conclude, on 20 November 2017 the Council adopted the regulation for an entry-exit system and the regulation amending the Schengen border code in relation to the Entry-Exit System. This system envisions registering the entry and exit of third country nationals (with or without visa) in order to avoid overstayers. The system applies to third country nationals admitted for a short stay (up to three months), covering both those that are subject to the visa requirement and those that are not. Entry/Exit System, on the contrary to stamping passports of third country nationals upon entry into and exit from Schengen area which is considered a rather unreliable method of establishing overstay[216], records information on the time and place of entry, biometric identifiers (face, fingerprints), the length of authorized stay, and automatically transmit alerts directly to the authorities, should a person be identified as an 'overstayer'. The above-mentioned data related to third country nationals are to be kept for border management purposes in a central database connected to national uniform interfaces for a period of five years for overstayers and three years for others. Furthermore, the Entry/Exit Regulation provides

214 Visa statistics: Schengen States receive 15.2 million applications for short-stay visas in 2016, at: https://ec.europa.eu/home-affairs/news/visa-statistics-schengen-states-receive-152-million-applications-short-stay-visas-2016_en (Accessed: January 2018).

215 Eurodac Annual Statistics April 2017, in: http://www.statewatch.org/news/2017/jun/eu-elisa-eurodac-stats-prel.pdf, (Accessed: January 2018).

216 Art. 10 Schengen Border Code. Stamps may be illegible or visa applicants may simply require new passport to hide previous overstay.

access to information stored in the System to border authorities, visa authorities and the authorities within the member states competent to check if a third country national fulfills the conditions of entry or stay. What is more, data collection by the Entry-Exit System are at the disposal of the designated authorities and Europol, to prevent, detect and investigate terrorist offenses or other serious crimes, according to conditions as set out in the regulation. To conclude, it is worth to emphasize that the regulation also provides interoperability between the Entry-Exit System and the Visa Information System (VIS) for those third country nationals who require a visa to cross the EU external border, which will ensure rapidity and efficiency at the border checks.

e) Automated Border Control System (ABC): The purpose of it is to minimize border checks for EU citizens. The idea, proposed in the EU Commission's Border Package (COM 2008 69), is connected to the introduction of European biometric passports, which are already being issued by EU member states and should be possessed by all EU citizens by 2019. The system is expected to work on a 'no enrollment' principle and will contain two biometric identifiers—face and, with the second generation, also fingerprints—which the system can read and check against EU and national databases at automated border gates. Technically speaking, ABC system involves the use of: a) physical barriers (single-door or double door e-Gates); b) full-page e-Passport readers: optical recognition of the biographic data page, the machine-readable zone (MRZ) and a radio frequency (RF) reader for communication with the chip; c) monitor displaying instructions; d) biometric capture device; e) system management hardware and software.[217]

(f) Registered Travelers System was proposed in the same Border Package (COM 2008 69) as the Automated Border Crossings. The automated gates, mentioned above, are also expected to be used by certain groups of pre-enrolled, 'low risk', third country nationals, who have been granted registered traveler status, despite the fact that they may be subject to visa requirements. Individuals could be granted registered traveler status after appropriate screening on the basis of common vetting criteria. To become a low-risk traveler, the third country national would need to have previously traveled to the EU and stayed for a while, which would give them a reliable travel history. Other criteria include proof of sufficient means of subsistence, absence of threat to public order, and holding a biometric passport.

---

217 „Best Practice Operational Guidelines for Automated Border Control (ABC) Systems", at: https://frontex.europa.eu/assets/Publications/Research/Best_Practice_Operational_Guidelines_for_Automated_Border_Control.pdf (Accessed: March 2020)

g) EU-lisa -the European Agency for the operational management of large-scale IT systems in the area of freedom, security and justice was established by Regulation (EU) No 1077/2011 of the European Parliament and of the Council of 25 October 2011 (OJ L 286, 01.11.2011, p. 1) which entered into force on 21 November 2011. The Regulation provided that the Agency will take up its main responsibilities from 1 December 2012. Bearing in mind the strategic goal of guaranteeing interoperability between the already established EU data systems within the field of EU border and immigration control, the main challenge for the Agency may be to leverage the complexity and capabilities of the second generation Schengen Information System (SIS II), the Visa Information System (VIS) and EURODAC under management. It is worth to mention in this context that EU-LISA is mandated to ensure that it applies the highest levels of information security and data protection to the information entrusted to it, guaranteeing that personal information is treated fairly, lawfully and correctly, in full compliance with the relevant data protection principles and legislation in force. On 29 June 2017, following an evaluation of the agency, as well as recent developments in the fields of migration and security, the Commission presented a proposal for a new legal mandate for eu-LISA so that it is better equipped to meet current and future challenges in the area of freedom, security and justice. On 21 November 2018, the new establishing regulation of eu-LISA was published in the Official Journal of the European Union; consequently, it entered into force on 11 December 2018. The reinforced Agency is due to develop and manage large-scale EU information systems such as the Entry/Exit System (EES), the European Travel Information and Authorisation System (ETIAS) and the upgraded European Criminal Records Information System (ECRIS-TCN); upgrade and maintain existing systems, such as the Schengen Information System (SIS), the Visa Information System (VIS) and Eurodac, for which it is already responsible; support Member States by providing greater ad-hoc technical and operational support to them.
h) European Border Surveillance System (Eurosur): EUROSUR aims to provide a common technical framework for the external border surveillance on the southern Mediterranean and eastern borders of the EU. It seeks to integrate the numerous national surveillance systems and to use the collected information in a more coherent manner, and share more expensive surveillance tools such as satellites and unmanned aerial vehicles (UAVs) (COM 2008 68 final). It is designed as a decentralized system of existing systems, which was established gradually in three phases (SEC 2009 1265 final): 1) Interlinking and streamlining existing surveillance systems and mechanisms at Member States level; 2) Development and implementation of common tools and applications for

border surveillance at EU level; 3) Creation of a common information sharing environment for the EU maritime domain. To conclude the European Border Surveillance System (Eurosur) became operable on the October 22, 2013.[218].

I) European Travel Information and Authorization System (ETIAS) - is due to collect information from visa free third country nationals, and ensure interoperability in terms of information and technological infrastructure with the EES and other EU information systems. ETIAS gathers information on these travelers prior to the start of their travel, to allow for advance processing. As a result, travelers cross the borders smoothly. The legal procedures to pass the ETIAS have started in 2016, and the system is expected to be in place by 2022.

To conclude this descriptive part, there is no doubt that the increasing number of information systems that have been or are being established to control migration flow reveals the ambition to set up one integrated European Union information system.[219] However, due to technical obstacles the above-mentioned ambitions have to be limited to the second best solution; namely, realizing synergy by promoting interoperability between the current and future information systems. In addition, this idea has already found its expression in the decision to establish EU-lisa, the agency whose main activity focuses on the management of the second generation Schengen Information Systems (SIS II), the Visa Information System (VIS) and EURODAC). The argument for harmonizing and integrating the information systems is economic in nature; the synergy and interoperability between them promises less costs, increased efficacy and effectiveness. On the other hand, Europe's effort to make the migration flow visible for the purpose of tracing illegal immigrants has been disputed by many pointing at risks of fundamental rights infringements. Cyber-fortress Europe by means of advanced technology not only does not stop illegal immigrants, but also indirectly leaves them no other choice than pursuing even more dangerous routes, causing fatalities among them.[220]

---

218 Regulation (EU) No 1052/2013 of the European parliament and of the Council of 22 October 2013 establishing the European Border Surveillance System (Eurosur), at: https://eur-lex.europa.eu/legal-content/EN/TXT/HTML/?uri=CELEX:32013R1052&from=EN#d1e1501-11-1 (Accessed: January 2020).

219 Bigo D. – Carerra S. – Gonzalez G. – Fuster E. –Guild P. – de Hert P. – Jeandesboz J.–Papaconstantinou V., T*owards a New EU Legal Framework for Data Protection and Privacy Challenges, Principles and the Role of the European Parliament,* European Parliament Study 2011, pp. 122–124.

220 Besters M. Brom F.W.A., *Greedy Information Technology: the digitalization of the European migration policy*, 2010, "European Journal of Migration and Law", Volume 12, Issue 4, 2010, pp. 455 – 470.

III Possible risks of fundamental rights infringements posed by the digitalization of the EU immigration and asylum policy

1 Introduction

While technology has been embraced without much debate as a core component of the EU's Area of Freedom Security and Justice (AFSJ) policies, it is crucial to ask what are the legal boundaries in the use of databases and biometrics in border surveillance and migration policy? This is explicitly evidenced in the June 2008 report from the Future Group on European home affairs, which considered that "[d]atabases and new technologies would play a central role in further developing Home Affairs policies [...] Even if technology can never completely replace the human factor, technological progress can provide the necessary means to optimize mobility, security and privacy simultaneously"[221]. In this context, it is worth to mention that the European Parliament (EP) focused in its study on data protection challenges posed by the increased processing (ongoing or envisaged) of personal data for law-enforcement purposes. Among these were mentioned: 1) the tendency to generalize of data processing meaning the shift towards dataveillance, pro-activity and profiling; 2) putting limitation purpose referring to the „life of data" in EU data-systems-the key principle of data protection at risk by means of the proliferation of data-systems and, as a result, tendency to consider technology as one-size-fits-all solution[222]. The latter was also shared by the European Data Protection Supervisor (EDPS) who emphasized that „[far] reaching proposals regarding large-scale IT systems has been 'programme-driven' rather than 'evidence-driven'"[223]; in other words, the main stimulus originated from some Member States, the European Commission as well as private sector, rather than was caused by the

221 Report of the High Level Advisory Group on Future of European Home Affairs Policy: (2008), at: http://register.consilium.europa.eu/doc/srv?l=EN&f=ST%20 11657 %202008 %20INIT, p. 11. (Accessed: March 2018).

222 Bigo D. – Carrera S. – Gonzalez G. – Fuster G. – Guild E. – de Hert P. – Jeandesboz J. – Papakonstantinou V. (2011): *Towards a New EU Legal Framework for Data Protection and Privacy Challenges, Principles and the Role of the European Parliament*, European Parliament Study, pp. 40–48.

223 Hustinx P. (2008): Round Table: *"Liberty and Security in Integrated Management of EU Borders"*, pp. 1–5.

demonstrated need. It is worth to underline that already in 2006 the EDPS had regretted that the European Commission's proposal for a regulation on SIS II had not been accompanied by an impact assessment study, on the argument that the first version of SIS was already in place. Furthermore, enormous pace at which large-scale IT systems proposals were tabled made it extremely difficult for stakeholders (European and national Parliaments, Data Protection Authorities (DPAs) including EDPS as well as civil society) to have a full overview. What is more, the notion that all these initiatives occured without the clear policy direction was shared by the Conference of European DPAs, which called upon the European institutions and the Member States to "first evaluate whether already existing legal measures were implemented and executed in an effective way", establishing the principle that a "new proposal should have been put forward only when clear evidence was available to support new actions"[224]. The impact of such practices on fundamental freedoms should not be underestimated. Especially that the smart borders initiative is likely to entail the creation of at least one centralized EU database containing biometric data, to which a currently unknown number of actors could have access; Eurosur, on the other hand, is said not to gather large amounts of personal or biometric data or include a central database[225]. It focuses, according to the language of the European Commission, on the surveillance of specific geographical areas (borders) and specific activities (illegal border crossings). Furthermore, according to the Commission, „the situational pictures will as a general rule not involve personal data but rather the exchange of information on incidents and depersonalized objects, such as the detection and tracking of vessels". However, bearing in mind the existence of Eurosur in the broader Common Information Sharing Environment which has an enormous potential for exchanging of personal data with third states and agencies, this database should be the cause of concern in the future in terms of fundamental rights violations (privacy rights). Not to mention, that smart border initiative as well as Eurosur can also have an indirect negative impact on the right to asylum.

Against the backdrop of the above described developments concerning migration technology, such standards as the right to privacy, the principle of non-discrimination as well as the two substantive standards relating to data protection law, namely: the purpose limitation principle, in other words requirement

224 *Towards a New Legal Framework for Data Protection and Privacy,* (2006/C 91/11).

225 Tzanou M., *The EU as an emerging 'Surveillance Society': The function creep case study and challenges to privacy and data protection*, in: "Vienna Online Journal on International Constitutional Law", 2010, pp. 407–427; see also: K. AAS, '*Crimmigrant' bodies and bona fide travelers: Surveillance, citizenship and global governance*', in: „Theoretical Crimminology", Volume: 15 issue: 3, 2011, pp. 331–346.

of necessity, and the prohibition on automated decision-making are either frequently neglected or their importance is all too easily trivialized[226]. Furthermore, the phenomenon of applying migration technology at all costs, is, according to Evelien Brouwer, reinforced by certain trends in nowadays information policy; in the first place, the new technological advances in gathering data on a large scale by means of central data bases and the application of Radio-Frequency Identification (RFID) chips and biometrics have enabled the ever closer and more systematic tracking of individuals' movements. Similar doubts were to be heard on the other side of the Atlantic where American Civil Liberties Union Foundation questioned acquisition and use by the public authorities of the marketed by Amazon facial recognition technology[227]. In this context, the question arises whether this new forms of monitoring of individuals can be reconciled with the rights to private life and protection of personal data as protected in Article 8 of the European Convention on Human Rights (ECHR), Council of Europe Convention 108 (in future its modernized version-108+, once it is ratified by the EU Member States) for the Protection of Individuals with regard to Automatic Processing of Personal Data; EU Human Rights Charter: articles 7 and 8 respectively or amendments to the Constitution of the United States of America. Secondly, information systems are thought by the policy makers to be used for multiple purposes; in other words, data collected for one specific goal are foreseen to be used for other objectives as well. This trend can be illustrated by the decision[228] to grant law-enforcement authorities access to data stored into Eurodac. Paradoxically, this originally established for the purpose of determining

226 E. Brouwer, *Legal Boundaries and the Use of Migration Technology*, in: „Migration and the New Technological Borders of Europe", H. Dijstelbloem and A. Meijer (Eds.), Palgrave Macmillian, New York 2011, p. 134.

227 According to an article featured at Amazon's website and authored by the representative of the Sheriff's Office titled „Using Amazon Rekognition to Identify Persons of Interest for Law Enforcement" by Chris Adzima (AWS AI Blog), June15, 2017, the sheriff's Office built a database using Rekognition and populated it with at least 300,00 mugshot photos, at: https://aws.amazon.com/blogs/ai/using-amazon-rekognition-to-identify-persons-of-interest-for-law-enforcement/, (Accessed: February 2019).

228 Regulation (EU) No 603/2013 of the European Parliament and of the Council of 26 June 2013 on the establishment of ·Eurodac· for the comparison of fingerprints for the effective application of Regulation (EU) No 604/2013 establishing the criteria and mechanisms for determining the Member State responsible for examining an application for international protection lodged in one of the Member States by a third-country national or a stateless person and on requests for the comparison with Eurodac data by Member States' law enforcement authorities and Europol for law

which state is responsible for an asylum application data base, became a source of knowledge for European Police Office (Europol)[229] while performing its tasks in the field of cross-border crime investigation; Thirdly, government agencies increasingly act automatically; on the basis of information from a range of databases, irrespective of the origin of these data. An obvious example here is the Schengen Information System (SIS) based on reciprocal recognition of decisions made at national level (and recorded within it) by the authorities of the Schengen member countries. Fourthly, one may observe that the usage of profiling - activity that leads to identification of the characteristics of a specific target group by means of comparing a range of information sources - allows - on the one hand - to apply specific measures to particular groups and as a result monitor them more efficiently - on the other-however, the selection process based on information concerning race, origin, or nationality, raises questions concerning its conformity with the non-discrimination principle enshrined in international law[230].

2 Digitalization of the EU migration policy versus fundamental rights standards

The fundamental rights risks connected with the digitalization of the European Migration and Refugee Policy are to be analyzed here on the basis of some exemplary judgments of the European Court of Human Rights (Strasbourg), Court of Justice of the European Union (Luxembourg) as well Member States judicial bodies that refer to the systematic collection and large-scale storage of data, including biometrics. In this context, it is necessary to explain two European legal orders whose jurisprudence does affect migration policy of the European Union and its member states.

In the first place, it is worth to mention that European Union and its institutions are not directly bound by the European Convention on Human Rights (ECHR) as such, still less by the case-law of the European Court of Human Rights (ECtHR). However, Article 6 § 3 of the Treaty on European Union refers to the ECHR as part of the principles of Community law. This is reflected in the case-law of the Court of Justice and the General Court of the European Union; they regularly refer to the ECHR and the Strasbourg case-law in their judgments but apply them

---

enforcement purposes, and amending Regulation (EU) No 1077/2011 establishing a European Agency for the operational management of large-scale IT systems in the area of freedom, security and justice.

229 OJ L 121, 15.5.2009, p. 37.

230 E. Brouwer, *Legal Boundaries and the Use of Migration Technology*, in: „Migration and the New Technological Borders ...", Op. Cit., pp. 135–136.

indirectly, as part of the general principles of the Union's law. Secondly, although the rights enshrined in the ECHR are not legally binding on the EU and its institutions (Commission, Council, European Parliament, Court of Justice, etc.), they do apply to the European Union member States, even when the latter are applying or implementing EU law. These circumstances may lead to the legal uncertainty and confusion about who, ultimately, is responsible for any breaches of ECHR rights. In addition, it is crucial to note that all 27 EU Member Countries are parties to the European Convention on Human Rights upon which the judgments of the above-mentioned court are issued. At the same time, however, it is the Charter of Fundamental Rights that is legally binding on the European Union and its member states while implementing EU law. In these circumstances the European Union jurisprudence applies many provisions of the Charter that are based on, but not identical to the European Convention of Human Rights Protection. To conclude, in order to avoid future contradictions in the case-law of - on the one hand- European Court of Human Rights and- on the other- the European Union Court of Justice, and, as a result, achieve a coherent system of fundamental rights' protection across Europe, the Lisbon Treaty stated that: „The Union shall accede to the European Convention for the Protection of Human Rights and Fundamental Freedoms. Such accession shall not affect the Union's competences as defined in the Treaties".

Let us now dwell on the structure of the European Convention on Human Right's article 8-*Right to respect for private and family life,* which stipulates that: "1. Everyone has the right to respect for his private and family life, his home and his correspondence; 2. There shall be no interference by a public authority with the exercise of this right except such as is in accordance with the law and is necessary in a democratic society in the interests of national security, public safety or the economic well-being of the country, for the prevention of disorder or crime, for the protection of health or morals, or for the protection of the rights and freedoms of others." Summarizing, in its first paragraph, Article 8 of the ECHR establishes the existence of a series of rights: a right to respect for private life, a right to family life, a right to inviolability of the home, and a right to confidentiality of correspondence. The ECtHR however often mentions these rights in conjunction with each other, for instance by referring jointly to the right to respect for private and family life, or to respect for private life and confidentiality of correspondence in combination. The second paragraph of Article 8 of the ECHR details the requirements of lawful interferences by public authorities with the described rights, which need to be 'in accordance with law' and 'necessary in a democratic society', and to pursue one of the explicitly enumerated aims. When adjudicating on Article 8 of the ECHR, the European Court of Human Rights (ECtHR) typically follows a two-step approach: first, it examines whether the issue at stake shall be regarded as an interference with any of the rights mentioned; second, it appraises whether the interference is to be considered legitimate or not. It is crucial to emphasize in this respect that the European Court of Human Rights has given to the wording of Article 8(1) of the European Convention of Human Rights a wide, generous interpretation[231], as an element of its general approach of regarding the ECHR as a living instrument to be interpreted each time in light of 'present- day conditions'.[232] This broad reading has allowed the Strasbourg Court to consider as interferences with the rights enshrined in the article 8 of the Convention measures related to the processing of data about individuals, and, vice versa. As a result, adjudication on this kind of measures has contributed to the progressive extension of ECtHR's construal of Article 8. As evidenced by the *Niemietz* ruling[233] the Court stressed that the right to respect for private life exemplified in the Article 8 of the ECHR includes to a certain degree the right for individuals to develop relationships with other human beings.[234] Furthermore, it was declared by the Court that it regarded as both impossible and unnecessary to attempt to define the notion of private life, but that in any case it would be too restrictive to limit the notion to an 'inner cycle' in which the individual may live his own personal life as he chooses excluding entirely the outside world. Hence, respect for private life must also comprise to a certain degree the right to establish and develop relationships with other human beings.[235] The case concerned the search of a lawyer's office in the context of criminal proceedings against a third party, raising the issue of the protection granted to profession or business activities. During the search, various cabinets and files had been examined, but no relevant documents had been found. In its judgment, the ECtHR made it clear that there was no reason of principle why the notion of private life should be taken to exclude professional or business activities, since it is precisely in the course of their working lives that the majority of people have a significant opportunity to develop relationships with others.[236] In addition, the

---

231 Nardell, Gordon Q. C., *Levelling up: Data privacy and the European Court of Human Rights* in: *Data protection in a profiled world*, eds. Serge Gutwirth, Yves Poullet, and Paul De Hert, Dordrecht: Springer 2014, p. 46.

232 *Tyrer v United Kingdom* [1978] Series A No. 26, App. No. 5856/72.

233 *Niemietz v Germany* [1992] Series A No. 251-B, App. No 13710/88.

234 *Niemietz* § 29. See also: (Sudre 2005, p. 402). This broad conception was partly based in a special use of the expression 'right to respect for private and family life' as referring to a nebulous notion that covers the right to develop interpersonal relations (Sudre 2005, pp. 403–404).

235 *Niemietz* § 29.

236 Ibid.

Court noted, in some cases it is not even possible to clearly distinguish which activities are part of a professional or business life, and which are not.[237] The ECtHR has since then regularly emphasized the wideness of the notion of private life, portraying it as a term 'not susceptible to exhaustive definition'.[238]

The 1987 *Leander* judgment[239] is said to be the cornerstone of the Strasbourg's case law on the processing of information about individuals, where the Court declared that the mere storing by the police of information relating to the private life of an individual amounts to an interference with the right to respect for private life,[240] and that this is so independently of the possible subsequent use of the data in question.[241] The case concerned a Swedish carpenter who wished to work at a museum adjacent to a restricted military security zone, but, after a personnel control procedure, and seemingly on the basis of a secret police file, was refused the job. In *Leander*, the ECtHR merely declared that it was uncontested that the data at stake in the particular case related to the private life of the individual,[242] which was true, because precisely one of the concerns raised by the applicant was that he had not been able to access the content of the secret file,[243] and this impossibility to access the data prevented any contestation regarding their nature. The Court, however, critically failed to explain in what was grounded such qualification of data as relating to somebody's private life[244]. Furthermore, it is to be acknowledged that *Leander* opened up the question of whether the category of 'information relating to private life' the mere storage of which can amount to an interference with Article 8 of the ECHR corresponded or not to the category of 'personal data' recognized in Convention 108, which covers any automated

237 Ibid.

238 *Bensaid v United Kingdom* [2001] RJD 2001-I, App. No. 44599/98, § 47.

239 *Leander v Sweden* [1987] Series A No. 116, App. No. 9248/81. See also: (Peers 2006, p. 507).

240 *Leander* § 48.

241 In *Leander*, the ECtHR was additionally concerned with the release of information.

242 *Leander* § 48.

243 De Schutter, Olivier. 2001. Vie privée et protection de l'individu vis-à-vis des traitements de données à caractère personnel. *Revue trimestrielle des droits de l'homme, in: "Revue trimestrielle des droits de l'homme"* - no. 45, p. 137–183 (2001), *p.153*; See also: De Hert, Paul, and Serge Gutwirth. 2013. *Anthologie de la vie privée: Compilation d'articles, de législation et de jurisprudence concernant la protection de la vie privée et des données à caractère personnel pour la Belgique jusque 1998*. Bruxelles: Academic and Scientific Publishers (ASP) & Commission Protection de la Vie Privée.

244 Gonzalez Fuster G., *The Emergence of Personal Data Protection as a Fundamental Rights of the EU* , Springer 2014, pp. 95–107.

processing of personal data, including their storage. It is worth to mention in this context that the Convention 108 applies to personal data qualified as pertaining to 'special categor(ies)' of data, such as personal data 'revealing racial origin, political opinions or religious or other beliefs, as well as personal data concerning health or sexual life', or relating to criminal convictions,[245] but also, generally, to data not falling under any of such categories, which are nonetheless 'personal' data, defined as any information relating to an identified or identifiable individual.[246] The issue whether the Court should rely or not on the provisions of Convention 108 had already been touched upon in the *Malone* judgment of 1984, in relation to the monitoring of telephone communications by the police, within the context of criminal investigations, through a technique called 'metering', and the related storage of information.[247] In *Malone*, it was concluded by the Court that there had been a violation of Article 8 of the ECHR in connection with these practices, but without explicitly referring to Convention 108. The judgment was however accompanied by the concurring opinion, signed by Judge Pettiti, in whose view it was impossible to isolate the issue of the interception of communications from the issue of data banks, because interceptions give rise to storing of the information obtained; in this context, Judge Pettiti referred to the principles established by Convention 108 as criteria relevant to assess whether or not a measure constitutes a violation of Article 8 of the ECHR.

---

245 The article 6 of the revised Convention, named afterwards as Convention 108 + reads as follows: 1. The processing of:–genetic data;–personal data relating to offences, criminal proceedings and convictions, and related security measures;–biometric data uniquely identifying a person; –personal data for the information they reveal relating to racial or ethnic origin, political opinions, trade-union membership, religious or other beliefs, health or sexual life, shall only be allowed where appropriate safeguards are enshrined in law, complementing those of this Convention; 2. Such safeguards shall guard against the risks that the processing of sensitive data may present for the interests, rights and fundamental freedoms of the data subject, notably a risk of discrimination.

246 Ibid. Article 2(a).

247 *Malone v the United Kingdom* [1984] Series A No. 82, App. No. 8691/79. Concerning 'metering', the Court took note of the fact that a meter check printer registers information that a supplier of a telephone service may in principle legitimately obtain, and that metering is therefore to be distinguished from interception of communications. The Court did not accept, however, that the use of data obtained from metering cannot give rise to an issue under Article 8 of the ECHR, as the records of metering contain information that is an integral element in the communications made by telephone. Consequently, release of that information to the police without the consent of the subscriber also amounts, in the opinion of the Court, to an interference with a right guaranteed by Article 8 of the ECHR (§ 84).

The lawful dilemma, whether in the expression information 'relating to the private life' of individuals the adjective private shall be read as opposed to public, or not, was discussed on the forum of European jurisprudence in the context of the *Friedl* case.[248] In 1994, the Commission of Human Rights looked into the case of an Austrian citizen who had participated in a demonstration to draw attention to the plight of the homeless. The police had taken pictures of him and stored them. The Commission of Human Rights noting that: a) there had been no intrusion of the 'inner circle' of the applicant's private life in the sense that he was not at home when the pictures were taken; b) the photographs were related to the public event, he was attending freely; c) they were taken to record the sanitary conditions of the demonstration;[249] d) no names were noted on the pictures, with participants remaining unidentified; e) no personal data or images had been entered into a data processing system,[250] concluded that the measure did not amount to an interference with Article 8 of the ECHR.[251] It has been, however, not asserted that any of these criteria excluded by itself the possible qualification of the measure as an interference with the right to respect for private life.

In 2000, the ECtHR put forward that the category of information 'relating to private life' (the storage of which can amount to an interference with the right protected by Article 8 of the ECHR) shall be understood in line with its broad reading of the notion of private life, which, it argued, corresponded also to the view sustained by Convention 108. In *Amann*,[252] the Court indeed recalled the principle established in *Niemietz* according to which there is no reason in principle to justify excluding activities of a professional or business nature from the notion of private life,[253] and maintained that this broad interpretation corresponds with that of Convention 108.[254] The *Amann* case concerned a seller of depilatory appliances, who once received a telephone call from the Soviet embassy in Berne for the order of a machine called Perma Tweez. The call was intercepted by the public prosecutor's office, who requested the intelligence service to draw up a file about the seller. Recalling its *Leander* case law, and after connecting it to *Niemietz* and Convention 108, the Court concluded

248 Commission (Plenary) *Friedl v Austria* [1994] RJD 31.

249 Ibid. § 49.

250 Ibid. § 50.

251 Ibid. 51.

252 *Amann v Switzerland* [2000] RJD 2000-II, App. No. 27798/95.

253 *Niemietz* § 29, and *Halford v United Kingdom* [1997] RJD 1997-III, App. No. 20605/92, § 42).

254 Amann § 65.

in the judgment that storing a card on the seller, on which he was described as 'a contact with the Russian embassy', and where it was pointed out that he did 'business of various kinds' with a certain company,[255] was to be regarded as containing details that 'undeniably' amounted to data relating to the applicant's private life.[256] The matter was further developed in another judgment of the same year, *Rotaru*,[257] where the defendant tried to argue that Article 8 of the ECHR was not applicable to the case on the grounds that the information stored related not to the applicant's private life, but to his public life.[258] In *Rotaru*, the applicant was a Romanian national complaining about information seemingly in possession of the Romanian Intelligence Service, and which he considered false and defamatory. The information had been revealed in a letter, and generally concerned his youth, covering also his political activities. The intelligence service had notably claimed he had participated in an extreme right-wing movement in the 1930s, apparently mistaking him with another individual of the same name. In its judgment in *Rotaru*, the Court referred to *Leander* and *Amann*, and explicitly pointed out that 'public information' can also fall with the scope of 'private life', concretely when systematically collected and stored in files held by the authorities, and that this 'is all the truer where such information concerns a person's distant past'.[259] The ECtHR then noted that the letter in question 'contained various pieces of information about the applicant's life, in particular his studies, his political activities and his criminal record, some of which had been gathered more than 50 years earlier',[260] and declared that 'such information, when systematically collected and stored in a file held by agents of the State', fell within the scope of private life for the purposes of Article 8 of the ECHR. In Rotaru it was made clear that the category of information relating to private life shall not be read as opposed to public information. As this was clarified, the question remained of determining what is exactly information relating to private life, the mere storage of which can deserve qualification as an interference with the rights established by Article 8 of the ECHR. Since then, the ECtHR has been throwing further light on the issue,

---

255 Ibid. § 66.

256 Ibid. § 67.

257 *Rotaru v. Romania* [2000] RJD 2000-V, App. No. 28341/95.

258 Ibid. § 42.

259 Ibid. § 43. See also: *Cemalettín Canli v Turkey* [2008] App. No. 22427/04, § 33. The case concerned a man who appeared in registers held by the police as former member of illegal organizations, despite having been acquitted of that offence.

260 Ibid. § 44.

often making use of criteria implicitly or explicitly associated to Convention 108.[261] In *P.G. and J.H.*,[262] for instance, the Court alluded to Convention 108 to develop the case law of *Rotaru* and to apply it to the recording of the applicants' voices when being charged and when in their police cell, commenting that '(p)rivate-life considerations may arise (...) once any systematic or permanent record comes into existence of (...) material from the public domain'.[263]

The 2008 *S and Marper* judgment[264] illustrates particularly well the variety of grounds that can justify the qualification of information as relating to private life for the purposes of considering that its mere storage amounts to an interference with the rights of Article 8 of the ECHR.[265] In *S and Marper*, the applicants complained about the retention by UK authorities of their fingerprints, cellular samples and DNA profiles after criminal proceedings against them were terminated. The Court found that the three types of data deserved protection, but for different reasons. Concerning cellular samples, the ECtHR noted that their retention had to be regarded 'per se' as interfering with the right to respect for private life, given the 'nature' (labelled as 'highly personal')[266] and the 'amount' of 'sensitive'[267] personal information they contained.[268] DNA profiles were described as containing less information, but as being able, nonetheless, to generate information going 'beyond neutral identification' (for instance, touching upon genetic relationships between individuals) when submitted to automated processing.[269] Finally, the storage of fingerprints was described as giving rise to important private-life concerns because they constituted data regarding identified or identifiable individuals held by public authorities with the aim of being permanently kept and regularly processed by automated means for criminal-identification purposes;[270] thus, not because of the nature of the

261 The ECtHR generally takes into account the context and the way in which information is used, and its nature. See also, for example: *Peck v the United Kingdom* [2003] RJD 2003, App. No. 44647/98.

262 *P.G. and J.H. v the United Kingdom* [2001] RJD 2001-IX, App. No. 44787/98.

263 Ibid. § 57. See also: *Segerstedt-Wiberg and Others v Sweden* [2006] RJD 2006-VII, App. No. 44787/98 (in particular, § 72).

264 *S. and Marper v the United Kingdom* [2008] RJD 2008, App. Nos. 30562/04 and 30566/04.

265 See, for instance: (González Fuster 2009).

266 *Marper* § 73.

267 Ibid. § 72.

268 Ibid.

269 Ibid. § 75.

270 Ibid. § 78–86. See also: (De Beer de Laer et al. 2010, p. 141).

data, but because of storage conditions. The Strasbourg Court later affirmed in *Khelili*[271] that *Marper* had detailed some of the principles applying to the storage of 'personal' information; 'personal' being advanced here as in 'personal data protection':[272] the judgment was issued in French, and the words used by the Court (*à caractère personnel*)[273] were words ostensibly rooted in European data protection.[274] The qualification of data as 'personal' did not, however, trigger immediately the qualification of their memorization as an interference under Article 8 of the ECHR: the Court declared that, in order to determine whether personal data engaged any aspects of private life, it was necessary to take into account the context in which the data had been collected and stored, their nature, the way they were used and treated and the results obtainable from the processing.[275]

The ECtHR case law built over the years upon *Leander* certainly appears to move towards the incorporation of the substance of Convention 108 into the interpretation of Article 8 of the ECHR. The degree of such incorporation is nevertheless debatable.[276] Ultimately, the case law evidences Strasbourg Court's reluctance to apprehend the assessment of whether a measure constitutes or not an interference with Article 8 of the ECHR in terms other than those present in that provision. The ECtHR has never declared that any automated processing of personal data shall per se be considered as an interference with Article 8 of the ECHR, but it remains unclear whether this should be interpreted as indicating that some processing activities are excluded from the scope of Article 8 of the ECHR or, perhaps, simply not included yet.

A category of data unquestionably portrayed by the ECtHR as deserving protection under Article 8 of the ECHR is the data related to health. In this area, the ECtHR has been particularly keen to vocalize the importance of 'data protection', and of Convention 108. It is highly questionable, nonetheless, to which extent health data have been granted protection in the name of general 'data protection' (understood as the legal notion developed by Convention 108, applicable to any automated processing of personal data), or in the name of exceptional provisions

---

271 *Khelili v Switzerland* [2011] App. No. 16188/07.

272 See also, for references to both personal data and sensitive data as in Convention 108: *M.M. v UK* [2012] App. No. 24029/07 § 188.

273 See, for instance, *Khelili* § 55.

274 The case concerned a woman who contested her description as prostitute in a police.

275 *Khelili* § 55.

276 On the partial recognition of data protection under Article 8 of the ECHR by the ECtHR, see also: (De Hert and Gutwirth 2009, p. 24 ff).

on special categories of data deserving reinforced protection (which are also covered by Convention 108). The case *Z v Finland*[277] serves as an instance of these ambiguities. It relates to the disclosure of the medical condition of the applicant, who was infected with HIV, in the context of proceedings concerning a sexual assault. In its judgment, the ECtHR underlined that 'the protection of personal data, not least medical data, is of fundamental importance to a person's enjoyment of his or her right to respect for private and family life' as guaranteed by Article 8 of the ECHR.[278] Despite this formal endorsement of 'the protection of personal data', eventually the Court justified the level of protection deserved by the information disclosed[279] not because it constituted 'personal data' in the sense of Convention 108, but because it was sensitive data, the disclosure of which 'may dramatically affect' the private and family life of individuals.[280] Additionally, the Court associated the protection in question with a principle 'of confidentiality',[281] and described it as consisting in safeguards to prevent some types of communication or disclosure,[282] even though 'data protection' in the sense of Convention 108 encompasses principles that go beyond confidentiality obligations.

I v Finland,[283] about the protection of patient records, added a new dimension to what is known as the doctrine of positive obligations in relation to the protection of personal data.[284] The case concerned an applicant, also diagnosed as HIV-positive, whose confidential patient records had been unlawfully consulted by her colleagues. The applicant complained that the district health authority had failed to provide adequate safeguards against unauthorized access to medical data. In this ruling, the ECtHR recalled that according to its own case law Article 8 of the ECHR does not merely compel States to abstain from interferences with the right to respect for private life, but that there may also be positive obligations inherent

277 *Z v Finland* [1997] RJD 1997-I, App. No. 22009/93.

278 Ibid. § 95. See also *M. S. v Sweden* [1997] RJD 1997-IV, App. No. 20837/92, § 51.

279 In *Z v Finland*, the Court enters into these considerations when examining whether the interferences with Article 8 of the ECHR can be considered 'necessary in a democratic society'. It was undisputed that the various measures of which the applicant complained constituted interferences (*Z v Finland* § 71).

280 Ibid. § 96.

281 Ibid. § 95.

282 Ibid.

283 *I. v. Finland* [2008] App. No. 20511/03.

284 P. de Hert and S. Gutwirth, *Data protection in the case law of Strasbourg and Luxembourg: Constitualization in action*, in: *Reinventing Data Protection?*, S. Gutwirth, Y. Poullet, P. de Hert, C. de Terwangne, and S. Nouwt (eds), Dordrecht-Springer 2013, pp. 3–44.

in an effective respect for private or family life,[285] and that these obligations may involve the adoption of measures designed to secure the respect for private life even in the sphere of the relations of individuals between them.[286]

As far as the refusal to grant individuals access to the information stored, thus depriving them of the opportunity to refute it, is concerned, it is also regarded by the ECtHR as an interference with the rights enshrined in Article 8 of the ECHR.[287] A landmark judgment regarding access to information is *Gaskin*,[288] of 1989. Circumstances of the case are as follows: the applicant, who had been taken into care as a child, wished to find out about his past to overcome some personal problems, but had been refused access to his file on the ground that it contained confidential information. The Strasbourg Court found that the applicant had an essential interest in accessing the information at stake, described as relating to the applicant's childhood and formative years and, thus, to his 'private and family life', and eventually established there had been a violation of Article 8 of the ECHR because decision denying the request for access had not been taken by an independent authority. In addition, some regard *Gaskin* as a leading case on the right of individuals, under Article 8 of the ECHR, to access information about them held by public authorities. It is to be acknowledged, however, that the Court considered the refusal of access as amounting to an interference not because of the nature of the data, or of the way in which the data were used, but because of the potential impact of the denial on the life of the applicant, and due to the fact that the act of accessing the data served an essential interest. In this sense, the Court explicitly emphasized that its judgment shall not be interpreted as providing general guidance on the question of whether general access rights to personal information could be derived from the article 8 of the ECHR[289]

As far as the European Union jurisprudence is concerned, the developments in migration technology are to a large extent covered by data protection law: General Data Protection Regulation that replaced the Directive 95/46/EC for the private sector and most of the public sector in the Member States, as well as Directive to replace the Council Framework Decision 2008/977/JHA for the area of criminal law enforcement.[290] As far as the processing of personal data for

285 *Airey v Ireland* [1979] Series A No. 32, App. No. 6289/73, § 32.

286 *X and Y v the Netherlands* [1985] Series A No. 91, App. No. 8978/80, § 23.

287 See also: *M.G. v the United Kingdom* [2002] App. No. 39393/98.

288 *Gaskin v the United Kingdom* [1989] Series A No. 160, App. No. 10454/83.

289 Ibid. § 37.

290 Proposal for a Regulation of the European Parliament and of the Council on the Protection of Individuals with Regard to the Processing of Personal Data and on the

the purpose of police or judicial cooperation in criminal matters is concerned, the SIS II Decision provides that the Convention of the Council of Europe of 28 January 1981 for the protection of individuals with regards to automatic processing of personal data is applicable.[291] In addition, the Framework Decision on data protection in police and judicial cooperation in criminal matters replaced in May 2018 by the Directive applies to the processing of data under the SIS II Decision, as well as the access of law enforcement staff to VIS and EURODAC[292]. While Europol and Eurojust are subject to the data protection rules contained in their founding decisions[293].

The National Supervisory Authorities (NSAs) under Directive 95/46/EC are responsible for supervising the data processing in Member States; the European Data Protection Officer (EDPO) bears this responsibility, according to the Regulation No 45/2001, at the EU level[294]. What is even more under the General Data Protection Regulation supervisory authorities in all of the Member States are provided with strong enforcement Powers[295]. It is crucial to note that the requirement for national data protection authorities to act in complete independence has already been confirmed by Court of Justice of the European Union three times: in its rulings in cases concerning Germany (C-518/07 of 9 March 2010) and Austria (C-614/10 of 16 October 2012) the Court underlined that data protection supervisory authorities have to remain free from any external influence, including the direct or indirect influence of the state. The mere risk of political pressure through state scrutiny is sufficient to hinder the independent performance of the supervisory authority's

---

Free Movement of such Data (General Data Protection Regulation), 25 January 2012, COM(2012) 11final, and Proposal for a Directive of the European Parliament and of the Council on the Protection of Individuals with Regards to the Processing of Personal Data by competent authorities for the purposes of Prevention, Investigation, Detection or Prosecution of Criminal Offences or the Execution of Criminal Penalties, and the Free Movement of Such Data, 25 January 2012, COM(2012) 10 final.

291 Art. 57 SIS II Decision.

292 Council Framework Decision 2008/977/JHA, OJ 2008 L 350/60.

293 Decision 2009/371/JHA, OJ 2009 L 121/37 (Europol) and Council Decision 2002/187/JHA, OJ 2002 L 63/1 (Eurojust). Only EURODAC Regulation makes this explicit in Art. 33 for data processing by Europol. See also: Jorrit J. Rijmpa Brave new borders. The EU's Use of new technologies for the management of migration and Asylum, in: "New technologies and EU Law" Ed. by Marise Cremona, pp. 216–219.

294 The EDPS has replaced the Joint Supervisory authority of SIS (Art. 115 CISA) and EURODAC (Art. 20 Council Regulation (EC) 2725/2000 (‚Dublin II Regulation')), OJ 2000 L 316/1: Art. 45 SIS II Regulation and Art. 31 EURODAC Regulation.

295 Arts 53 and 79 Proposal for General Data Protection Regulation.

tasks. Consequently, in the case C-288/12 the Court ruled that the abrupt termination of the Hungarian Data Protection Commissioner's term in office by the government constitutes an infringement of the Article 16 of the Treaty on Functioning of the EU and Article 8 of the Charter of Fundamental Rights.

Furthermore, independence of the data protection supervisory authorities is of particular importance in the context of third state law enforcement transfer. In addition, the issue of data protection guarantees in countries with different legal systems is mirrored in the case *Schrems v. Data Protection* Commissioner, in which the Court was faced with the question, whether the economically related safe harbor framework[296] enabling the transfer of Facebook data of EU citizens to the US, where these data are in fact accessed by US law enforcement and secret service authorities, was still in accordance with EU fundamental rights[297]? The Advocate General's opinion was delivered on the 23rd of September 2015; he proposed that the Commission's Safe Harbor Decision should have been declared invalid and even referred to a possible violation of the essence of the rights enshrined in Article 7 (Respect for private and family life) of the Charter through the US intelligence services accessing the content of data transferred[298]. Consequently,

296 Following the terrorist attacks on 11 September 2001, the United States enacted a statue and accompanying regulations, requiring all air carriers operating passenger flights to and from the US to provide access to certain Passenger Name Records (PNR) information to US Customs and Border Protection-a component of the US Department of Homeland Security. In June 2002, the Commission informed the US authorities that these requirements could conflict with European and Member States's legislation on data protection. As a result, the EU and the US entered negotiations aimed at reaching agreement on sharing PNR data while securing adequate level of protection; the current (2018) EU-US PNR agreement on the transfer of air passengers' data for flights from the EU to the US entered into force on 1 July 2012. The first joint review of the Agreement was carried out in Washington one year later after its entry into force (1 July 2012) on 8 and 9 July 2013; on 19 January 2017 the European Commission presented the second implementation report on the EU-US PNR Agreement; in: European Commission Press release: europa.eu/rapid/press-release_IP-17-99_en.htm (Accessed: December 2019).

297 CJEU, Case C-362/14, Schrems v. Data Protection Commissioner, Reference for a preliminary ruling from High Court of Ireland made on 25 July 2014; See also: F. Boehm, EU PNR: European Flight Passengers under General Suspicion-the Envisaged European Model of Analyzing Flight Passenger Data, in: „*Computers, Privacy and Data Protection: an Element of Choice*, S. Gutwirth Y. Poullet, P. de Hert, R. Leenes (Eds.), Springer Dordrecht Heiderberg New York 2011, pp. 171–199.

298 CJEU, Case C-362/14, Schrems v. Data Protection Commissioner, Opinion of the Advocate General Bot on 23rd of September 2015, § 177.

the CJEU issued its ruling on October 6, 2015, agreeing with the Advocate General and invalidating Safe Harbor. Furthermore, the court emphasized that: 1) national data protection authorities have the right to investigate the adequacy of data transfers under the EU-US Safe Harbor arrangement or any other arrangements concluded pursuant to an adequacy decision by the European Commission for that matter, and 2) the Safe Harbor arrangement should be invalid due to the lack of adequacy.

As far as the SIS, VIS and EURODAC are concerned, they do contain in their founding regulations further 'specifications' to the above presented rules; the data subject has to be informed of his/her inclusion in the system[299]. An individual has a right to request access, correction, and deletion of unlawfully stored data[300]. In addition, the request can be made in any Member State, although the actual change would have to be carried out by the Member State that entered the data. From the point of view of the protection of a data subject and the potentially serious consequences of incorrect inclusion of personal data in one of the systems, it seems, according the former Data Protection Supervisor (DPS) - Peter Hustinx- unnecessarily restrictive to allow only the courts of the Member States that entered the data to rule on the accuracy and the legality thereof[301]. Finally, all founding regulations provide for remedies against decisions on access, correction, and deletion before a competent authority or court[302]. Not to mention about the fact that all regulations contain rules on liability and penalties for the unlawful processing of data[303]. Furthermore, there is no doubt that the large-scale collection and storage of personal data, including biometric data, constitutes an interference with the right to private life under under article 8 of both the European Convention on Human Rights and Charter of Fundamental Rights as well as the Council of Europe Convention 108 for the Protection of Individuals with regard to Automatic Processing of Personal Data to be followed in future by the modernized Convention 108+. Specifically, the European Court of Human Rights (ECtHR) held that 'the mere storage of data relating to the

299 Art. 42 SIS II Regulation; Art. 29(1)–(3) EURODAC Regulation; Art. 37 VIS Regulation.

300 Art. 41 SIS II Regulation; Art. 29(4)–(13) EURODAC Regulation; Art. 38 VIS Regulation.

301 P. Hustinx, *EU Data Protection Law: The Review of Directive 95/46/EC and the General Data protection Regulation*, in: „New Technologies and EU Law", Op. Cit., pp. 123–173.

302 Art. 43 SIS II Regulation; Art. 29(14) and (15) EURODAC Regulation; Art. 40 VIS Regulation.

303 Arts 48 and 49 SIS II Regulations; Arts 37 and 51 EURODAC Regulation; Arts 33 and 36 VIS Regulation.

private life of an individual amounts to an interference within the meaning of Article 8'[304]. The subsequent use of the stored information has no bearing on that finding[305]. In addition, the Court of Justice of the European Union has already held that whether the information is sensitive or not and whether or not persons concerned have been inconvenienced in any way is irrelevant.

One of the first cases partly dealing with data protection in the law enforcement (LE) sector after the adoption of the Lisbon Treaty was the *Schwarz* case (C-291/12), known also as the *Passport Case,* which concerned the storing and subsequent use of fingerprints records in passports; interestingly, the Court while dealing with the merits of this case applied the exception clause to limitations to protection of personal data and the respect of private life. The case originated in the German court where Mr. Schwarz argued that the Article 1(2) of the Passport Regulation 2252/2004 which obliged Member States to include in their passports and travel documents a facial image, as well as fingerprints in interoperable formats, infringed Articles 7 (Respect for private and family life) and 8 (Protection of personal data) of the Charter of Fundamental Rights (CFR)[306]. The court argued that there was a legitimate aim for the inclusion of biometric data in a passport since this *sophisticated technology* would make forgery more difficult and as a result would facilitate the work of border guard authorities aimed at countering irregular migration.[307] This reasoning would probably apply to the SIS II, VIS and EURODAC Regulation, as well as Entry-Exit System. As the court held in the case of *Wattson and Belmann,* EU law does not prevent Member States from adopting measures that enable authorities to have an exact *knowledge* of population movements affecting their territory. Where this applies to EU citizens, it a *fortiori* applies to third country nationals. However, that does not mean that the collection and storage of individualized personal information in a register is per se necessary, as only anonymous information is required in order for such an objective to be attained. Interestingly, the Court diminished the argument that fingerprints are not always reliable to the detriment of their usefulness in reducing the likelihood

304 *Leander v. Sweden, supra* note 138, at para 48;ECtHR, *S. Marper v. United Kingdom* (Application no 30562/04 and 30566/04), 4 December 2008, ECtHR (2008) 1581, at § 67.

305 ECtHR, *Amann v. Switzerland,* (GC) (Application no. 27798/95), 16 February 2000, at § 69; *S. and Marper v United Kingdom, supra note 141, at* § 81.

306 Case C-291/12, Schwarz, Judgment of 17 October 2013 (ECLI:EU:C:2013:670)

307 *Schwarz,* at§ 41.

of irregular entry[308]. In addition, the Court also considered that the only possible alternative to taking fingerprints would be iris-scanning, but recognized at the same time that this technology of identification is not as advanced and not necessarily less repressive than taking fingerprints[309] As regards the question whether the measure was the least restrictive, the Court in *Schwarz* held that the taking of fingerprints was not of intimate nature nor such as to cause particular physical or mental discomfort[310]. This conclusion, however, does not seem in line with earlier case law, e.g. *Österreichischer Rundfunk* - a case concerning the communication and publication of salaries and pensions of staff of a public body exceeding a certain level, together with the names of the recipients. The court while deciding that the collection of data by name relating to an individual's professional income, with a view to communicating it to third parties, falls within the scope of Article 8 of the ECHR, underlined that it does not matter whether the information communicated is of a sensitive character or whether the persons concerned have been inconvenienced in any way. Furthermore, the Court also reiterated that the term „private life" must not be interpreted restrictively; in particular, respect for *private life* comprises the right to establish and develop relationships with other human beings; furthermore, there is no reason to justify excluding activities of a professional or business nature from the notion of „private life"[311].

Moreover, the issue of compatibility of the databases with the fundamental right to private life and the right to the protection of one's personal data, has taken on a new significance especially in the law enforcement sector resulting in harmonization of the Member Sates' data retention rules after the CJEU's key judgment, that concerned the validity of the directive 2002/58/EC which had at its ancillary goal the prevention and prosecution of crime[312]. It obliged providers of publicly available electronic communications services or of public communications networks to retain, for a prescribed period, data relating to a person's private life and to his communications. Moreover, it provided access

308 Ibid, § 43.

309 Ibid. at § 51 and 52.

310 *Schwarz*, at § 48.

311 Joined cases C-465/00, C-138/01 and C-139/01, *Österreichischer Rundfunk*, EU:C;2003:294, at 73; case of *Amann v. Switzerland*, ECHR, at § 65.

312 Directive 2006/24/EC 2006 L 105/54 ('Retention Directive'), Joined Cases C-293/12 (*Digital Rights Ireland*) and C-594/12 (*Kärtner Landesregierung*), Judgment of 8 April 2014.

to these data by competent national authorities (Data Retention case)[313]. It originated from two requests for preliminary ruling under Article 267 TFEU made by: 1) the High Court (Case C-293/12) in reference to proceedings between Digital Rights Ireland Ltd. and Minister for Communications, Marine and Natural Resources, Minister for Justice, Equality and Law Reform, Commissioner of the Garda Síochána, Ireland, the Attorney General, regarding the legality of national legislative and administrative measures concerning the retention of data relating to electronic communications; 2) Austrian Constitutional Court (Case C-594/12) as a response to constitutional actions brought before that court by the Government of the Province of Carinthia and by Mr. Seitlinger, Mr. Tschohl and 11 128 other applicants regarding the compatibility with the Federal Constitutional Law (Bundes-Verfassungsgesetz) of the law transposing Directive 2006/24 into Austrian National law. In other words, the High Court (Ireland) and the Verfassungsgerichtshof (Constitutional Court, Austria) asked the Court of Justice to examine the validity of the directive, in particular, in the light of two fundamental rights under the Charter of Fundamental Rights of the EU, namely the fundamental right to respect for private life and the fundamental right to the protection of personal data. In its preliminary ruling, the court observed, in the first place, that the data to be retained make it possible, in particular, (1) to know the identity of the person with whom a subscriber or registered user has communicated and by what means, (2) to identify the time of the communication as well as the place from which that communication took place and (3) to know the frequency of the communications of the subscriber or registered user with certain persons during a given period. As a result, those data, taken as a whole, may provide very precise information on the private lives of the persons whose data are retained, such as the habits of everyday life, permanent or temporary places of residence, daily or other movements, activities carried out, social relationships and the social environments frequented[314]. Similar assumption could be drawn, albeit to lesser and differing degrees, of the information stored in the VIS as well as Entry-Exit System. What is even more, the wide-ranging retention and subsequent use without the user being informed

313 The preliminary ruling issued by the CJEU concerned the validity of Directive 2006/24/EC of the European Parliament and of the Council of 5 March 2006 on the retention of data generated or processed in connection with the provision of publicly available electronic communications services or of public communications networks and amending Directive 2002/58/EC (OJ 2006 L 105, p.54).

314 Joined Cases C-293 and 594/12, ibid., at § 27.

would be liable to create feeling of constant surveillance[315]. The interference with Articles 7 and 8 of the CFR was therefore particularly serious. At the same time, it authentically satisfied an objective of genuine interest, namely the fight against international terrorism and serious crime[316].

Summarizing, in order to sustain its judgment in the Data Retention case the Court of Justice of the European Union reasoned that the directive: 1) covers, in a generalized manner, all individuals, all means of electronic communication and all traffic data without any differentiation, limitation or exception being made in the light of the objective of fighting against serious crime; 2) fails to lay down any objective criterion which would ensure that the competent national authorities have access to the data and can use them only for the purposes of prevention, detection or criminal prosecutions concerning offenses; 3) does not make the access to the data dependent on the prior review by a court or by an independent administrative body; and 4) imposes a period of data retention of at least six months, without making any distinction between the categories of data on the basis of the persons concerned or the possible usefulness of the data in relation to the objective pursued (C-293/12 and C-594/12).

As a result, in the Data Retention case the Court of Justice of the European Union in its judgment (8 April 2014) declared the data retention directive to be invalid by stating that this directive entailed a wide-ranging and particularly serious interference with the fundamental rights to respect for private life and to the pro tection of personal data. Particularly mentioned are the cases Leander v. Sweden, Rotaru v. Romania, Weber and Saravia v. Germany, Liberty and Others v. United Kingdom, M.K. versus France and S. and Marper v. United Kingdom. The latter is of specific importance since the facts and circumstances of that case is similar to the data retention situation and is concerned with the mass collection and storage of data for lawenforcement purposes. The first applicant, Mr S., was arrested in January 2001 at the age of eleven and charged with attempted robbery. His fingerprints and DNA samples were collected but he was subsequently acquitted. The second applicant, Mr Marper, who also had his fingerprints and DNA samples taken, was arrested in March 2001 and charged with harassment of his partner. Before a pretrial review took place, he and his partner had become reconciled thus the charge was not pressed and in June 2001 the case was formally discontinued. As a result, both applicants asked for their fingerprints and

315 Ibid., at § 37, with reference to § 52 and 72 of the Advocate General's opinion.

316 *Ibid,* at § 41–44. This in addition to internal market objective, as had already been recognized by the Court in the Case C-301/06, *Ireland v. European Parliament and the Council,* (2009) ECR I-593 (ECLI:EU:C:2009:68), *at paragraphs* 71–74.

DNA samples to be destroyed, but in both cases the police refused. Hence, in the S. and Marper Case it has been investigated whether the storage by the National DNA Database of cellular samples, fingerprints and DNA profiles to be used by the UK Police for criminal investigations, was lawful? In its conclusion the Court emphasized that "(...) blanket and indiscriminate nature of the powers of retention of the fingerprints, cellular samples and DNA profiles of persons suspected but not convicted of offenses, fails to strike a fair balance between the competing public and private interests and that the respondent State has overstepped any acceptable margin of appreciation in this regard. In other words, the retention at issue constitutes disproportionate interference with the applicants' right to respect for private life and cannot be regarded as necessary in a democratic society". In addition, the Court " observed that the protection afforded by Article 8 of the Convention would be unacceptably weakened if the use of modern scientific techniques in the criminal-justice system were allowed at any cost and without carefully balancing the potential benefits of the extensive use of such techniques against important private-life interests. Any State claiming a pioneer role in the development of new technologies bore special responsibility for striking the right balance in this regard".

Furthermore, following the *Digital Rights Ireland* judgment of 2014 invalidating the EU's Directive 2006/24/EC on data retention on the grounds that a general obligation to retain certain communications data constituted a serious interference with the fundamental rights to respect for private life and to the protection of personal data, and that national rules effecting such obligation were not limited to what was strictly necessary for the purpose of fighting serious crime, two references were made to the Court in relation to the general obligation imposed, in Sweden and in the UK, on providers of electronic communications services to retain the data, relating to those communications, retention of which was required by the invalidated directive[317]. In the first place, the telecommunications company Tele2 Sverige informed the Swedish Post and Telecom Authority that it had decided that it would no longer retain data due to the fact that the applicable Swedish law (Chapter 6 of Sweden's Law on Electronic Communications) no longer conformed

317 Analysis of Joined Cases: C-203/15 Tele2 Sverige AB v Post-och telestyrelsen and C-698/15 Secretary of State for the Home Department v Tom Watson and Others by Global Freedom of Expression, Colombia University, at: https://globalfreedomofexpression.columbia.edu/cases/joined-cases-tele2-sverige-ab-v-post-och-telestyrelsen-c-20315-secretary-state-home-department-v-watson/ (Accessed: March 2020).

to European fundamental rights law. Tele2 Sverige also informed that it intended to erase those previously recorded (Case C-203/15). As a result, Sweden's National Police Board made a formal complaint to the Swedish Post and Telecommunications Authority (PTS) arguing that Tele2 Sverige's decision would have serious negative consequences for law enforcement. The PTS ordered Tele2 Sverige to resume retention of communications data. Subsequently, legal proceedings were instituted and the Stockholm Administrative Court of Appeal which found arguments both in favor of and against the compatibility of Sweden's Law on Electronic Communications and EU Directive 2002/58. Secondly, in the Case C-698/15, Mr Tom Watson, Mr Peter Brice and Mr Geoffrey Lewis brought actions challenging the UK rules on the retention of data which enabled the Secretary of State for the Home Department to require public telecommunications operators to retain all the data relating to communications for a maximum period of 12 months, with the provision that retention of the content of those communications is excluded.

Consequently, in references for a preliminary ruling made by the Kammarrätten in Stockholm (Administrative Court of Appeal, Stockholm, Sweden) and the Court of Appeal (England and Wales) (Civil Division) (UK), the CJEU was requested to state whether national rules that impose on providers a general obligation to retain data and which make provision for access by the competent national authorities to the retained data, where, inter alia, the objective pursued by that access is not restricted solely to fighting serious crime and where access is not subject to prior review by a court or an independent administrative authority, are compatible with EU law, in particular the directive on 'privacy and electronic communications'[318] read in the light of Articles: 7 (right to privacy) , 8 (right to the protection of personal data) as well as the Article 52 (1) of the Charter of Fundamental Rights of the European Union which states that: "*Any limitation on the exercise of the rights and freedoms recognised by the Charter must be provided for by law and respect the essence of those rights and freedoms. Subject to the principle of proportionality, limitations may be made only if they are necessary and genuinely meet objectives of general interest recognised by the Union or the need to protect the rights and freedoms of others*". More precisely, the national courts asked whether Article 15 of the Directive allowing Member States (MS) to adopt

318 Directive 2002/58/EC of the European Parliament and of the Council of 12 July 2002 concerning the processing of personal data and the protection of privacy in the electronic communications sector (Directive on privacy and electronic communications) (OJ 2002 L 201, p. 37), as amended by Directive 2009/136/EC of the European Parliament and of the Council of 25 November 2009 (OJ 2009, L 337, p. 11)

legislative measures providing for the retention of data for a limited period of time justified on the grounds of national security (i.e. State security), defence, public security, and the prevention, investigation, detection and prosecution of criminal offences or of unauthorised use of the electronic communication system should be interpreted as precluding national legislation that provided, for the purpose of fighting crime, for general and indiscriminate retention of all traffic and location data of all subscribers and registered users with respect to all means of electronic communication.

In its response, the Court of Justice of the European Union had to examine, in the first place, whether and to what extent EU Member States' national legislation on the retention of traffic and location data and access to that data by national authorities, for the purpose of combating crime, fell within the scope of EU law, and of Directive 2002/58/EC in particular. This Directive excluded from its scope "activities of the State" in specific fields, such as criminal law, public security, defence, State security. However, the Court stated that the Directive applied when the state activity involved providers of electronic communications services, and therefore the processing of personal data by those providers. The Court then focused on the main question that had been referred by the national courts, namely how to interpret Article 15 of Directive 2002/58 so as to allow MS to adopt legislative measures providing for the retention of data for a limited period of time when this was justified on grounds such as national security, defense, public security and the prevention, investigation, detection and prosecution of criminal offences for the unauthorized use of an electronic communication system, and when such restriction constituted a necessary, appropriate and proportionate measure. The Court affirmed that the Directive on privacy and electronic communications was designed "*to offer users of electronic communications services protection against risks to their personal data and privacy that arise from new technology and the increasing capacity for automated storage and processing data*". [para. 83] Indeed, the confidentiality of communications was a pillar of the Directive and implied that, as a general rule, any person other than the user was prohibited from storing the traffic data related to electronic communications without the consent of the user concerned, The Court stressed that the only exceptions were those set out in Article 15 and that these must be interpreted strictly and could not be allowed to become the rule.

Furthermore, CJEU recognized that national legislation imposing an obligation on providers of electronic communications services to retain traffic data when necessary in order to make that data available to the competent national authorities, raised questions relating to compatibility not only with the rights to privacy and data protection enshrined in Articles 7 and 8 of the Charter, which were expressly referred to in the questions for a preliminary ruling, but also with the right to freedom of expression guaranteed in Article 11 of the CFR. The Court emphasized the importance of the right to privacy, data protection and freedom of expression in any democratic society. "*That fundamental right [freedom of expression], guaranteed in Article 11 of the CFREU, constitutes one of the essential foundations of a pluralist, democratic society, and is one of the values on which, under Article 2 TEU (Treaty on the European Union), the Union is founded*". [paras. 92-93] The Court then proceeded to analyze the limitations that can be imposed on the exercise of the rights and freedoms recognized by the CFR, namely that they had to be provided by law and had to respect the essence of those rights. In other words, they must be proportionate, necessary and meet objectives of general interest recognized by the EU or the need to protect the rights and freedoms of others. As a result, the Court stated that the legislation under consideration provided for the general and indiscriminate retention of all traffic and location data of all subscribers and registered users relating to all means of electronic communication, and that it imposed on providers of electronic communications services an obligation to retain that data systematically and continuously, with no exceptions. Indeed, "*the data which providers of electronic communications services must therefore retain makes it possible to trace and identify the source of a communication and its destination, to identify the date, time, duration and type of a communication, to identify users' communication equipment, and to establish the location of mobile communication equipment. That data includes, inter alia, the name and address of the subscriber or registered user, the telephone number of the caller, the number called and an IP address for internet services. That data makes it possible, in particular, to identify the person with whom a subscriber or registered user has communicated and by what means, and to identify the time of the communication as well as the place from which that communication took place. Further, that data makes it possible to know how often the subscriber or registered user communicated with certain persons in a given period*." [para. 98] In light of this, national authorities were able to completely reconstruct a user's private life, such as residence, everyday habits, movements, activities, social relationships, social environments frequented. The interference was then "very far-reaching and must be considered to be particularly serious. The fact that the data is retained without the subscriber or registered user being informed is likely to cause the persons concerned to feel that their private lives are the subject of constant surveillance". [para.100] In particular, the Court noted that this retention could have an effect on the use of means of electronic communication and, consequently, on the exercise by the users of their freedom of expression.

Summarizing, the Court declared that the interference allowed by Directive was very serious and could only be justified if the objective was to fight serious crime, such as organized crime and terrorism. However, it went on, that in itself did not mean that such a fight justified national legislation providing for the general and indiscriminate retention of all traffic and location data Indeed, the laws affected all persons using electronic communications services, even those persons who were not in a situation likely to give rise to criminal proceedings. It was therefore evident that such restrictions on fundamental rights were not limited to what it was strictly necessary. The Court pointed out that while the conditions for restrictions may vary according to the nature of the measures taken for the purposes of prevention, investigation, detection and prosecution of serious crime, the retention of data must continue nonetheless to meet objective criteria that established a connection between the data to be retained and the objective pursued. In particular, such criteria must be shown to define the extent of that measure and, thus, the public affected. In conclusion, the Court set out guidelines on the procedure to be followed by national authorities to ensure that those conditions were fully respected. Hence, except in cases of a validly established urgency, it was essential that the national authorities' access to retained data was subject to prior review carried out either by a court or by an independent administrative body, and that the decision of that court or body should have been made following a reasoned request by the authorities submitted within the framework of procedures for the prevention, detection or prosecution of crime. [para. 120] Moreover, the competent national authorities to whom access to the retained data had been granted, had to notify the persons affected, under the applicable national procedures, as soon as that notification was no longer liable to jeopardize the investigations being undertaken by those authorities. That notification was necessary to enable the persons affected to exercise their right to a legal remedy. The Court said that Member States must ensure that there was an independent review to ensure compliance with the level of protection guaranteed by EU law for the processing of personal data. This control was expressly required by Article 8(3) of the CFR and constituted an essential element of respect for the protection of individuals in relation to the processing of personal data, in accordance with the principles established in Digital Rights Ireland and Schrems[319].

---

319 Digital Rights Ireland and Schrems (insert footnote: case 498/16, at: http://curia.europa.eu/juris/document/document.jsf;jsessionid=239E641DD87C6B5BB6CDC4CFC7536040?text=&docid=198764&pageIndex=0&doclang=en&mode=lst&dir=&occ=first&part=1&cid=560500 (Accessed: March 2020).

If that were not so, the Court stressed, persons whose personalities data was retained would be deprived of the right, guaranteed in Article 8(1) and (3) of the Charter, to lodge with the national supervisory authorities a claim seeking the protection of their data [para.123] Accordingly, the ECJ held that, firstly, Directive 2002/58, read in the light of Articles 7 and 8 of the CFREU, must be interpreted as precluding national legislation which, for the purpose of fighting crime, provided for the general and indiscriminate retention of all traffic and location data of all subscribers and registered users relating to all means of electronic communication. Secondly, Directive 2002/58 must be interpreted as precluding national legislation that permitted national authorities access to the retained data, unless the objective pursued by that access, in the context of fighting crime, was restricted solely to fighting serious crime, was subject to prior review by a court or an independent administrative authority, and required the data to be retained within the EU.

To conclude, both cases: C-291/12 Michael Schwarz v Stadt Bochum, and Joined Cases C-293/12 (Digital Rights Ireland) and C-594/12 (Kärtner Landesregierung) questioning the obligation under Directive 2006/24/EC to retain data obtained in the supply of telecommunication services ('Retention Directive') are of importance when assessing to what extent the storage of personal data in the EU's centralized databases for borders, migration, and asylum can be justified under the rules of the Charter. In the context of legal boundaries in the use of databases and biometrics in border surveillance and migration policy, it is crucial to mention about such substantive standards relating to data protection law as the requirement of necessity, the purpose limitation principle and the prohibition on automated decision-making[320].

The requirement of necessity, as one of legal boundaries in the use of databases and biometrics in border surveillance and migration policy, is mirrored in the Court's stance in the case C-524/06 of Mr. Huber. This Austrian national, who moved to Germany in 1996 in order to carry on business there as a self-employed insurance agent claimed that he had been discriminated against because personal data concerning him were stored in the centralized register that contained certain personal data relating to foreign nationals who were resident in Germany for a period of more than three months; while, this kind of database did not existed for German nationals. What is more, the

320 See also: Jorrit J. Rijpma, *Brave New Borders: The EU's Use of New Technologies for the Management of Migration and Asylum*, in: *New Technologies and EU Law*, (M Cremona ed.), Oxford University Press 2017, pp. 197–237.

register was used for statistical purposes. However, access to it was open for the security and police services as well as judicial authorities in exercising their powers in relation to the prosecution and investigation of criminal activities that threaten public security. As a result, Mr. Huber unsuccessfully requested that those data be deleted. While looking at this case the Court of Justice of the European Union ruled that: in the first place, the above mentioned register complied with EU data protection law concerning processing of personal data as long as it contained only data which are necessary for the application by those authorities of that legislation and if its centralized nature enables that legislation to be more effectively applied as regards the right of residence of Union citizens who are not nationals of that State. Secondly, as regards the storage and processing of those data for statistical purposes, the Court observed that Community law does not exclude the power of Member States to adopt measures enabling the national authorities to have an exact knowledge of population movements affecting their territory. Those statistics presuppose that certain information would be collected by those States. However, the exercise of that power does not, of itself, mean that the collection and storage of individualized personal information of the kind undertaken in the register at issue is, of itself, necessary. Consequently, the Court decided that such processing of personal data does not satisfy the requirement of necessity laid down in the directive. Thirdly, the court held that while the objective of the register involves the prosecution of crimes and offenses committed irrespective of the nationality of their perpetrators and at the same time the register at issue did not contained personal data relating to nationals of the Member State concerned; use of these data for the purposes of fighting crime was contrary to the principle of non-discrimination and hence contrary to Community law.

The prohibition on automated decision-making in the framework of Schengen Information System is mirrored in the case, *Commission* v. *Spain*[321] where the CJEU examined the refusal of entry of two Algerian nationals married to Spanish nationals issued by the Spanish authorities on the grounds that both were already subject of an alert which had been introduced into the Schengen Information System (SIS) by Germany. In addition, in the context of EU border control regime and the rights and duties of individuals under EU law as well as international law one may distinguish some twenty different categories of third-country nationals, each with different rights that vary according to the ties they have with EU Member States: 1) Persons with rights derived from EU free

321 C-503/03, 31 January 2006, OJ C 86, 8 April 2006.

movement provisions, such as family members of citizens of EU Member States; 2) Persons with rights derived from international agreements: family members of citizens of the European Economic Area (EEA) and Switzerland; 3) Turkish citizens and their family members;4) Citizens of countries which have concluded bilateral or multilateral agreements with the EU (over 100 countries); 5) Short and long term-term immigrants; within this category can be found family members of third-country national sponsors; long-term residents in the EU; researchers; students; seasonal workers; Blue card holders (highly qualified non-EU workers and their families) equipped by the EU with the special residence and work permit – „Blue Card" that facilitates access to the labor market, entitles its holders to socio-economic rights, favorable conditions for family reunification and facilitated movement around the EU[322]; 6) Persons in need of protection such as asylum seekers, refugees, beneficiaries of subsidiary or temporary protection as well as victims of human trafficking; in this context it is worth to emphasize that EU law and the ECHR prohibit the rejection at borders of persons at risk of persecution or other serious harm (principle non-refoulement)[323].

---

322 EU Blue card scheme was drafted in 2009 by means of the Directive 2009/50/EC; however, due to the fact that the current scheme has proven insufficient and unattractive since only 31 % of highly-educated migrants to OECD countries choose the EU as a destination; 69 % opt for other destinations, e.g. USA, which compete economically with the EU, the European Commission issued a proposal to repeal the above mentioned Directive (Commission Staff Working document. Impact Assessment-Accompanying the document: *Proposal for a Directive of the European Parliament and the Council on the conditions of entry and residence of third-country nationals for the purposes of highly skilled employment and repealing Directive 2009/50/EC.* Namely, in May 2015 when the Agenda on Migration was put forward, the Commission also launched a public consultation the Blue Card Directive with the aim of its modernization and introducing such improvements as: less stringent admissions criteria, such as lower salary threshold and shorter required length of work contracts, better family reunification conditions, facilitated mobility, and the abolishment of parallel national schemes. The results were published on 6 April 2016. In September 2016, the Commission also launched so-called fitness check of the 2003 Long-Term Residents Directive and 2011 Single Permit Directive. On 7 December, the commission presented a roadmap to deal by June 2018 on the comprehensive migration package in which it aims for an agreement on the blue Card file between the Council and the Parliament by June 2018. See: *Legislative Train Schedule. Towards a new policy on migration,* at:http://www.europarl.europa.eu/legislative-train/theme-towards-a-new-policy-on-migration/fiche (Accessed: January 2020).

323 Moreover, the Treaty of Lisbon provided for a duty of the EU to accede to the ECHR. However, when the negotiated agreement was put to the Court of Justice for opinion,

Last, but not least category of the third-country nationals under EU law consists of migrants in an irregular situation; in other words those who stay illegally on the territory of the European Union.

Bearing in mind the above-mentioned categories of third-country nationals in the case C-503/03 duties and rights of two Algerian nationals married to Spanish nationals are to be derived from the European Union law; namely, provisions related to free movement of family members of the citizens of the EU Member States within the area of the European Union. Consequently, the court reasoned as follows: 1) the Schengen Agreement (OJ L 239, 22 September 2000) providing for the gradual abolition of controls at common borders is accompanied by a „CISA" - Convention implementing the Schengen Agreement that enabled the signatory States to abolish checks at internal borders and as a result establish a single external border; 2) In addition, the Schengen Information System (SIS) was set up so that national authorities could exchange data concerning the identity of individuals and descriptions of objects sought; 3) As a result, article 96 CISA provides that individuals may be entered into SIS database by a Member State if the state decides according to its national criteria that an individual may likely pose a threat to public security and safety. However, one has to bear in mind that different member states have different conceptions of what constitutes risk. As a result, in line with the principle of a mutual recognition somebody may be excluded by all states, even where she or he satisfies the exclusion criteria of only one. Once an alert against a person has been issued in the SIS, entry is refused automatically. Refusal is automatic whether or not the alien is the spouse of a national of a Member State. But a third-country national who is a member of the family of a Community citizen (with the entry into force of the Lisbon Treaty: European Union citizen) is at the same time covered by Community (with the entry into force of the Lisbon Treaty: European Union law) on freedom of movement. Admittedly, the right to enter and stay in the territory of another Member State is not unconditional, as a prohibition thereof is possible on grounds of public policy or public security. But, the court noted, the public policy exception is a derogation from the fundamental principle of freedom of movement for persons that must be interpreted strictly. In particular, its scope cannot be determined unilaterally by the Member States. It is thus clear according to the Court of the European Union that the concept of public policy for the purposes of freedom of movement of persons does not correspond to that in

---

it ruled (in December 2015) that the agreement did not provide for sufficient protection of the EU's specific legal arrangements and the Court's exclusive jurisdiction. For the time being, no new accession agreement has been drafted (2017), but both the Parliament and the Commission underline the need for EU accession.

Article 96 of the CISA, under which an alert in the SIS for the purposes of refusing entry may be issued irrespective of any specific assessment of the threat represented by the person concerned. In this particular case C-503/03 Spanish authorities had not analyzed the situation to ascertain whether the two Algerian nationals married to Spanish nationals who were subjected to SIS alerts originally introduced by the German authorities, constituted a genuine, present and sufficiently serious threat. Another important reason why member states are not permitted to use the information stored in the European Systems unchecked is the possible infallibility of these data acquired by means of biometric identification. However, the widespread reliance on technological solutions aimed at guarding the borders diminishes the value of *knowledge* and information exchange on migrants on the routes to the detriment of the *power* of digital borders at the disposal of particular authority[324]. Hence, the Court held that the Spanish responsible bodies had failed to fulfill its obligations especially that the Schengen States have facilities for rapidly verifying whether the threat to public policy meets these conditions: the network of Sirene Bureaux was established to conduct such verifications, and a response by the national authorities consulted must be given within twelve hours[325].

Another example of the SIS alerts misuse constitutes the case of Mr. Moon, the founder and leader of the religious organization called Unification Church and his wife who were reported as 'inadmissible' in the SIS after an initial alert introduced in the system by the German authorities in 1995 on grounds of public order[326]. Namely, according to the German government the activities of the leaders of the Unification Church would pose a threat to „personal development of young people" and their public performances could lead to „violent reactions" (heftigen Reakcionen) in Germany.[327] As a result, the Moons appealed their being reported in the SIS in several national jurisdictions (Germany, Belgium, and France). Finally, the entry ban after having been dealt with in courts of first and second instance for 12 years, was removed by the judgment of the German Constitutional Court which ruled that the SIS alert which was based on Article 96 (2) CISA, required the availability of "substantial grounds" (gewisse

324 Kuster B. Tsianos V.S., *How to liquefy a Body on the Move: Eurodac and the Making of the European Digital Border*, in: *EU Borders and Shifting Internal Security. Technology, Externalization and Accountability*, Springer International Publishing Switzerland 2016, pp. 45–63.

325 C-503/03 Commission v Spain, judgment of 31.1.2006.

326 Brouwer E., *The Other Side of the Moon: The Schengen Information System and Human Rights: A Task for National Courts*, in: *CEPS Working Documents*, No. 288, April 2008.

327 See: Federal Administrative Court: Judgement BVerwG, 10.07.2001, Az. 1 C 35.00.

Erheblichkeit) that the presence of the third-country national poses a threat to public policy or security. For this conclusion, the Court referred to the examples listed in Article 96 (2) including the fact that the person has been convicted or that there are serious grounds to believe that he or she will commit serious crimes in future. According to the Constitutional Court, during the procedure before the administrative courts it was not clarified why the visit of Mr. and Mrs. Moon implied such risk. To conclude, the case highlights how dataveillance - the practice of monitoring digital data relating to personal details or online activities-can have far-reaching fundamental freedoms and rights implications; in the Moons' case this was freedom of religion and freedom of movement.

In this context, it is crucial to pay attention to the fact that the Moon's claim for legal redress for their having been reported in the SIS in several national jurisdictions, have been disputed in some EU Member States; the Dutch Minister of Immigration held the view that the decision to report a third-country national in the National Schengen Information System (NSIS) was not an administrative decision and, as a result, the third country national who disputed the lawfulness of the SIS alert could not appeal against it. This view has been rejected by the Dutch courts afterwards. This can be evidenced in The Hague Court's decision concerning eight Polish applicants who asked the Dutch authority to delete the reports concerning them in the NSIS. The applicants, working illegally in Dutch greenhouses, were registered in the NSIS on grounds of having been repeatedly expelled or have evaded expulsion. Since the Dutch authority had refused to delete their SIS reports, the Polish workers appealed against this refusal, but their appeal was said to be inadmissible because the applicants should have used the procedure under the Dutch Data Protection Law. However, in the final judgment of the President of the Court of The Hague, the opposite conclusion was reached; the right to judicial remedies as provided for in Article 111 CISA was referred in this case. As a result, the temporary measure to suspend the SIS alert was granted until four weeks after the final decision, at the applicant's request, because it had been found that there was at least a reasonable doubt about whether the disputed SIS report was in conformity with Article 96 CISA. To conclude, despite the judgments, in which Dutch courts recognized the direct legal effects of a SIS alert, the Dutch ministerial authorities maintained the view that the SIS report is a practical measure against which no right of appeal is possible[328].

328 In June 2005, the Aliens circular 2000 was amended, describing the procedures to be followed with regard to individual remedies against alerts registered in the NSIS: *Wijziging Vreemdelingencirculaire, Decision 2005/29*, Staatscourant,

As far as the Visa Information System is concerned, in the case C-84/12 Koushkaki - an Iranian national whose Schengen visa application to Germany was refused due to significant doubt as to his intention to return to Iran before the expiry of the visa, the CJEU in his preliminary ruling, that had been requested by the Administrative Court in Berlin, concluded that the Member State cannot refuse to issue the applicant a Schengen visa unless one of the grounds for refusal of a visa listed in the Visa Code: a) false or counterfeit travel document; b) incapability of providing justification for the purpose and conditions of an intended stay by an applicant as well as proof of sufficient means of subsistence; c) presence of the applicant for three months during the current six-month period on the territory of the Member States on the basis of a uniform visa or a visa with limited territorial validity; d) issuance of an alert in the SIS for the purpose of his/her refusing entry; e) applicant may constitute a threat to public policy, internal security or public health, as defined in Article 2(19) of the Schengen Borders Code, or to the international relations of any of the Member States, in particular where an alert has been issued in one of national data bases for the purpose of refusing entry on the same grounds; f) he/she does not provide proof of holding adequate and valid travel medicine insurance; g) final visa refusal ground, existence of reasonable doubts as to the authenticity of the supporting documents submitted by the applicant or the veracity of their contents, the reliability of the statements made by the applicant or his intention to leave the territory of the Member States before the expiry of the visa applied for[329]. The authorities have wide discretion in the examination of that application within the provision of the Visa Code, with a view to ascertaining if one of those grounds for refusal can be applied to the applicant. In addition, when deciding on the application, the authorities must be satisfied that there is no reasonable doubt that the applicant intends to leave the territory of the Member States before the visa expires. This must be determined in the light of the general situation in the applicant's country of residence and of the applicant's individual characteristics.

Automatic return of persons, implemented by the Italian border authorities by the means of the EURODAC - the instrument of the Dublin system which serves to determine which European Union Member State is responsible for

---

23 June 2005, no. 119. See § A3/9.6.3.3. In this text in the *Aliens Circular*, it was again explicitly stated that a national decision to report a SIS alert into NSIS is not an administrative decision. It does stress, however, that „procedures against a refusal to withdraw such a SIS report should be in accordance with Article 111 CISA".

329 Regulation (EC) No 810/2009 of the European Parliament and of the Council of 13 July 2009 establishing a Community Code on Visas (Visa Code), OJ L 243/1 § 32.

examining an asylum application lodged in one of the Member States by a third-country national- was deliberated by the European Court of Human Rights in the case Sharifi and Others v. Italy and Greece (application no. 16643/09), where the plaintiffs having been handed over to ferry captains with the aim to remove them back to Greece, were deprived in this way of any procedural and substantive rights. It is to be acknowledged that under Eurodac Regulation (EU) No. 603/2013 all asylum seekers and migrants in an irregular situation apprehended in connection with an infrequent border crossing-except of children under the age of 14 years - must provide their fingerprints that are stored afterwards in the large-scale database called Eurodac. Although taking fingerprints for Eurodac does not in itself determine the identity of a person, it contributes to the identification since a link may be established between an asylum applicant and a past Eurodac entry. In case of a match in Eurodac, the authorities can request the personal data from the Member State that first entered the person into Eurodac, based on the Article 34 of the Dublin Regulation. In addition, Article 1(3) of the Eurodac Regulation allows the Member State of origin to check the fingerprints taken for the purpose of Eurodac against other databases set up under its national law, such as national databases on foreigners. This may also result in the identification of the person. Under certain conditions, Article 20 of the Eurodac Regulation and Articles 21 and 22 of the VIS Regulation allow fingerprints from asylum seekers to be searched in the Visa Information System (VIS). Therefore, at least in these situations and in line with Recital 5 of the Eurodac Regulation, taking fingerprints for Eurodac might also serve to determine or verify a person's identity. Further exchanges of information with the Member State in which a match was obtained could also identify the nationality of the asylum seeker or third country national[330]

To conclude, the ECHR underlined that no form of collective and indiscriminate returns could be justified by reference to that system (Dublin-EURODAC). What is more, it was, according to the Court, the responsibility of the State carrying out the return to ensure that the destination country offered sufficient guarantees in the application of its asylum policy to prevent the person concerned being removed to the country where she/he may face persecution ('non-refoulement' Geneva Convention 1951- ratified by the all EU Member States).

Summarizing, information sharing, including the exchange of personal data, in the European Union especially in the areas related to law enforcement and judicial cooperation, such as the Area of Freedom, Security and Justice (AFSJ),

---

330 *Fundamental rights implications of the obligation to provide fingerprints for Eurodac*, Fundamental Rights Agency 05/2015, Vienna, pp.1–10.

has become an essential tool in the internal security policy of the EU[331]. Personal data are therefore constantly exchanged, not only between Member States and with third countries, but also between EU bodies[332].One of the areas of the EU policies that relies heavily on the use of technology including through large-scale databases is management of immigration and asylum. The number of these established throughout the years has recently caused concerns over - on the on hand - interoperability[333] between EU information systems in the area of borders and security - on the other - fundamental rights infringements, as has been evidenced in this chapter, linked to the right to private life (Article 7 of the EU Charter of Fundamental Rights (the Charter) and the protection of personal data (Article 8 of the Charter). Furthermore, the actual broader availability of data can in itself have additional implications-positive or negative-on, for instance, the right to an effective remedy (Article 47) or the prohibition of torture and inhuman or degrading treatment or punishment (Article 4), liberty and security of person (Article 6) integrity of the person (Article 3) the right to asylum (Article 18) and prohibition of collective expulsion (Article 19) rights of the child (Article 24) and equality before the law (Article 20)[334]. To conclude, the above presented judgments of the European jurisprudence can be also framed in the so called dilemma of *knowledge* -understood in the context of this paper as minimal personal information obtained by an administrative body for the purpose of migration control - and *power* - interpreted here as competences and restrictions, e.g. data minimization, purpose/storage limitation imposed on executive bodies by the EU Data Protection Law in the context of the EU immigration and asylum policy.

---

331 Boehm F., *Information Sharing and Data Protection in the Area of Freedom, Security and Justice. Towards Harmonized Data Protection Principles for Information Exchange at the EU level, Springer Berlin Heidelberg 2012,* pp. 321–368.

332 In this context, it is worth to mention that one of the most important tools for the achievement of the AFSJ provided for in the Title V TFEU is a reinforced police and judicial cooperation (Articles 82–89 TFEU), which is carried out in no small part by sharing and exchanging personal data. Furthermore, article 87 TFEU clarifies that the EU shall establish police cooperation involving all the Member States' competent authorities, including police, customs and other specialized law enforcement services.

333 In 2019 the Council adopted two regulations: 1) on border and visa; 2) police, judicial cooperation and migration, establishing a framework for interoperability between EU information systems in the area of justice and home affairs, at: https://data.consilium.europa.eu/doc/document/PE-30-2019-INIT/en/pdf; https://data.consilium.europa.eu/doc/document/PE-31-2019-INIT/en/pdf (Accessed: March 2020).

334 *Fundamental rights and the interoperability of EU information systems: borders and security, European Union Agency for Fundamental Rights,* Vienna 2017, p. 7.

IV Between knowledge and power – use of technology for the management of immigration policy: European Union versus United States of America

1 Introduction

Nowadays, in the age of globalization innovative means of transport and telecommunication have - on the one hand - increased peoples' capabilities and aspirations to migrate - on the other - stimulated especially after September 11 2001- terrorist threats around the world. That has found its expression in the words of Tom Ridge, former US Secretary of Homeland Security: „As the world community has become more connected through the globalization of technology, transportation, commerce and communication the benefits of globalization available to peace loving, freedom loving people were available to the terrorists as well"[335]. Hence, in the climate of insecurity the threat of terrorism was being used to justify restrictions imposed on human rights standards, among them on the right to privacy. These circumstances were ostentatiously described by M. Ignatieff as *„the end of human rights era"*[336]. Bearing in mind this context, one may ask a question concerning the appropriate balance between security priorities and human rights standards especially data protection guarantees while guarding borders. This part of the book is focused on this dilemma by contrasting the use of technology for regulation of migration and asylum policy by the European Union and the United States of America.

First of all, it is worth to emphasize, that in its response to global terrorism and transnational crime after September 11 2001 border control have emerged as a preferred policy choice by the United States[337].What is even more, the threat of terrorism coming through U. S. borders was being discursively constructed by the elites to securitize the American boundaries as conduits for terrorist

---

335 Transcript of Secretary of Homeland Security Tom Ridge at the Center for Transatlantic Relations at Johns Hopkins University 2004, at: http://www.dhs.gov/dhspublic/display?theme1⁄444& content1⁄43994&print1⁄4true>, (Accessed: February 2018).

336 Ignatieff M., Will the Quest for Security Kill the Human Rights Era?, in: "International Herald Tribune" 6 February 2002, p. 3.

337 Ackleson J., Securing Through Technology? "Smart Borders" after September 11th, in: Technology and Terrorism, D. Clarke (ed.), Routledge New York 2017, pp. 55–68.

movement.[338] This tendency can be illustrated by the official statement of the Attorney General John Ashcroft who had stressed that in this new war, our enemies' platoons infiltrate our borders quietly, blending in with visitors and tourists, students and workers.[339] Regardless of the fact that no evidence existed that the 9/11 terrorists entered the United States from Mexico or Canada. In fact, most of those who committed the 9/11 attacks entered on tourist or student visas legally and then violated the conditions of their admittance. As a result, the new controversial rules followed according to which foreigners, arriving at airports and seaports, who fit the profile of potential terrorist would have their fingerprints matched electronically against federal databases. The Bush administration was a pioneer in launching the "Smart Borders" program that was later copied by the European Union[340], designed to screen for terrorist incursions into the United States at air and land ports of entry; consequently, the system that tracked virtually all of the 35 million annual visitors to the United States was operable by 2005[341]. This approach was widely heralded as a reasonable first step in regaining control over illegal immigration in the United States. Using a variety of technologies, including surveillance, biometrics, and inter-linked information technology (IT) databases, the stated goal was to identify problematic entrants-either persons or cargo (e.g., terrorists and their weapons)-while at the same time facilitating the quick entry of legitimate goods and travelers. In the wide sea of information flowing across globalized borders "secured through technology"-utilizing tools to identify valuable knowledge about threats- became priority. At the same time, the *power* of these technological solutions invoked questions of efficacy and

338 The Congressional Immigration Reform Caucus: "The time is right to call for troops on the border in order to protect our national security interests."; Representative Tom Tancredo (R-Colorado): "The defense of the nation begins with the defense of its borders." The U.S. State Department: "The threat posed by our open borders is a diffuse and insidious threat." See also, „Technology and Terrorism", Francis T. Cullen (Ed.), Routledge, London and New York 2017.

339 Schmitt E., Traces of Terror: Immigration, Ashcroft Proposes Rules for Foreign Visitors, in: "International New York Times", June 6, 2002, p. 3.

340 In February 2013, the Commission tabled a Smart Borders package consisting of three proposals: (1) a Regulation for an Entry/Exit System (EES) for the recording of information on the time and place of entry and exit of third country nationals traveling to the Schengen area; (2) a Regulation for a Registered Traveler Program (RTP) to allow third country nationals who have been pre-vetted to benefit from facilitation of border checks at the Union external border; (3) a Regulation amending the Schengen Borders Code in order to take into account the establishment of the EES and RTP.

341 E. Schmitt, Traces of Terror, Ibid.

democratic values. These were however silenced by the border security policy constructed in response to September 11 terrorist attacks. "Constructed" in this context refers not only how physical security--such as agents, fortifications, surveillance, and the like--were deployed, but also to the nature of the social environment in which actors, like government elites and federal agencies, formulated solutions and then took actions against perceived "threats" or „risks." In this context, it is worth to compare European versus American threat perception defined in their security strategies. In the European Security Strategy terrorism "arises out of complex causes: (…) the pressures of modernization, cultural, social and political crises, and the alienation of young people living in foreign societies"[342]. Hence, the European Union as civilian *power* is well equipped to tackle such threats using "mixture of intelligence, police, judicial, military and other means"[343]. United States of America, on the other hand, concentrates on military means by emphasizing in its strategy commitment to fight global terrorism defined as politically motivated violence perpetrated against innocents, with or without the support of international community by acting preemptively against global terrorism[344], what constitutes breach of international law, namely, Article 2 § 4[345].

Hence, U.S. borders were seen as a conduit for terrorist movement, regardless of the fact that there was little clarity about whom the United States was really at war with. Consequently, successive American presidents George W. Bush-Barack Obama, Donald Trump - have lumped disparate and often competing militants into simplified categories - „terrorists", „violent extremists" or just „enemy" who would be found, stopped and defeated[346]. To illustrate, the Bush administration claimed to have defeated the Taliban seven times from 2002 through 2005. The military

---

342 "*A Secure Europe in a Better World*"-European Security Strategy, Brussels, 12 December 2003, p. 3.

343 I. Manners, *Normative Power Europe: A Contradiction in Terms*?, in: "Journal of Common Market Studies", Volume 40, Issue 2, June 2002, pp. 235–258.

344 Compare: "*The National Security Strategy of the United States of America*", September 2002, p. 6.

345 All members shall refrain in their international relations from the threat or use of force against the territorial integrity or political independence of any state, or in any other manner inconsistent with the Purposes of the United Nations.

346 Micah Zenko, *Bush and Obama Fought a Failed 'War on Terror.' It's Trump's Turn*, in: "International New York Times", Aug. 25, 2017, https://www.nytimes.com/2017/08/25/opinion/trump-afghanistan-war-on-terror.html (Accessed: May 2018); *President George W. Bush address to a Joint Session of Congress and the American People,* September 20, 2001, at:https://www.washingtonpost.com/wp-srv/nation/specials/attacked/transcripts/bushaddress_092001.html? (Accessed: January 2020).

and counterterrorism officials however were confronted with a different reality. It is to be acknowledged, however, that Barack Obama being inaugurated as the first president to take office in the Age of Terrorism inherited two struggles-one with Al Qaeda and its ideological allies, and another that divided his country over issues like torture, prosecutions, and security. In such a reality Obama rejected the phrase "war on terror" altogether in favor of the expression: "a number of vital challenges confronting America".[347] In contrast, President Donald Trump claimed in his Inaugural Address that he „would eradicate" „radical Islamic Terrorism" completely from the face of the earth. Furthermore, while describing terrorist groups as monolithic enemy the successive American administrations repeated a disproved belief: that terrorists require „safe havens" from which to conduct attacks, and therefore were more inclined to increase deployment of troops in combat zones. This was based on a fundamental-and inexcusable-misunderstanding about the Sept. 11 attacks, where the hijackers passed undetected through border checkpoints 33 times and enjoyed the safe havens of southern Maryland, San Diego and Oklahoma City.

Crucial to note is the fact that in the "antiterrorist crusade" scientific community was due to "(...) serve on the front lines of this war, by developing new technologies that would make America safer[348]. In the first place, at the United States House subcommittee hearing in February 2002, a panel of commercial information technology experts and management consultants were asked to give technical advice on how the war on terror might be fought using risk profiling techniques. The hearing concluded that technologies designed to classify populations according to their degree of threat were long available in the private commercial sector and should be deployed at the service of border security. Indeed, the invited panel of experts stated clearly that 'our enemies were hiding in open and available information' and that, had surveillance and profiling techniques been in place, the events of 9/11 'could have been predicted and averted'. Secondly, the federal government response to terrorism was also largely vested in the newly established Department of Homeland Security (DHS). Officials of this institution have placed border security high on its priority list, and in its discourse strongly linked border control and terrorism. In the words of the new secretary Tom Ridge, U.S. boundaries were described as "a conduits for terrorists, weapons of mass destruction, illegal migrants, contraband, and

347 *Obama's War on Terror* by Peter Baker, "International New York Times" January 4 2010, at: https://www.nytimes.com/2010/01/17/magazine/17Terror-t.html?searchResultPosition=1 (Accessed: March 2020)

348 G. W. Bush, "*Anti-Terrorism Technology Key to Homeland Security,*" Remarks at Argonne National Laboratory (22 July 2002), at: https://georgewbush-whitehouse.archives.gov/news/releases/2002/07/20020722-1.html (Accessed: January 2020)

other unlawful commodities... [thus] the new threats and opportunities of the 21st century demanded a new approach to border management." As a result, Ridge declared deployment of more technology as the solution to create, in his words, a "smart...seamless border."[349] Technology was thus a major emphasis in the legislation that established the Department of Homeland Security. The bill set up a Directorate of Science and Technology whose focus was development of a „...national policy and strategic plan for...efforts to identify and develop countermeasures for...emerging terrorist threats" including the importation of weapons and terrorists. The bill also included a complex web of priorities for research, development, and technology transfer to law enforcement and the private sector.[350] In order to „(...) harness the creative genius of the entire research and development community, especially the private sector...to confront the full range of terrorist threats to the homeland."[351], new governmental and non-governmental (e.g., university) centers were authorized for the development and transfer of such technologies.[352]

Furthermore, it was the Patriot Act („Uniting and Strengthening America by Providing Appropriate Tools Required to Intercept and Obstruct Terrorism") signed into law by the President Bush on October 26, 2001 that gave security agencies increased resources to fight terrorism, at home and abroad and the law enforcement officials' expansive powers. As far as the former is concerned, the Bush administration's fiscal 2003 budget proposed to spend $11 billion on border security, $2.2 billion more than in 2002.[353] While over $50 billion in Fiscal Year (FY)03 were foreseen for investments in government-wide information technology, funding for technology for homeland defense in particular topped $722 million for FY03, a 214 percent increase over the previous year.[354]; the latter consisted of the huge number (from 2001-the half of the 2005: 178) of executive orders issued by the president uncontrolled by the congress. In order to assess

349 Office of Homeland Security, "*Securing America's Borders Fact Sheet: Border Security*", in: http://www.whitehouse.gov/news/releases/2002/01/20020125.html, (Accessed: 25 January 2002)

350 Homeland Security Act (H.R. 5710) 107th Congress, 2d sess., 13 November 2002, section 71.

351 Tom Ridge, statement on the Department of Homeland Security, House Select Committee on Homeland Security (15 July 2002)

352 Homeland Security Act, Ibid, sect. 84,89.

353 Kevin G. Hall, "Security Will Tighten on Mexican Border: U.S. Plans New Safeguards", "Miami Herald", 6 March 2002.

354 Henry Stimson Center, U.S. Homeland Security: A Look at the Financial Year 2003 Homeland Security Budget Request, at: https://www.files.ethz.ch/isn/31134/FollowingtheMoney.pdf, (Accessed: May 2018)

the scale of antidemocratic provisions introduced in the USA Patriot Act, one may compare it with its predecessor-the foreign Intelligence Surveillance Act (FISA) passed in 1978. This Act allowed the U.S. government to spy on foreign governments and foreign nationals. It prescribed procedures for requesting judicial authorization for electronic surveillance and physical searches of persons engaged in espionage or international terrorism against the U.S. on behalf of a foreign power. In contrast to this provision, while in FISA one may observe a consistent attempt to protect U.S. persons from surveillance making a target of it „foreign agent"; government spying on American citizens, according to USA Patriot Act that speaks about „any U.S. person", became common practice. Continuing this comparison, „terrorist activity" being the central point of surveillance under FISA, became in Patriot Act „any domestic criminal activity". To conclude, while the point of FISA was to allow electronic surveillance for the purpose of prosecution; in Patriot Act, the aim of surveillance becomes information gathering. Interestingly, in July 2015 in response to Charlie Hebdo attacks the French Intelligence Act, which resonated with the USA Patriot Act as far as uncontrolled surveillance is concerned, was passed[355] by the National Assembly with 438 votes in favor and just 86 against. It introduced in France state of emergency and, as a result, enabled intelligence agencies to record any calls, text messages and internet activity using the so called "black boxes" (complex algorithms installed to detect a pattern of suspicious behavior online). Moreover, in a declared officially state of emergency authorities became capable of executing wireless phone taps, installing hidden cameras as well as using geolocation measures. In addition, in France as well as throughout Europe states have enacted anti-incitement and public disorder laws aimed at broadening authority to prohibit and punish speech that may have highly attenuated links to terrorist activity[356].

355 Aputtzo M. Erlanger S., *Patriot Act Rises in France, and is Ridiculed, „International New York Times"*, January 16, 2015, p.3.

356 Marie Boyne Shawn, *Free Speech, Terrorism, and European Security: Defining and Defending the Political Community, in: „Pace Law Review" Volume 30, Issue 2, 2010,* pp. 417–483; for example, in 2003, Belgium amended its criminal code to include the crime of incitement. The provision states: Any person who, either by views expressed in meetings or public places or by writings, printed matter, images or emblems of any kind displayed, distributed, sold or put on sale or public view, directly provoked others to commit the crime or offense, without prejudice to the penalties imposed by law on authors of provocations to commit crimes or offenses, even if such provocations were not acted upon; See also: *A War on Terror? The European Stance on a New Threat, Changing Laws and Human Rights Implications,* Wade M. Malijević A. (Eds.), New York, Dordrecht, Heidelberg, London 2010.

Opponents of this French version of the Patriot Act manifested their dissatisfaction with the new security measures by means of petition signed by over 100,000 people raising awareness that "mass surveillance is part of an intolerable and oppressive machine, which is by nature the seed of totalitarianism"[357]. However, on the 3rd October 2017 under president Macron many of the above mentioned heightened security measures envisioned by the state of emergency (2015), that have given local police and administrative authorities power to monitor, arrest or detain suspects without judicial oversight, were approved by the French Parliament in the framework of anti-terrorism laws[358].

Answering to the terror-related challenges Western countries (European Union & USA) attempted to reinforce their knowledge about the cross-border movement of people by employment of scientific technologies and managerial expertise in the politics of border management. More and more sophisticated technological tools, used for exercising of biopower such that the bodies of migrants and travelers themselves became sites of multiple encoded boundaries, consisted of: bone scanners, speech-recognition utilities and last but not least biometrics. The latter defined as technologies that measure and analyze human body characteristics, such as fingerprints, eye retinas and irises, voice patterns, facial patterns and hand measurements or DNA for authentication purposes, to be stored in databases afterwards. Accordingly, the US Patriot Act defined a set of practices for biometric applications that afforded their almost unlimited use in the investigation and identification of terrorism. In effect, the US VISIT system converged the data from integrated databases with biometric identifiers such as electronic fingerprints, facial and gait recognition, and iris scans. What is more, as information sharing and secure borders were citizens' strategic priorities, the emphasis on risk profiling embodied within US VISIT was merely an initial step in motivating population to monitor suspicious or risky groups. According to this concept, as Butler has put the problem, 'when the alert goes out, every member of the population is asked to become a "foot soldier"' in the war on terror, observing the behavior of fellow passengers on a train, new neighbors in town, 'and anyone who looks vaguely Arab in the dominant racial imaginary'[359]. Yet, there were apparently no questions raised as to the implications of such

357 Zimmermann J., co-founder of La Quadrature du Net: „France in the Era of Mass Surveillance! We must resist!", in: https://www.laquadrature.net/en/france-in-era-of-mass-surveillance-we-must-resist (Accessed: April 2018).

358 www.assemblee-nationale.fr/15/ta-pdf/0164-p.pdf, (Accessed: May 2018).

359 Butler, J., *Precarious life: The powers of mourning and violence*, London: Verso 2004, p. 39.

citizen profiling for the Arab Americans and other groups who have found that risk profiling is racial and ethnic targeting[360]. This tendency was to be observed on the other site of the Atlantic in the wake of the July 2005 London bombings, when the Chief Constable of London transport police called for increased vigilance on the part of commuters and tourists, simultaneously urging that stop and search powers should be 'targeted' and 'should not waste time on white old ladies' (*Plan to Improve*, 2005). In addition, the 'Life Savers' hotline number was downloaded to mobile phones with the message that 'people should consider whether the behavior of those they encounter, through work or socially, gives them any reason to think they might be planning terrorist attacks' (*Home Office*, 2005). Being drawn into the everyday armory of the war on terror citizens have at their disposal technological innovations-personal products to fight the war on terror, such as the Town Compass LLC marketed by the Seattle IT company. Their 'Most Wanted Terrorists' database was available as a free download to pocket PCs and smart phones as part of a 'terrorism survival' bundle. Hence, by means of Town Compass 'people could have the photos and descriptions at their fingertips at all times in case they spotted a suspicious person, easily comparing the person to the photo without endangering themselves'. Should the vigilant citizen succeed in identifying a suspicious person, the download came complete with one-touch dialing to the FBI and full details of available rewards.

Though the implementation of biometric gateways has been beset by difficulties, the seductive allure of biometrics, similar to that one observed in the legislation of the European Union (see: chapter II) has taken a strong hold in the governmentality of mobility. This, among others, can be evidenced in number of agreements completed by American officials in January 2005 with the Dutch government to deploy biometric systems aimed at accelerating movement of 'trusted travelers' whilst restricting that one of higher risk groups. In addition, while opening the new registered traveler programs at Schiphol airport, Secretary Ridge emphasized the possibilities for the categorization of air passengers via biometrics: *we can design border security initiatives to both enhance homeland security and facilitate global commerce and travel.* Within these programs, we see not only the intertwinement of physical identifiers with information systems, but

360 Edley C., The new American dilemma: Racial profiling post-9/11, in: *The war on our freedoms: Civil liberties in an age of terrorism*, R. Leone, & G. Anrig (Eds.), New York: Public Affairs 2003; C. Nagel, Geopolitics by any other name: Immigration and the politics of assimilation, in: „Political Geography" 21(8), 2002, pp. 971–987; L. Amoore, *Biometric borders: Governing mobility in the war on terror*, in: "Political Geography", 25 (2006) pp. 336–351.

also the annexing of patterns of behavior, and their associated identities, that can be afforded smooth movement across borders. The use of air miles databases, for example, is coupled to the biometric submission of an iris scan to produce the identity of a 'trusted traveler'.[361] In a sense, the US Air Transportation Association's registered traveler projects, together with the Netherlands' Privium Plus, have much in common with the historical practices of what is called 'risk pooling' in studies of the insurance industry.[362] By categorizing patterns of behavior as 'low risk' (whether in the profiling of claims history in insurance, or via frequent flier history in airline security), authorities group together for common treatment individuals who are classified and encoded with a similar category of risk in this case expedited passage through security checks. Whereas the trusted traveler biometrics tend to emphasize membership of (or inclusion in) a group based on pre-screening checks such as citizenship and past travel patterns, untrusted traveler biometrics are based on ongoing surveillance and checks on patterns of behavior. As a result, while for the trusted traveler the biometric submission is usually the end of the matter, the passport to 'borders lite' (if not to a borderless world), the risky traveler's biometric submission is only the beginning of a world of perennial dataveillance where the border looms large.

In these circumstances, after the attacks of 9/11/2001 transatlantic information sharing, including the exchange of more complex and sensitive personal data, has become an essential tool in the security policy of the European Union &United States of America. Nevertheless, fostering closer U.S.-E.U. cooperation was fraught with plethora of conflicts: security versus privacy, US versus EU antiterrorist legislation; EU versus US legal privacy regime: European Parliament versus Council and Commission; 'commercial processing' of data versus 'law enforcement processing'; and data protection versus data mining. It is worth to emphasize that in two landmark decisions, the Court of Justice of the European Union has acknowledged a specific right to be forgotten (Google/Spain)[363] as a new fundamental right and has also invalidated the Safe Harbor Agreement (mainly the Commission's adequacy decision 520/2000/EC) between

361 Department of Homeland Security, 2005, p. 1.

362 Ewald F., *Insurance and risk*, in: *The Foucault Effect: Studies in Governmentality*, G Burchell (ed.), 1991.

363 C-131/12, Google Spain SL, Google Inc v Agencia Española de Protección de Datos (AEPD), Mario Costeja González, ECLI:EU:C:2014:317 (CJEU) (2014).

the EU and the US (Schrems/Ireland[364]) for various reasons, not at least due to nonconformity of some US-surveillance measures with the constitutional privacy rights in Europe.

Right to be forgotten debate on both sides of Atlantic exemplifies the crucial differences in approach to human rights, specifically to data protection rights and privacy protection. The reaction to the proposals for the right to be forgotten in the US was quite dramatic. Headlines such as *'More crap from the EU'* by Jane Bambauer writing in Harvard's Info/Law blog17 and *"Why Can't Europe Just Forget the Ridiculous Idea of a 'Right To Be Forgotten*"-by Mike Masnick in TechDirt[365] created an atmosphere of distrust between the transatlantic allies. What was seen by those proposing it on the European side to be further development of data protection standards, was presented in the US as the biggest threat to free speech on the internet in the current decade[366]. Closer examination, however, evidences that this right looks more like a right to delete; the name 'right to be forgotten' comes to an extent from one part of the right's origins, the old French- le droit à l'oubli - and Italian - dritto al oblio - were much more about 'forgetting' - about the rights of criminals with spent convictions to have those convictions 'forgotten' and not taken into account in how they are dealt with by the media and by potential employers and so forth. The new right framed in the General Data Protection Regulation equipped an individual with the right to delete/erasure especially in the context of dealing with personal data held on social networks.[367] Nevertheless, one of key objections came from the Professor Jeffrey Rosen who assumed that not only would the right to be forgotten allow people to have control over data that they themselves have placed on the internet, but also it would allow them to control data about them that other people have created or posted. Personal data, as Rosen correctly noted, is broadly defined as 'any information relating to a data subject'. That, then, brings the 'free speech' issue to a focus. In these terms, if someone posts a 'story' about you, that story becomes 'personal data', and hence, using the right to be forgotten, you appear to have a 'right' to demand the deletion

364 C-362/14 Maximillian Schrems v Data protection Commissioner, ECLI:EU:C:2015:650 (CJEU) (2015).

365 Accessible at: https://www.techdirt.com/articles/20120129/23085517583/why-cant-europe-just-forget-ridiculous-idea-right-to-be-forgotten.shtml, (Accessed: June 2018).

366 General Data Protection Regulation, Article 17.

367 In addition, 'right to be forgotten' is accompanied by the article 15, which gives the data subject the right to access the personal data, and Article 16, which grants a right to rectify inaccurate data.

of that story. Looked at from this perspective, the right to be forgotten may indeed be recognized as a tool of censorship, an attempt to allow the rewriting of history—and in direct contradiction of the all-important First Amendment of the US Constitution. Interestingly, while considering the case Google v. AFPD by the Court of Justice of the European Union the above mentioned reasoning was shared by the advocate General Niilo Jääskinen in his advisory opinion; "Google had no responsibility to remove any links ('right to be forgotten') on its search engine based on a privacy claim[368] due to the fact that suppressing legitimate and legal information already in the public domain would interfere with freedom of expression and undermine the objectivity of information on the Internet".[369] The CJEU, however, rejected the Advocate General's argument and recognized a broad right to be forgotten under Spain's implementation of Directive 95/46/EC.[370] It has been emphasized, in the first place, that "Google as an indexer of information was processing personal data and therefore subject to the Directive's obligations for data controllers. Google's argument that imposing a duty to remove personal data violated the principle of proportionality, and that such removal must be addressed to the publisher of the website because the publisher was responsible for making the information public was also rejected. Furthermore, court reasoned that search engines make access to this information effortlessly available, because they enable users to obtain information about a data subject by simply typing the subject's name".[371] What is more, due to their preeminent role in organizing data, search engines like Google are far more likely to interfere with the data subject's right to privacy than the original website publisher; information is *power*, and *information/knowledge* about people is *power* over people. To conclude, 'the right to be forgotten' was heralded in US as the biggest threat to free speech on the Internet in the coming decade; this particular right, as many claimed, could make Facebook, Google, Apple, Microsoft, etc. - businesses with great lobbying *power* - liable for the EU data protection breaches and as a result American enterprises may be fined if they fail to remove photos that people post about themselves and later regret, even if the photos have been widely distributed already.

The argument over the free speech/privacy balance may appear simplistic on the surface, but it is crucial to understand how deeply the attitudes presented by both sides are ingrained in cultural differences between the US and the EU. Apart from the depicted beneath discrepancies, the defense of free speech by

368 Opinion of Advocate General Jääskinen, § 138.
369 Ibid § 120–34.
370 Google Spain SL, Case C-131/12.
371 Ibid § 80.

the American side may serve as some kind of cover for US protection of its own business interest; as well as privacy could be perceived as a sort of clandestine EU attacks on US businesses in order to promote and protect existing and future European enterprises[372].

The European Union and the United States of America share a common heritage in their views on democracy, the rule of law, and fundamental freedoms. It is the EU, however, that has played a major role in the global privacy debate since 1990s. Many countries have followed and also implemented data and privacy protection laws mirroring some of the EU provisions. Data Protection Directive followed by the General Data Protection Regulation have sought to establish de facto international benchmarks for corporate information processing[373]. Both, The European Union and United States of America address privacy from similar foundations, based on principles of autonomy, dignity and restraint on government *power*. They have many common interests, including increasing the transparency of data processing on the Internet, facilitating the assertion of privacy rights by individuals, and restraining government surveillance. What is more there has been cooperation between the EU and the US on privacy issues; such as in the drafting of the 1980 and 2013 versions of the Organization for Economic Cooperation and Development (OECD) Guidelines on the Protection of Privacy and Transborder Flows of Personal Data (OECD Guidelines).

2 Data and privacy protection in the United States of America

Describing the US privacy regime, legal scholar Gregory Shaffer noted: 'data privacy regulation in the United States is fragmented, ad hoc, and narrowly targeted to cover specific sectors and concerns.'[374]. Indeed, US privacy law can be found in a number of different sources: the US Constitution, the Supreme Court case

---

372 Bernal P., *The EU, the US and Right to be Forgotten*, in: *Reloading Data Protection. Multidisciplinary Insights and Contemporary Challenges*, S. Gutwirth, R. Leenes, P. de Hert (eds.), Dordrecht 2014, pp.61–78.

373 Scheer D., *For Young Eyes Only-Europe's new High-Tech Role: Playing Privacy Cop to the World*, in: "Wall Street Journal", Oct. 10, 2003, pp.10–12.

374 Shaffer Gregory C., *Globalization and Social Protection: The impact of EU and International Rules in the Ratcheting up of U.S. Data Privacy Standards*, in: "Yale Journal of International Law" (2000) 25, p. 22.

law, federal legislation, state legislation and the theory of torts[375]. As far as the definition of the term "privacy" is concerned, in EU law there is a distinction between "privacy" and "data protection". By contrast, in the US the protection of an individual's "private space", the collection and use of "personally identifying information", and other related topics tend to be subsumed under the term "privacy". This is an example of using the same terms to mean different things that is one of the causes of misunderstandings between the two sides[376]. Furthermore, continental law is avidly protective of many kinds of "privacy" in many realms of life, whether the issue is consumer data, credit reporting, workplace privacy, etc[377]. This approach is a sort of World War II heritage when Europeans experienced disastrous abuses of their personal records[378]. Privacy protection in the US is based on concepts of autonomy and liberty articulated in the US Constitution and the Bill of Rights. Specifically, protection of privacy is mainly based on the First Amendment (protection of free speech and freedom of assembly), the fourth Amendment (protection from unreasonable searches and seizures), and the Fifth Amendment (privilege against self-incrimination). The Fourth Amendment, in particular, according to the US Supreme Court aims at 'protecting personal privacy and dignity against unwarranted intrusion by the State'.[379] It contains two clauses: the first, the substantive clause, protects against certain government activities; the second, the procedural clause, regulates government *power* through the process of obtaining a warrant[380]. It can be obtained when there is a 'probable cause' for conducting a search or seizure[381]. Applicability of the Fourth Amendment might be illustrated by the

---

375 Tzanou M., *The War Against Terror and Transatlantic Information Sharing: Spillovers of Privacy or Spillovers of Security?'*, in: „Utrecht Journal of International and European Law", Vol. 31, No. 80, pp. 87–103, February 2015.

376 *Privacy Bridges. EU and US privacy experts in search of transatlantic privacy solutions,* in: 37th International Privacy Conference, Amsterdam 2015, at:http://privacybridges.mit.edu/sites/default/files/documents/PrivacyBridges-FINAL.pdf (Accessed: February 2018).

377 Whitman James Q., *The Two Western Cultures of Privacy: Dignity versus Liberty,* in: "Yale Law Journal" Vol. 113, Issue 6, pp. 1153–1221.

378 Bignami F., *European versus American Liberty: A comparative privacy analysis of anti-terrorism data mining,* in: "Boston College Law Review" Vol. 48, pp. 609–698.

379 *Schmerber v. California* (1966) 384 U.S. 757.

380 Solove Daniel J., *'Digital Dossiers and the Dissipation of Fourth Amendment Privacy', in:* "Southern California Law Review" Vol. 75, July 2002, pp. 1084–1167.

381 Solove D. and Schwartz P., *Information Privacy Law* 3rd edition, Wolters Kluwer Law & Business, Aspen Publishers 2009, p. 237.

Katz v. United States case[382], where the Supreme Court established that the protection of the Fourth Amendment against government intrusion applied when an individual had a 'reasonable expectation of privacy.'[383] Justice Harlan, in his concurring opinion in Katz, articulated the twofold requirement, known as the 'reasonable expectation privacy test'[384] that triggers the application of the Fourth Amendment: 'first, that a person have exhibited an actual (subjective) expectation of privacy and, second, that the expectation be one that society is prepared to recognize as "reasonable."[385] This means, according to Justice Harlan, that 'conversations in the open would not be protected against being overheard, for the expectation of privacy under the circumstances would be unreasonable.'[386] A similar statement was made by the majority opinion, which held that 'what a person knowingly exposes to the public, even in his own home or office, is not a subject of Fourth Amendment protection.'[387] On this basis, the Court has found that US citizens lack a reasonable expectation in anything they say to a friend,[388] their bank records,[389] and their garbage.[390]

The above-described reasoning was applied by the Court on phone records in Smith v. Maryland.[391] The police, without a warrant, asked the telephone company to install a device to record the numbers dialed from the defendant's home.[392] The Court agreed that there was no reasonable expectation of privacy regarding the numbers someone dials on her phone, because '*[t]elephone users... typically know that they must convey numerical information to the phone company; that the company has facilities for recording this information; and that the phone company does in fact record this information for a variety of legitimate business purposes. Although subjective expectations cannot be scientifically gauged, it is too much to*

---

382 The decision has been characterized as 'the most important judicial decision on the scope of the Fourth Amendment.' *See* Slobogin Ch., *Privacy at Risk: The New Government Surveillance and the Fourth Amendment, Chicago University Press 2007.*

383 Katz v. United States [1967] 389 U.S 347.

384 Slobogin Ch. and Schumacher Joseph E., '*Reasonable Expectations of Privacy and Autonomy in Fourth Amendment Cases: An Empirical Look at Understandings Recognized and Permitted by Society*', in: „Duke Law Journal" 42 (1993), pp.727–775.

385 Katz v. United States (n 43).

386 Ibid.

387 Ibid.

388 United States v. White [1971] 401 U.S. 745.

389 United States v. Miller [1976] 425 U.S. 435, 437.

390 California v. Greenwood [1988] 486 U.S. 3.

391 Smith v. Maryland [1979] U.S 735.

392 Solove, 'Digital Dossiers …, Op. Cit., p. 1134.

believe that telephone subscribers, under these circumstances, harbor any general expectation that the numbers they dial will remain secret'.[393] Smith v. Maryland established, therefore, a general rule, according to which, '*if information is in the hands of third parties, then an individual can have no reasonable expectation of privacy in that information, which means that the Fourth Amendment does not apply*'.[394] This decision is to be found illuminating for the Passenger Name Records (PNR) case that is due to be described in this chapter. Applying the Smith v. Maryland reasoning, PNR data cannot be covered by the Fourth Amendment protection since travelers cannot enjoy any reasonable expectation of privacy of data they, themselves, give to the airline companies in order to effectuate the ticket reservation.

At the federal level, statutes are '*narrowly tailored to specific privacy problems*'.[395] The most significant and the only federal omnibus piece of privacy legislation is the Privacy Act of 1974.[396] The Privacy Act embodies fair information principles in a statutory framework governing the means by which federal agencies collect, maintain, use, and disseminate personally identifiable information. The Privacy Act applies to information that is maintained in a 'system of records.' A system of records is a group of any records under the control of an agency from which information is retrieved by the name of the individual or by some identifying number, symbol, or other identifying particular assigned to the individual. While the Privacy Act applies to government records, it is ambiguous as to whether it applies to '*commercial data brokers who supply information to the government*'.[397] Furthermore, the Privacy Act applies to US citizens and lawful permanent residents. Safeguards guaranteed by this Act were extended administratively by the EU-US PNR agreements to EU citizens concerning their PNR data. However, the Privacy Act is significantly limited by the so-called 'routine use' exception, according to which information may be disclosed by the Department of Homeland Security for any 'routine use' if disclosure is 'compatible' with the purpose for which the agency collected the information.[398] Finally, another important

393 Smith v. Maryland (n 51).

394 Also known as third-party doctrine. See Solove, 'Digital Dossiers ..., Op. Cit. p. 1135.

395 Solove D., 'Privacy and Power: Computer Databases and Metaphors for Information Privacy', in: 53 „Stanley Law Review", 2001, pp. 1393–1440.

396 Pub. L. No. 93–579, 88 Stat. 1896 (2000) (codified at 5 U.S.C. § 552a).

397 Hoofnagle Ch., 'Big Brother's Little Helpers: How Choice Point and Other Commercial Data Brokers Collect, Process, and Package Your Data for Law Enforcement' (2004) 29 N.C.J. Int'l L. & Com. Reg., pp. 595–637.

398 Daniel Solove, '*A Brief History of Information Privacy Law*', in: Proskauer on Privacy, GWU Law School Public Law Research Paper No. 215 1, 2006, pp. 1–46; Paul

piece of federal legislation is the Freedom of Information Act (FOIA) adopted in 1966. FOIA permits any person (regardless of nationality or country of residence) access to the US federal agency's records, except to the extent such records (or a portion thereof) are protected from disclosure by an applicable exemption under the FOIA. In the 2007 PNR Agreement, FOIA was also extended to apply to individuals traveling with European airlines. According to DHS, PNR data were not disclosed to the public, but to the data subjects or their agents in accordance with US law.

3 Clashes between two western cultures of privacy

It has been argued on both sides of the Atlantic, that '*the drama played out between the United States and the European Union over PNR-data transfers, Terrorist Finance Tracking Program (TFTP) as well as National Security Agency Database is a prominent example of the clash between conflicting philosophies on privacy protection*'.[399] In the middle of 2006, two significant issues, both involving privacy and specifically data protection, came to the forefront of U.S. efforts in the War on Terror[400]. First, in May 2006, the European Court of Justice (ECJ) annulled the agreement between the United States and the European Union regarding the transfer of airline passenger information-or passenger name records (PNR)-from the European Union to

Schwartz, '*Privacy and Participation: Personal Information and Public Sector Regulation in the United States*' (1995) 80 Iowa L. Rev. 553 (1994) pp. 557–613; Daniel Solove, '*The Origins and Growth of Information Privacy Law*' (2003) 748 PLI/PAT, p. 29.

399 Rizer A., '*Dog Fight:Did the International Battle over Airline Passenger Name Records Enable the Christmas-Day Bomber?*' Catholic University Law Review Volume 60 Issue 1, Fall 2010, pp. 77–105. According to Rasmussen, 'The dispute between the United States and European Union over the transfer of PNR data is a prima facie conflict of laws dispute.' Rasmussen R.,'*Is International Travel per Se Suspicion of Terrorism? The Dispute between the United States and the European Union over Passenger Name Record Data Transfers*', in: Wisconsin International Law Journal 28 (2008), pp. 551–90; See also: M. Tzanou, *The War against Terror and Transatlantic Information Sharing: Spillovers of Privacy or Spillovers of Security?*, in: "Utrecht Journal of International and European Law" 31 (80) 2015, pp. 87–103.

400 Matthew R. Van Wasshnova, *Data Protection Conflicts between the United States and the European Union in the War on Terror: Lessons learned from existing system of financial information exchange*, in: "Case Western Reserve Journal of International Law" Vol. 39, Issue 3, 2007–2008, pp. 827–865.

the United States[401]. The second major issue arose on June 24, 2006 when the "New York Times" uncovered a secret U.S. government financial record surveillance program called the Terrorist Finance Tracking Program (TFTP)[402].

The origins of the Passenger Name Records agreement (PNR) which denotes "the travel record for a person, as used by airline and travel agency databases" can be traced back to the 19 November 2001 US Aviation and Transportation Security Act (ATSA). This US domestic legislation requested airlines flying from, to or through the US to share, before every departure, their passenger name records[403] data with authorities in the Customs and Border Protection Bureau (CBP) and the Transportation Security Administration (TSA). As a result, European commercial airlines were forced by means of the ATSA to either violate the Data Protection directive or pay substantial penalties as a result. Although the Data Protection Directive did not apply to the processing of personal data in operations concerning public security, defense, and Member State security[404], the PNR were "*collected for a commercial purpose (flying abroad), and only subsequently exploited for national security information ...*". Hypothetically, if the data had been collected only for security purposes, they likely would have fallen under the security exemption that the national privacy laws have created for security and policing issues. The high penalties facing European companies stemming from the US unilateral decision put significant pressure on the Commission to resolve this legal limbo by negotiating a temporary settlement with the US in a high-level meeting on 17–18 February 2003. Evidently, the most difficult problem was to overcome the generally known "inadequacy" of the US legal scheme for the protection of privacy in comparison with European standards. The parties did not reach an agreement that fully reconciled the provisions of ATSA with the Data Protection Directive, what was mirrored in the Joint Statement[405]. Ten months later, on December 16, 2003, in a Communication to the European Council and Parliament, the Commission presented its approach to the transfer of

401 Joint cases Case C-317/07 and C-318/04, European Parliament v. Council of the European Union (C-317/04) and European Parliament v. Commission of the European Community (C-318/04), 2006 E.C.R. I-4721.

402 Lichtblau E. & Risen J., *Bank data sifted in Secret by U.S. to Block Terror*, in: "New York Times", June 23, 2006, at A1.

403 A Passenger Name Record is the generic name given to the files created by airlines for each journey any passenger books. They are stored in the Airlines' reservation and departure control databases.

404 Council Directive 95/46/EC, art. 3(2), 1995 O.J. (L 281) 1, (EC).

405 The Joint Statement detailed the initial data protection undertakings agreed to by U.S. Customs and confirmed the parties' intention to pursue talks with a view of

PNR data to the United States[406]. The legal framework, in the first place, called for a "light" bilateral agreement between the United States and the European Union and an "adequacy finding" by the Commission. Secondly, a series of "undertakings" with the United States was outlined, whereby the United States had agreed to: (1) limit its PNR requests to a closed list of thirty-four items, (2) delete all categories of sensitive data, (3) use the data only to prevent and combat terrorism and related crimes, (4) retain the PNR data for no more than three and a half years, (5) receive and handle representations from E.U. data protection authorities on behalf of E.U. citizens who have outstanding complaints with the Department of Homeland Security, and (6) participate with an E.U. team led by the Commission in an annual joint review. The Communication detailed the characteristics of a "push" system of data transfers, which meant that the airlines would transmit the data to U.S. authorities, as opposed to the practised at that time "pull" system, which allowed the United States access to the airline reservation systems, and envisioned "switching to 'push' with filters" by the middle of 2004. Finally, the Communication advocated that a multilateral approach to the PNR data transfer problem was to be developed and recommended that the International Civil Aviation Organization (ICAO) was "the most appropriate framework" for bringing forth a multilateral initiative.

On May 14, 2004, the Commission, under Article 25(2) of the Data Protection Directive and in line with the Joint Statement and the Communication, found that U.S. Customs ensured an adequate level of protection for PNR data transferred from the European Union.[407] Despite strong opposition from European Data Protection authorities, privacy rights advocates and the European Parliament's (EP) LIBE Committee (Civil Liberties, Justice and Home Affairs Committee)[408] on May 17, 2004, the E.U. Council approved the conclusion of the PNR data processing and transfer agreement and on May 28, 2004 the United States and the European Union signed a definite agreement on the processing and transfer of the

---

allowing the Commission to make an "adequacy finding" declaring U. S. data protection safeguards adequate in accordance with Article 25(6) of the Data Protection Directive.

406 *Communication from the Commission to the Council and the Parliament, Transfer of Air Pas*senger Name Record (PNR) Data: A Global EU Approach, *COM* (2003) 826 final (DEC. 12, 2003).

407 Commission Decision on the Adequate Protection of Personal Data Contained in the Passenger Name Record of Air Passengers transferred to the United States' Bureau of Customs and Border Protection 2004/535/EC, art. 1,2004 O.J.(L 235) 11, 13 (EC).

408 A 24 October 2002 opinion from the Article 29 Data Protection Working Party criticized the legality and proportionality of the US requests and raised concerns over the adequacy of data protection in the USA. Similar criticisms were voiced by the

PNR data (Original Agreement).[409] For the most part, the Original Agreement contained the provisions set forth above in the Communication, except that there was no mention of a multilateral approach under the ICAO nor did it mention an expiration date for the "pull" system of PNR data transfers.[410] It is to be acknowledged in this context that the Commission's approach to the transmission of passenger's data for security purposes has been fundamentally shaped by its 2003 Communication '*Transfer of Air Passenger Name Record (PNR) Data: A global EU approach*'. This document outlined the core elements of an EU policy in this area, namely, *the 'EU's approach cannot be limited to responding to the authorities of others'*. It also claimed that by 2007 '*the EU will have developed its own policy on the use of PNR'. Furthermore, it was also postulated that the principle of reciprocity should be the base of 'any possible information exchange with US authorities'*. The Commission aimed with this document at consolidating its central position as the main EU negotiator in this area by insisting upon a global approach to this problem through international standards agreed at the International Civil Aviation Organization. Thus, the Commission had consistently worked on a European PNR policy for four years in parallel to the negotiation process. In fact, the Commission organized several meetings and consultations under the PNR negotiations, which were further expanded with a questionnaire sent out in December 2006 to relevant stakeholders and a February 2007 meeting in Brussels with state representatives. This time Member States were clearly more receptive. By 2007 only UK, France and Denmark had enacted national PNR legislation. It is, however, worth to mention, that there emerged contestation from within the EU's institutional structure; the position of the EU negotiating agents (i.e. the Commission and the Presidency) differed from such EU actors as i.e. European Parliament, Article 29 Working Party, the European Data Protection Supervisor that had been kept excluded from the negotiations. Whilst the former have been willing to compromise and cooperate with the US, the latter have worked closely together to challenge some of the American demands. Under their perspective, the EU's acquiescing and mirroring of US policies had the potential to erode European citizens' civil liberties and

European Parliament in March 2003 when overwhelmingly voting in favor of a very critical resolution drafted by Civil Liberties (LIBE) Committee. Moreover, a coalition of privacy and civil liberties organizations in Europe launched a campaign in May 2003 against the transfer of data.

409 Press Release, European Commission, *International Agreement on Passenger Name Records (PNR) Enters into Force*, (May 28, 2004), available at: http://ec.europa.eu/comm/externalrelations/us/news/ip04_694.htm (Accessed: May 2017)

410 Council Decision 2004, Op. Cit.

privacy rights[411]. The fact that these measures were seen as being imposed from outside has strengthened such contestation. This can be exemplified by the response of the European Parliament represented by its President Pat Cox who, on July 27, 2004, who appealed to the CJEU for annulment of the May 17, 2004 Council decision and of the Commission's decision on the adequacy of United States' data protection, contending *"that adoption of the decision on adequacy was ultra vires, that Article 95 EC does not constitute an appropriate legal basis for the decision approving the conclusion of the agreement and, in both cases, that fundamental rights have been infringed"*[412]. On May 30, 2006, the CJEU joined the actions against the Council (C-317/04) and the Commission (C-318/04) and without addressing the ultra vires or fundamental rights infringement claims, annulled both the Council decision and the Commission's decision on adequacy and gave the parties time until September 30, 2006 to work out a new agreement.[413] It is crucial to mention, that a few months before the Judgment, the European Union adopted the data retention directive[414], which created an obligation for communications and Internet service providers to retain traffic and location data for the purpose of the investigation, detection and prosecution of serious crime. The directive did not however deal with the access and actual use of the retained data

---

411 As an example, the European Parliament 12 July 2007 Resolution criticized the deal for being *'substantively flawed'* by 'open and vague definitions and multiple possibilities for exception'. *See:* European Parliament (2007).A 17 August 2007 opinion from the Article 29 Data Protection Working Party also claimed that 'the new agreement leaves open serious questions and shortcomings' and that 'safeguards provided for under the previous agreement have been markedly weakened'. *See*: Article 29 Data Protection Working Party (2007).

412 Press Release, European Court of Justice, The Court Annuls the Council Decision Concerning the Conclusion of an Agreement Between the European Community and the United States of America on the Processing and Transfer of Personal Data and the Commission Decision on the Adequate Protection of Those Data, (May 30, 2006) (citation omitted), available at: http://curia.europa.eu/en/actu/communiques/cp06/aff/cpO60046en.pdf (Accessed: January 2020)

413 Joined cases: Case C-317/07 and C-318/04, European Parliament v. Council of the European Union (C-317/04) and European Parliament v. Commission of the European Communities (C-318/04), 2006 E.C.R. 1-4721.

414 Directive 2006/24/EC of the European Parliament and of the Council of 15 March 2006 on the retention of data generated or processed in connection with the provision of publicly available electronic communications services or of public communications networks and amending Directive 2002/58/EC, at:http://eur-lex.europa.eu/LexUriServ/LexUriServ.do?uri=OJ:L:2006:105:0054:0063:EN:PDF (Accessed: May 2018)

after they have been accessed by competent authorities in the field of law enforcement. According to the European Data Protection Supervisor '*the rules on the access, the use and the exchange of the data were inseparable from the obligation itself to retain the data*'.[415] Furthermore, the fact that the data retention directive did not regulate how the data subject could be protected after the data were accessed by law enforcement authorities and further used, '*made it even more urgent to establish a legal framework for data protection in the third pillar*'.[416] It is worth to mention in this context, that the legal basis of the data retention directive has been challenged by the Irish Government[417] who claimed that it should have been adopted under the third pillar. The application filed by Ireland followed the reasoning of the Court in the PNR Judgment which, as mentioned above, considered as the purpose for the transfer of the PNR data not their collection from the airline companies within commercial activities, but their 'processing for operations concerning public security and the activities of the State in areas of criminal law'.[418] In addition, Ireland contained that, the sole or, alternatively, the main or predominant purpose of the Directive was to facilitate the investigation, detection and prosecution of serious crime, including terrorism [and consequently] the only permissible legal base for the measures contained in the Directive was Title VI of the Treaty on European Union ('TEU'), in particular Articles 30, 31(1)(c) and 34(2)(b).The aforementioned examples illustrate that the limits between data collected and used in the first and the third pillar were not always clear. Data collected within commercial activities can be processed according to the rules set out in the data protection directive and they can further be transferred to or accessed by law enforcement authorities for public security reasons. The growing involvement of the private sector in law enforcement entails that personal data move from the one pillar to

---

415 Opinion of the European Data Protection Supervisor on the proposal for a Directive of the European Parliament and of the Council on the retention of data processed in connection with the provision of public electronic communication services and amending Directive 2002/58/EC (COM(2005) 438 final).

416 Ibid.

417 Judgment of the Court (Grand Chamber) of 10 February 2009. Ireland v European Parliament and Council of the European Union.

Action for annulment - Directive 2006/24/EC - Retention of data generated or processed in connection with the provision of electronic communications services - Choice of legal basis. Case C-301/06.

418 Ibid.

another[419] and the distinction in pillars results in a situation where although the data are the same, the protection offered by the European legal system is different. In this vein, in the case against the Commission (C-318/04), the CJEU reasoned that even though the PNR data may be viewed as being collected first by the airlines for commercial purposes (the sale of an airplane ticket for a supply of services), the Commission's decision on adequacy concerned data processing regarded as necessary for safeguarding public security and for law enforcement purposes. Since Article 3(2)63 of the Data Protection Directive excludes data processing for operations concerning public security, defense, and Member State security from the scope of the Data Protection Directive, the CJEU held that the Commission's decision on adequacy did not fall within the scope of Data Protection Directive and it must therefore be annulled[420]. Furthermore, in the case against the E. U. Council (C-317/04), the Parliament argued that Article 95 of the Treaty Establishing the European Union does not constitute an appropriate legal basis, for the Council's decision. Specifically, the Article 95(1) provides, in pertinent part, as follows: "[t]he Council shall ... adopt the measures for approximation of the provisions laid down by law, regulation or administrative action in Member States which have as their object the establishment and functioning of the internal market."[421] The Parliament further argued that Article 95 "cannot justify [c]ommunity competence to conclude the [Original] Agreement" because the Original Agreement relates to data processing operations which "are excluded from the scope of the [Data Protection] Directive."[422] Although Article 25 of the Data Directive allows personal data to be transferred to a third country provided that the country ensures an adequate level of protection, the ECJ held Article 95 EC, even read "in conjunction with Article 25 of the Data Protection Directive, cannot justify Community competence to conclude the Agreement" because as determined in Decision C-318, the PNR data transfer to the United States is outside the scope of the Data Protection Directive.[423] Thus, the E.U. Council did not have appropriate legal basis for its decision.

To conclude, both parties - the European Union and United States of America - as has been already mentioned, were ordered by the Court of Justice of the

419 *Opinion of the European Data Protection Supervisor on the Final Report by the EU-US High Level Contact Group on information sharing and privacy and personal data protection*, in: OJ C 128, 6.6.2009, pp. 1–12.

420 European Parliament, 2006 E.C.R. 1-4721, para 63.

421 Treaty Establishing the European Community, art. 95, Nov. 10, 1997, 1997 O.J. (C340) 3, 213.

422 European Parliament, 2006, Op. Cit., § 67–68.

423 Ibid. at § 63–67.

European Union to negotiate until September 30, 2006 a new agreement. As a result, an interim agreement was reached on October 16, 2006 (Interim Agreement), which subsequently expired on July 31, 2007.[424] However, before the Interim Agreement expired, the European Union and United States negotiators finalized a revised agreement (Revised Agreement), signed on July 23, 2007 in Brussels, and July 26, 2007 in Washington, D.C. The Revised Agreement consisted of three elements: (1) "*an agreement signed by both parties*"; *(2) "[a] letter by [the U.S. Department of Homeland Security] giving assurances on the way it intends to protect PNR data"; and (3) "[a] reply letter from the [European Union] . . . confirming that on the basis of the assurances, it considers the level of protection of PNR data in the United States as adequate"*.[425] Furthermore, it was foreseen that the Agreement expires seven years after the "date of signature," unless the parties mutually agree to replace it or if one of the parties terminates the agreement, at any time, through diplomatic channels. In order to abide by the annulment decisions, the Council-first in the Interim Agreement and then in the Revised Agreement—changed the legal basis of the E.U.-U.S. PNR agreement from the Treaty Establishing the European Community or "first pillar" to the Treaty on European Union or "third pillar"[426] As a result, the Revised Agreement fell under the competence of the European Union, as opposed to the European Community. As far as the substance of the document is concerned, to the dismay of the European Parliament and the Article 29 Working Party, the Revised Agreement did not improve standards related to airline passenger privacy.[427]

---

424 Agreement between the European Union and United States of America on the Processing and Transfer of Passenger Name Record (PNR) Data by Air Carriers to the United States Department of Homeland Security, U.S.-E.U., Oct. 27, 2006, 2006 O.J. (L 298) 29, 29–31 [hereinafter Interim Agreement]; The Council adopted the Interim Agreement on October 16, 2006. Council Decision 2006/729/CFSP/JHA 2006 O.J. (L 298) 27(EU).

425 Article 29 Data Protection Working Party, Opinion 5/2007 on the Follow-Up Agreement Between the European Union and the United States of America on the Processing and Transfer of Passenger Name Record (PNR) Data by Air Carriers to the United States Department of Homeland Security Concluded in July 2007, at 5, available at: http://ec.europa.eu/justice home/fsj/privacy/docs/wpdocs/2007/wp138_en.pdf (Accessed: Nov. 15, 2017).

426 See: Interim Agreement, in: European Parliament Doc. (B6-0393) 4 (2006) at §. 11.

427 See, e.g., European Parliament. Doc. (B-6-0393) (2006) (addressing issues in the draft version of the Revised Agreement that were included in the final version of the Revised Agreement); Opinion 5/2007 supra note 91, at 2–4.

On the one hand, the Revised Agreement did incorporate some important safeguards that were lacking in the previous two agreements. For instance, the document extended the privacy protections found in the Privacy Act of 1974 and the Freedom of Information Act to non-U.S. citizens and provided the system of redress for persons seeking information about or correction of PNR.[428] In addition, the Revised Agreement provided assurances from the Department of Homeland Security that it "would provide to airlines a form of notice concerning PNR collection and redress practices to be available for public display [and]... would work with interested parties in the aviation industry to promote greater visibility of this notice.'[429] Finally, the Revised Agreement adopted the "push" system of transmitting PNR.[430] On the other hand, however, the above described Agreement weakened many of the safeguards provided for under the previous two agreements. First, it extended the retention period from three and one-half years to fifteen years, with the possibility of it being further prolonged.[431] Second, the Department of Homeland Security was allowed to use sensitive PNR data elements-"personal data revealing racial or ethnic origin, political opinions, religious or philosophical beliefs, trade union membership, and data concerning health or sex life of the individual"-in exceptional cases, "where the life of a data subject or of others could be imperiled or seriously impaired".[432] Third, while the Revised Agreement seemed to reduce the number of PNR elements transferred to U.S. authorities from thirty-four to nineteen,[433] this change was a mere subterfuge as the Revised Agreement grouped all but one of the thirty-four elements

428 Agreement Between the European Union and the United States of America on the Processing and transfer of Passenger Name Record (PNR) Data by Air Carriers to the United States Department of Homeland Security, U.S.-E.U., Oct. 27, 2006, 2006 O.J. (L 298) 29, pp. 29–31 [hereinafter Interim Agreement]. The Council adopted the Interim Agreement on October 16, 2006. Council Decision 2006/729/CFSP/JHA2006 O.J. (L 298) 27(EU).

429 Ibid.

430 Id. at 23–24.

431 Under the Revised Agreement, data is stored in an active analytical database for seven years and then moved to dormant, non-operational status for eight years, where it can be "accessed only with approval of a senior [Department of Homeland Security] official … and only in response to an identifiable case, threat, or risk." Id. at 23. After the fifteen-year period has expired, the Department of Homeland Security expects that the data will be deleted, and the Revised Agreement states that "questions of whether and when to destroy PNR data ... will be addressed ... as part of future discussions." Ibid.

432 Id.

433 See id.; Opinion5/2007, supra note 91.

into one of nineteen new data sets.[434] Fourth, and finally, the Revised Agreement required the airlines to transfer new PNR data including additional baggage and frequent flyer information, that were not required under the previous agreements.[435] As a result, and as part of the Container Security Initiative (CSI) scheme, the American government demanded major European ports to establish dedicated shipping terminals and allow the deployment of US custom officers to screen containers identified as posing a potential risk for terrorism.[436] A December 2004 Council Regulation on the inclusion of digital facial images and fingerprints on passports also came as a result of American legislation requiring states participating in the US VWP to use passports with biometric features.[437] In parallel to these measures, the US demanded European airlines in December 2003 to accept the deployment of Sky Marshals on particular transatlantic flights under the threat of revoking their licenses[438]. Finally, an August 2007 US law forced foreign travelers to give US authorities at least 48 hours' notice of their plans to visit the country[439].

---

434 Id.

435 Revised Agreement, at 21–22.

436 Concerned about being cut off from the lucrative American market, major ports member states such as France (Le Havre), Netherlands (Rotterdam) or Belgium (Antwerp) conducted secret bilateral negotiations with US authorities. Thus, the Commission was forced to intervene to protect its competences under the Community pillar leading to the April 2004 Custom cooperation accord, which subsumed all previous bilateral accords and expanded the program to almost 20 ports in 10 member states. *See*: OJ L 304 of 30 September 2004. See also: Javier Argomaniz, When the EU is the ‚Norm taker': the Passenger Name Record's Agreement and the EU's Internationalization of US border Security Norms, in: „Justice and Home Affairs: A Different Security for the European Union?", edited by Sarah Wolff, Nicole Wichmann, Gregory Mounier, Routledge New York 2010, pp. 117–134.

437 In spite of European compliance, and in a politically sensitive decision, the US VISIT program was extended since September 2004 to those 15 member states which were under the VWP; allowing US authorities to collect biometric identifiers (two digital fingerprints and a photograph) from European visitors upon arrival to the US for their storage in a database.

438 US demands clashed with some member states' strict regulations against armed personal in-flight. Member states also found particularly irksome US authorities' lack of interest in contacting their allies to communicate their unilateral demands (some governments learnt about the measure from the media) and the vagueness of their requirements. Even so, EU transport ministers agreed on 12 October 2006 on European legislation allowing armed officers on board.

439 As a response to the US government's disregard of the repeated appeals to reconsider these measures, the Commission has prepared plans to mirror this system with an

On 27 April 2016, the co-legislators adopted the directive on the use of passenger name record (PNR) data for the prevention, detection, investigation and prosecution of terrorist offences and serious crime[440]. The aim of the directive, was to enhance EU's internal security and to harmonise national laws by setting-up an EU system to collect flight passenger data. Consequently, all air carriers flying on routes covered by the directive have to provide PNR data to Member States' law enforcement authorities[441]. The adoption of a common EU PNR system as part of the European security strategy[442] has long been debated: the European Commission proposed[443] a directive in 2011 (following an earlier proposal in 2007[444] on which the Council reached a general approach[445] in 2012. However, the European Parliament's Committee on Civil Liberties, Justice and Home Affairs (LIBE) rejected it in 2013[446] questioning its necessity and proportionality. Following the early 2015 Paris attacks and subsequent calls for an EU PNR scheme from different quarters (such as the European Council and the EU Counter-terrorism

---

electronic traveler authorization scheme similarly requiring foreigners, including US citizens, to give notice of their plans. *See*: Financial Times (2007) Travelers from US face EU crackdown, 7 August, at: https://www.ft.com/content/f490402c-4518-11dc-82f5-0000779fd2ac, (Accessed: May 2018).

440 *EU Passenger Name Record (PNR) directive: an overview*, at: https://www.europarl.europa.eu/news/en/press-room/20150123BKG12902/eu-passenger-name-record-pnr-directive-an-overview (Accessed: March 2020).

441 Completing the adoption of an EU PNR Directive, at: https://www.europarl.europa.eu/RegData/etudes/ATAG/2016/580886/EPRS_ATA(2016)580886_EN.pdf (Accessed: March 2020).

442 *The European Agenda on Security*, at: https://ec.europa.eu/home-affairs/sites/homeaffairs/files/e-library/documents/basic-documents/docs/eu_agenda_on_security_en.pdf (Accessed: March 2020).

443 Proposal for a Directive of the European Parliament and of the Council on the use of Passenger Name Record data for the prevention, detection, investigation and prosecution of terrorist offences and serious crime, (COM 20011/31 final), Brussels 2.2.2011, at: https://eur-lex.europa.eu/legal-content/EN/TXT/HTML/?uri=CELEX:52011PC0032&from=EN (Accessed: March 2020).

444 Proposal for a Council Framework Decision on the use of Passenger Name Record (PNR) for law enforcement purposes, (COM 654 2007 final), Brussels 6.11.2007, at: https://eur-lex.europa.eu/legal-content/EN/TXT/HTML/?uri=CELEX:52007PC0654&from=EN (Accessed: March 2020).

445 General Approach of the Council, at: https://ec.europa.eu/commission/presscorner/detail/en/PRES_12_172 (Accessed: March 2020).

446 *EP's report on the Proposal*, at: https://www.europarl.europa.eu/RegData/etudes/ATAG/2016/580886/EPRS_ATA(2016)580886_EN.pdf (Accessed: March 2020).

Coordinator), the proposal gained momentum again, as a means to counter the phenomenon of foreign fighters[447]. After several debates on a revised report presented in February by rapporteur Timothy Kirkhope (ECR, UK), on 15 July the Committee adopted a second report[448] enabling the opening of negotiations with the Council. The November Paris attacks gave impetus to a compromise, subsequently endorsed by the Council and backed by LIBE in December2015. The draft directive was initially rejected by the European Parliament's Committee on Civil Liberties, Justice and Home Affairs (LIBE) in April 2013, over privacy concerns. Members of the EP questioned the necessity and proportionality of the proposed EU scheme, and the length of the data retention period. Furthermore, following the annulment of the data retention directive by the Court of Justice of the European Union, the EP stressed the need to assess the Court of Justice's ruling before taking any new steps. On the grounds of privacy concerns, the Parliament also referred the *EU Canada PNR* agreement to the Court of Justice.

However, the proposal has gained momentum following the terror attacks on European soil, as well as concerns over threats to the EU's internal security posed by Europeans returning home after fighting in conflict zones for terrorist purposes. Convinced of the EU PNR's potential added value for EU counter-terrorism policy, the European Council several times called on Parliament to swiftly adopt its position on the issue and to finalise work with the Council.In a resolution on anti-terrorism measures adopted on 11 February 2015, the Parliament committed itself to work towards the finalisation of an EU PNR directive by the end of 2015. At the same time, it encouraged the Council to make progress on the data protection package, in order for the trilogues on both the EU PNR directive and data protection package to take place in parallel. In further resolutions on the European agenda on security (9 July 2015) and on the prevention of radicalisation (25 November 2015), the Parliament reiterated its commitment but also stressed that the PNR directive should comply with fundamental rights and data protection standards and be free from any discriminatory practices. The necessity to include mechanisms for the exchange of information and cooperation between Member States in any new security tools, such as the PNR, was also emphasised.A revised European Parliament report was presented to the LIBE Committee in February 2015. More than 800 amendments were introduced and views on the proposal remained quite

447 https://www.europarl.europa.eu/EPRS/EPRS-Briefing-548980-Foreign-fighters-FINAL.pdf (Accessed: March 2020).

448 EP Second Report, at: https://www.europarl.europa.eu/doceo/document/A-8-2015-0248_EN.html?redirect (Accessed: March 2020)

divergent as regards, in particular, privacy, necessity and proportionality issues. After several debates, the LIBE Committee adopted a final report in July 2015. In its report, the LIBE Committee adopted the following recommendations:only non-EU flights should be covered by the directive; the use of PNR should only be justified for a narrow list of serious crimes, such as trafficking in human beings, sexual exploitation of children, drug trafficking, trafficking in weapons, munitions and explosives, money laundering and cybercrime, as well as terrorist offences; the directive should include strong data protection safeguards, including an obligation to appoint a data protection officer in each Passenger Information Unit (PIU), prohibition to use sensitive data, stricter conditions for transfer of data to third countries and obligation to inform passengers about collection of their data and their rights;the data retention period would be of 30 days and then up to five years in 'masked out' form;PNR data should be shared between Member States and with Europol, with a possibility to create a 'one-stop shop' for information exchange. During the trilogue negotiations which followed, the EP negotiators sought to ensure that strict personal data protection safeguards were included and that the draft complied with the proportionality principle. The Parliament and the Council agreed on a compromise text in December 2015. Most EP recommendations, namely on data protection safeguards, were taken into account. The issue of the data retention period was one of the most controversial aspects, with the Council wishing to keep 'unmasked' data for two years. The EP managed to strike a compromise on a retention period of six months. Member States were also to be allowed (but not obliged) to include intra-EU flights. Moreover, the Parliament insisted on including a review clause into the agreed text: the Commission will have to carry out a review of the EU PNR directive two years after its transposition into national laws and could present a proposal to amend it. The Directive was finally adopted in early April 2016. Consequently, Directive (EU) 2016/681 of 27 April 2016 was published in the Official Journal on 4 May 2016.; Member States were obliged to transpose the directive to their legal orders within two years.

These and other initiatives reinforce the impression that some of the most significant EU measures in recent years in the field of border management have come as a result of direct US pressure or unilateral decisions. In other words, US forceful norm promotion, although creating friction in transatlantic relations, has ultimately been met by European compliance what can be exemplified by a secret Bush administration Terrorist Tracking Program (TFTP) initiated weeks after the Sept. 11 attacks. It may well be thought to illustrate the Bush administration's desire to exploit powerful technological tools to prevent another terrorist strike, and to break down longstanding legal or institutional barriers to the government's access to private information about Americans and others inside the United States. What is more, TFTP program was described by officials as the biggest and most far-reaching of several secret efforts to trace terrorist financing. Much more limited agreements with other companies have provided access to Automated Teller Machine (ATM) transactions, credit card purchases and Western Union wire payments, the officials said. Due to the fact that the 11 hijackers had helped finance their plot by moving money through banks; nine of them, for instance, funneled money from Europe and the Middle East to SunTrust bank accounts in Florida, the priority of the TFTP was to cut off the flow of money to Al Qaeda. By means of it counterterrorism officials, relying on Executive powers under the International Emergency Economic Powers Act enacted October 28 1977 (IEEPA)[449], have gained access to trace transactions of people suspected of having ties to Al Qaeda by reviewing records from the world's largest financial communication network-the Society for Worldwide Interbank Financial Telecommunication (SWIFT)- a Belgian cooperative based in Brussels, owned and operated by a consortium of financial institutions that routes about $6 trillion daily between banks, brokerages, stock exchanges and other institutions. Most routine financial transactions confined to this country were not in the data-base. Although, information is not provided in real time — Swift generally turns it over several weeks later. The records mostly involve wire transfers and other methods of moving money overseas and into and out of the United States. The cooperative's message traffic allowed investigators, for example, to track money from the Saudi bank account of a suspected terrorist to a mosque in New York. While conducting clandestine searching the database Customers' names, bank account numbers and other identifying information could be retrieved. The program, however, was a significant departure from typical practice in how the government acquired Americans' financial records. Treasury officials did not seek individual court-approved warrants or subpoenas to examine specific transactions, instead relying on broad administrative subpoenas for millions of records from the cooperative, known as Swift. While considering possible obstacles to legalize the above mentioned practice, lawyers in the Treasury Department and the Justice Department paid attention to the Right to Financial Privacy Act restricting government access to Americans' banking records passed by Congress (1978) in reaction to the Supreme Court's judgment (1976) according to which Americans had had no constitutional right to privacy for their records held by banks or other financial institutions. After an initial debate, Treasury

449 International Emergency Economic Powers Act, 50 U.S.C. §§ 1701–07 (2000), at: https://fas.org/sgp/crs/natsec/R45618.pdf (Accessed: September 2019)

Department lawyers, having been consulted with the Justice Department, concluded that the privacy laws applied to banks, not to a banking cooperative like Swift. It has been also emphasized that the law protected individual customers and small companies, not the major institutions that route money through Swift on behalf of their customers.[450] Underlying the government's legal analysis was the International Emergency Economic Powers Act, which president George W. Bush invoked after the 9/11 attacks. The law gave the president, what legal experts described as, broad authority to "investigate, regulate or prohibit" foreign transactions in responding to "an unusual and extraordinary threat." In addition, although the Terrorist Tracking Program was at first viewed as an urgent, temporary measure, it had become permanent tool of invigilation nearly five years later without specific Congressional approval or formal authorization. While many of those transactions have occurred entirely on foreign soil, officials have also been keenly interested in international transfers of money by individuals, businesses, charities and other groups under suspicion inside the United States. At the same time, however, awareness, among American as well as European officials realizing the potential for abuse, raised. Consequently, Swift executives agreed to continue providing the data only after top officials, including Alan Greenspan, then chairman of the Federal Reserve, intervened. As a result, the program targets were narrowed and more safeguards were provided. One of them was an outside auditing firm that verified that the data searches were based on intelligence leads about suspected terrorists. In addition, Swift executives insisted that the data be used only for terrorism investigations and had narrowed the scope of the information provided to American officials over time.

As far as legal liability is concerned, it has to be acknowledged that due to the fact that Swift was based overseas and had offices in the United States, it was governed by European and American laws. Several international regulations and policies imposed privacy restrictions on companies that were generally regarded as more stringent than those in this country. As far as the United States law is concerned, it establishes some protections for the privacy of Americans' financial data, but they are not ironclad. A 1978 measure, the *Right to Financial Privacy Act* already mentioned above, has a limited scope and a number of exceptions, and its role in national security cases remains largely untested. In these circumstances, Swift

450 Other state, federal and international regulations place different and sometimes conflicting restrictions on the government's access to financial records. Some put greater burdens on the company disclosing the information than on the government officials demanding it.

program was believed to have been exploiting a "gray area" in the law and that a case could have been made for restricting the government's access to the records on Fourth Amendment and statutory grounds. Officials, on the other hand, presented evidence that the Swift data provided clues to money trails and ties between possible terrorists and groups financing them. Among the successes was the capture of an Al Qaeda operative, Riduan Isamuddin, better known as Hambali, believed to be the mastermind of the 2002 bombing of a Bali resort; the Swift data identified a previously unknown figure in Southeast Asia who had financial dealings with a person suspected of being a member of Al Qaeda. In the United States, as documented by intelligence officials avoiding to give the details about the secret program, Swift data were used in investigations into possible domestic terrorist cells as well as inquiries of Islamic charities suspected of having links to extremists such as a Brooklyn man Uzair Paracha. He while working at a New York import business, aided Al Qaeda operative in Pakistan by agreeing to launder $200,000 through a Karachi bank. In addition, the Bush administration has pursued steps that might have provided some enhanced legal standing for the Swift program. In late 2004, Congress authorized the Treasury Department to develop regulations requiring American banks to turn over records of international wire transfers.

When the details of the secret Terrorist Financial Tracking Program (TFTP) were initially released by the "New York Times"[451] foreign officials from across the globe, but especially in the European Union, raised concerns as to whether the program violated their countries' privacy laws. Following the press revelation of the TFTP, the European Parliament expressed concern about the transfer of data to the US Treasury, and any secret operations on EU territory without EU citizens and their representatives being informed. Consequently, it called on the European Data Protection Supervisor to ascertain if the European Central Bank had met its obligations under Regulation (EC) 45/2001[452]- as it has been found out later, the European Central Bank knowing of TFTP, did not notify European data protection authorities - and demanded that Member States check for legal lacuna at local levels, and ensure that data protection legislation covered central banks. The Parliament also urged the Commission to take measures

451 Lichtblau E. and Risen J., *Bank Data Is Sifted by U.S. in Secret to Block Terror*, in: "International New York Times", June 23, 2006; at: https://www.nytimes.com/2006/06/23/washington/23intel.html, (Accessed: May 2018)

452 The ECB is a member of the Central Banks of the Group of Ten (G-10) countries that conduct collective oversight of SWIFT.

to ensure that cases like SWIFT would not occur in the future.[453] In turn, the Commission requested the Belgian authorities to conduct an investigation. As a result, the Belgian College of Intelligence and Security[454] requested an Opinion from the Belgian Commission for the Protection of Privacy, which had already made the decision to investigate the SWIFT case based on the press reporting and a complaint from Privacy International. Consequently, the 2006 report from the Belgian Privacy Commissioner found that SWIFT had broken Belgian law, and that there was a conflict between European and US law. Furthermore, it was suggested in the document that SWIFT had made errors in judgment while responding to the subpoenas, resulting in "hidden, systematic, massive, and long-term violation of the fundamental European principles as regards data protection".[455] The Commissioner stated that SWIFT should have complied with Belgian law relating to the notification of processing and transfers of data to countries outside the EU; should have followed the principles of proportionality, limited retention period and protection levels. Whilst SWIFT had notified G-10 banks of the program, the banks had not in turn notified privacy commissioners. Despite the findings of its initial report, the Belgian Data Protection Authority (DPA) lacked the power to fine or censure SWIFT, which would have been the responsibility of the Belgian public prosecutor. Interestingly, this institution took the decision not to pursue any legal action against SWIFT despite the wishes of the Belgian Data Protection Authority (DPA), and the Opinion of the Article 29 Working Group. Belgian Prime Minister Guy Verhofstadt, on the other hand, favored negotiation between the EU and US to achieve legal certainty for companies involved in international data transfer.

Following the Belgian report, the European Data Protection Supervisor (EDPS), Peter Hustinx, criticized the European Central Bank for failing to prevent the transfer of information, or to notify other parties such as European governments and authorities about the scheme.[456] Specifically, the EDPS criticized the ECB for continuing use of the SWIFT service after becoming aware of the subpoena process since February 2002.[457] Surprisingly, despite the concerns

453 European Parliament resolution on the interception of bank transfer data from the SWIFT system by the US secret services (P6_TA-PROV(2006)0317).

454 A committee chaired by the Prime Minister, with representatives of the Belgian intelligence services, police, Ministry of Foreign Affairs, the college of Attorneys General and the National Security Authority.

455 Commission de la protection de la vie privée, 26 Sep 2006.

456 European Data Protection Supervisor, Op. Cit., 1 Feb 2006.

457 EDRI, "SWIFT Found in Breach of Belgian Privacy Laws", *EDRI-gram*, 4.19, 11 Oct 2006.

that the program violated E.U. data protection laws, the Article 29 Working Party, 'an independent E.U. advisory body on data protection and privacy, waited until November 22, 2006 to issue an Opinion 10/2006 on the processing of personal data by the Society for Worldwide Interbank Financial Telecommunication denouncing SWIFT's activities with respect to the TFTP participation.' In its analysis, the Article 29 Working Party concluded that "SWIFT violated the Directive and called for it to cease all infringements." What is more, Opinion 10/2006's first and most important finding was that SWIFT represented a data controller under Article 2 of the Data Protection Directive.[458] SWIFT, on the other hand, contended that it served only as a data processor under the Act.[459] It is worth to remind in this place that under the Data Protection Directive, a *controller* means *the natural or legal persona, public authority, agency or any other body which alone or jointly with others determines the purposes and means of the processing of personal data*, while a *processor* means "*a natural or legal person, public authority, agency or any other body which processes personal data on behalf of the controller*".[460] The distinction is important because as the definitions indicate, a data processor processes information on behalf of the controller; therefore, the processor's duties under the Data Protection Directive are limited as compared to those of the data controller.[461] The Article 29 Working Party, however, held that SWIFT acts as a controller in both its normal secure messaging services and its processing of the subpoenaed data, and thus is responsible for complying with the Data Protection Directive, as a controller, even before the

458 General Data Protection Regulation, which came into force on May 25 2018 having replaced the Data Protection Directive, defines data controllers and data processors in its article 4; European Union Article 29 Working Party, Press Release on the SWIFT Case, (Nov. 23, 2006), available at http://ec.europa.eu/justice-home/fsj/privacy/news/docs/PRSwiftAffair_23 11 06 en.pdf (Accessed: January 2020) See also: Connorton Patrick M., *Tracking Terrorist Financing Through SWIFT: When U.S. Subpoenas and Foreign Privacy Law Collide*, in: "Fordham Law Review" Volume 76, Issue 1, pp. 283–322.

459 SWIFT Supports Calls for Debate to Move beyond Data Privacy to Security and Public Safety (Nov. 9, 2006), https://www.swift.com/about-us/swift-and-data, (containing SWIFT's response to the Belgian Privacy Commission's Advisory Opinion of September 27, 2006), (Accessed: January 2019).

460 Council Directive 95/46/EC, art. 2(d)-(e), 1995 O.J. (L 281) 1, 11–12 (EC).

461 A data processor still must comply with the provisions of the Data Protection Directive. See, e.g., art. 16 ("Any person acting under the authority of the controller or of the processor, including the processor himself, who has access to personal data must not process them except on instructions from the controller, unless he is required to do so by law.").

information was sent to the U.S. authorities. As such, the Article 29 Working Party called for SWIFT to cease its Data Protective Directive infringements.

To conclude, the SWIFT issue did result in negotiations between the EU and the US. The US Treasury made representations to the Council in which it committed to processing personal data originating in EU Member States in compliance with specific data protection principles. The Article 29 Working Party was kept informed of these discussions, but was not a participant in them. The resulting Terrorist Finance Tracking Programm (TFTP) agreement between the US and the EU entailed that information would only be obtained from SWIFT for counter-terrorism purposes, and it would not be kept longer than necessary. The Commission, in consultation with the US Treasury, the President of the Permanent Representatives Committee, and the President of the Committee of Civil Liberties, Justice and Home Affairs of the European Parliament, would have appointed an "eminent European" to independently monitor compliance with the agreement, and report to the Commission, that will in turn inform the Council and Parliament.[462] In reference to the changes in SWIFT's architecture resulting from the negotiation process it is crucial to note that there occurred subsequent disagreement between the European Commission and Parliament over the details of the negotiated treaty with the US regarding access to European financial transaction data, based on privacy, proportionality and reciprocity.[463] As a result, the Commission envisaged a new version of the bilateral EU-US international agreement between the EU and the US that required transfer to the US Treasury of relevant financial data necessary for the Treasury's Terrorist Finance Tracking Program. The key breakthrough, in the first place, was the intention with legal backing to develop an EU data extraction system equivalent to the US "Terrorism Finance Tracking Program" (TFTP) what automatically precluded the need to transfer data in bulk to the USA, by processing it in Europe. Secondly, Article 11 required the Commission to consider setting up such a system (it promised MEPs it would table a proposal within 12 months). Thirdly, the revised agreement gave Europol the "eminent European" role and the responsibility for determining if

462 Council of the European Union, Processing and protection of personal data subpoenaed by the Treasury Department from the US based operation center of the Society for Worldwide Interbank Financial Telecommunication (SWIFT), 11291/2/07 REV 2, Luxembourg, 28June 2007.

463 European Parliament, "European Parliament votes down agreement with the US", Press Release, 11 Feb 2010, at: http://www.europarl.europa.eu/sidesgetDoc.do?type=IMPRESS&reference=20100209IPR68674&language=EN, (Accessed: May 2018)

requests from the US for SWIFT data comply with the terms of the agreement. To conclude, The EDPS was invited to consult on the second draft agreement.[464]

After an extensive review of the TFTP initiated in early 2007, on 10 December 2008, the Belgian Data Protection Commission concluded that the SWIFT program complied with all applicable Belgian legislation. The Commission cited a number of measures SWIFT had undertaken to ensure the adequate protection of personal data, including joining a transatlantic framework ensuring that European data transferred to the US would be protected under similar standards as in Europe, and a proposed change to SWIFT's messaging architecture to allow for all intra-European messages to be processed and stored only in European facilities. In February 2009 after a year-long review conducted by French investigative judge Jean-Louis Bruguière, the European Commission confirmed that the US Treasury had *from the outset* been vigilant in respecting appropriate *safeguards in the handling of personal data obtained from SWIFT under subpoena*. The report of judge Bruguière, also issued to the European Parliament's Civil Liberties Committee, further found that the TFTP was targeted, narrowly focused, used exclusively for counterterrorism purposes, and had *generated significant value in the fight against terrorism, notably in Europe*. Following the announcement that SWIFT would shut down its American servers and store all relevant data in Europe, the European Commission declared in July 2009 its intention to negotiate with the US a new access agreement. A new storage center was to be opened in Switzerland starting 1 January 2010. Since SWIFT would no longer store any data on US soil, they were outside the jurisdiction of the Treasury's subpoena, and without the new access agreement the TFTP would effectively grind to a halt. To prevent a disruption in the flow of data, the European Commission attempted to approve a temporary agreement negotiated with the administration of the newly elected president Barack Obama (January, 20th 2009); finally, the permanent Agreement that would have formalized the SWIFT data flow was negotiated by the European Commission, approved by the Council of the European Union, rejected, however, by the European Parliament in making use of their new powers under the Lisbon Treaty. Eventually, the revised version of the SWIFT agreement was approved by the EP on 8 July 2010 to be signed by the US and the EU on June 28, 2010 (EU-US TFTP agreement took effect on 1 August 2010).[465]

---

464 European Parliament examines SWIFT II agreement, Justice and home affairs - 02-07-2010, at:http://www.europarl.europa.eu/sides/getDoc.do?type=IM-PRESS&reference=20100205BKG68527&language=EN, (Accessed: May 2018).

465 The European Commission has produced two subsequent reports on the implementation of the agreement in 2011 and 2012.The first report concluded that the agreement had been implemented in accordance with the provisions, but recommended greater

In this context, it is worth to note that the negative attitude of the European Parliament was to a certain extent caused by the British court's release on 11 February 2010 of previously secret and politically damaging information on the treatment of the former Guantanamo detainee by US interrogators. These facts constituted a challenge to Donald Trump's predecessor - president Barack Obama who already as a senator criticized the reauthorization of the Patriot Act and whose prominent goal heralded in 2007 presidential campaign was to resign from the „war on terror" rhetoric; furthermore, he accused the Bush administration of putting forward a false choice between liberty and security as well vowed to end the illegal wiretapping of American citizens. While being in office, however, and commenting the disclosure of the National Security Agency's secret programs such as PRISM Barack Obama - inaugurated as the first president to take office in the Age of Terrorism, fighting with Al Qaeda and its ideological allies, and at the same time attempting to reconcile his divided country over issues like torture, prosecutions, surveillance, security - stressed that "*it's important to recognize that you can't have 100 percent security and also then have 100 percent privacy and zero inconvenience. We are going to have to make some choices as a society. And what I can say is that in evaluating these programs, they make a difference in our capacity to anticipate and prevent possible terrorist activity*"[466]. To the dismay of general public it has been proved, however, that the National Security Agency

---

public information about the functioning of the scheme. The second review looked in greater depth at the functioning of the agreement. The review team was satisfied that recommendation in the first review had been carried out by the time of the second, and stated that the sensitive program is well protected and scrupulously managed. See: *European Commission, Report on the joint review of the implementation of the Agreement between the European Union and the United States of America on the processing and transfer of Financial Messaging data from the European Union to the United States for the purposes of the Terrorist Finance Tracking Program*, Brussels, 16 March 2011, at: https://ec.europa.eu/home-affairs/sites/homeaffairs/files/news/intro/docs/commission-report-on-the-joint-review-of-the-tftp.pdf (Accessed: January 2020), European Commission, Report on the second joint review of the implementation of the Agreement between the European Union and the United States of America on the processing and transfer of financial messaging data from the European Union to the United States for the purposes of the Terrorist Finance Tracking Program, SWD(2012) 454 final, Brussels, 14 Dec 2012, at: http://ec.europa.eu/dgs/home-affairs/pdf/20121214_joint_review_report_tftp_en.pdf (Accessed: May 2018)

466 *Obama's Remarks on Health Care and Surveillance*, at: "International New York Times", June 7, 2013; https://www.nytimes.com/2013/06/08/us/obamas-remarks-on-health-care-and-surveillance.html (Accessed: January 2020 2018).

had been collecting the telephone records of millions of US customers of Verizon, one of America's largest telecoms providers, under a top secret court order which required Verizon on an "ongoing, daily basis" to give the NSA information on all telephone calls in its systems, both within the US and between the US and other countries.[467] The NSA, as part of a program secretly authorized by President Bush on 4 October 2001, implemented a bulk collection program of domestic telephone, internet and email records. A furore erupted in 2006 when "USA Today" reported that the NSA had "*been secretly collecting the phone call records of tens of millions of Americans, using data provided by AT&T, Verizon and BellSouth* and was *analyzing calling patterns in an effort to detect terrorist activity*".[468] In 2008, after the program had come to light, Congress legalized a form of it by enacting Section 702 of the FISA law. That law enabled the program to expand to Silicon Valley firms, not just telecoms, and to all foreign intelligence purposes, not just counterterrorism. Hence, under president Obama, the document evidenced, a similar program has been implemented by means of the secret Foreign Intelligence Surveillance Court's (FISA) order as amended by the Patriot Act of 2001, passed in the wake of the 9/11 attacks[469]; the communication records of millions of US citizens were being collected indiscriminately and in bulk – regardless of whether they were suspected of any wrongdoing. Although the information acquired did not include the content of any communications or the name of any subscriber, being related exclusively to call details, such as a telephone number or the length of a telephone call, such metadata could have provided authorities with vast knowledge about a caller's identity. Particularly when cross-checked against other public records, the metadata could reveal someone's name, address, driver's license, credit history, social security number and more. Furthermore, government analysts were able to work out whether the relationship between two people was ongoing, occasional or a one-off. In this line, it is crucial to acknowledge that president Obama, similarly to

467 The secret Foreign Intelligence Surveillance Court (FISA) granted the order to the FBI on April 25th 2013, giving the government unlimited authority to obtain the data for a specified three-month period ending on July 19 2013.Under the terms of the blanket order, the numbers of both parties on a call are handed over, as is location data, call duration, unique identifiers, and the time and duration of all calls. The contents of the conversation itself are not covered.

468 NSA collecting phone records of millions of Verizon customers daily, in: "The Guardian" 6 June 2013, at: https://www.theguardian.com/world/2013/jun/06/nsa-phone-records-verizon-court-order (Accessed: January 2020) .

469 See also: Weisman J. and Stainhauer J., *Patriot Act Faces Revisions Backed by Both Parties*, in: "International New York Times", April 30, 2015, p.11.

his predecessor George W. Bush, unveiled the "*Big Data Research and Development Initiative*" aimed at extracting knowledge and insights more efficiently from large and complex collections of digital data. The initiative administered by the White House Office of Science and Technology Policy was announced as the tool to: 1) Advance state-of-the-art core technologies needed to collect, store, preserve, manage, analyze, and share huge quantities of data; 2) Harness these technologies to accelerate the pace of discovery in science and engineering, strengthen national security, and transform teaching and learning; 3) Expand the workforce needed to develop and use Big Data technologies.[470]

Prism scandal, however, caused a storm reaction of European political elites and the European Union officials; among them Commissioner Viviane Reading who in 2013 used this opportunity to announce the European Commission's Data Protection Reform contained in four key building blocks:1) a clear provision on the territory where the rules apply, expressed in the following words of the Commissioner: *it has to be made certain that companies from outside Europe abide by E.U. data protection laws when they offer and sell products and services to consumers in the Union. If you want to play in our backyard, you have to play by our rules;* 2) a broad definition of personal data-this should include not just the content of e-mails and phone calls, for example, but related traffic data as well, such as information on where something was sent from or how long somebody spent talking on the phone; 3) the rules cannot be limited to those companies that collect citizens' data. Rather, processors of those data— such as cloud providers —have to be also covered by data protection rules because, as the Prism scandal showed, they also present an avenue for those who want to access data. Hence, the E.U. needs specific rules on the obligations and liability of those processors. Finally, safeguards against the unfettered international transfer of data have to be guaranteed. The rules must ensure that E.U. citizens' data are transferred to non-European law enforcement authorities only in situations that are well defined, exceptional and subject to judicial review. It is time, Commissioner Reding called, that governments as well as members of the European Parliament show their commitment to protecting citizens' data.[471]

---

470 White House Press Release: *Obama Administration Unveils "Big Data" Initiative: Announces $200 Million in New R&D Investments*, at:https://obamawhitehouse.archives.gov/the-press-office/2015/11/19/release-obama-administration-unveils-big-data-initiative-announces-200, (Accessed: January 2018).

471 Reding V., *Protecting Europe's Privacy,* in: "International New York Times", 17 June 2013, p. 4.

In late 2012, on the other side of the Atlantic, the Congress extended the FISA law, enacted in 2008 in order to legalize a form of a once-secret warrantless surveillance program created after the terrorist attacks on Sept. 11, 2001. For five years without changes, the government was permitted to collect without a warrant, communications from United States companies like Google and AT&T of foreigners abroad — even when those targets were talking to Americans. Furthermore, in 2018, the pending expiration of Section 702 was forcing lawmakers to address its substance for the first time since the 2013 leaks about N.S.A. programs by its former contractor Edward J. Snowden. Civil libertarians and conservative skeptics of government *power* worked together to push for new limits, while intelligence and law enforcement agencies and their backers in Congress from across party lines — and in both the Obama and Trump administrations — tried to hold the line. In this context, it worth to underline that before voting to extend the law, known as Section 702 of the FISA Amendments Act, the House rejected an amendment that would have imposed a series of new safeguards. That proposal included a requirement that officials obtain warrants in most cases before hunting for, and reading, emails and other messages of Americans that were swept up under the surveillance. Supporters of those changes contended that the overhaul was needed to preserve Fourth Amendment privacy rights in the internet era. But intelligence and law enforcement officials argued that it was unnecessary, and dangerous, to limit security officials from being able to freely gain access to information the government already possessed.

To conclude, the post-Snowden privacy movement secured its largest victory in 2015 when Congress voted to end and replace one of the programs that Mr. Snowden exposed, under which the N.S.A. had been secretly collecting logs of Americans' domestic phone calls in bulk. To contrast, the vote in 2018 in both houses of the United States Congress in favour of National Security Agency's warrantless surveillance program extension for six years with minimal changes, might be perceived as the end of a debate over 21st-century surveillance and privacy rights that broke out in 2013[472]. Today, (2020) the European Union is seen as the leader on privacy, especially due to its General Data Protection Regulation that has just gone into effect in its 27 member countries. Paradoxically development of the EU migration policy and control of migratory movements by means of electronic devises collecting data

472 Ch. Savage E. Sullivan N. Fandos, *House extends surveillance law, rejecting new privacy safeguards*, in: "International New York Times", January 11 2018, at: https://www.nytimes.com/2018/01/11/us/politics/fisa-surveillance-congress-trump.html?searchResultPosition=1 (Accessed: January 2020)

of individuals on a large scale resulted in infringements of privacy rights. In the United States of America, on the other hand, the privacy debate under President Donald Trump has been recently concluded with the decisions made by the both houses of Congress to extend National Security Agency's warrantless surveillance program for another six years. In addition, it is to be acknowledged that in 2016, the Federal Communications Commission (FCC) imposed similar to European standards requirements on the companies that provide internet service, forcing them to offer an explicit "opt in" for having personal data collected, and to protect the information that was collected. Two years later, however, Congress, not without any influence of Internet service providers such as Comcast and AT&T and companies that use their connections, like Facebook and Google, passed a law signed by President Trump, that not only repealed the protections but also prohibited the F.C.C. from ever again imposing such safeguards. The same coalition of corporate interests succeeded in discouraging California from passing a state privacy law similar to the 2016 F.C.C. requirements[473].

473 Wheeler T., *Can Europe lead on Privacy?*, in: "International New York Times" April 1 2018, at: https://www.nytimes.com/2018/04/01/opinion/europe-privacy-protections.html (Access: May 2018); Savage Ch., *Congress Approves Six-Year Extension of Surveillance Law*, in: "International New York Times" January 18, 2018, at: https://www.nytimes.com/2018/01/18/us/politics/surveillance-congress-snowden-privacy.html (Accessed: January 2020)

Final remarks

The evolution of the European Union approach to the management of immigration and asylum has been to the large extent stimulated by the technological achievements such as biometrics and the exchange of information between national and EU authorities via large scale databases such as: SIS, VIS, Eurodac, EU-lisa, Eurosur, Entry-Exit System, Registered Traveler Program. However, the aim of the author was to emphasize that the digitalization of the EU immigration and asylum policy poses risks of fundamental rights infringements especially when law enforcement authorities have uncontrolled access to such databases. These practices undoubtedly distort the balance between *knowledge*-understood here as minimal personal information obtained by an administrative body for a particular purpose-and-*power* interpreted here as competences and restrictions imposed on executive bodies by the EU Data Protection Law/Charter of Fundamental Rights in the context of the EU immigration and asylum policy, e.g.: data minimization, purpose limitation, storage limitation, right to private life (Article 7) and the protection of personal data. Not to mention that broader availability of data can in itself have additional implications either positive or negative on liberty and security of a person (Article 6) or right to asylum (Article 18) and prohibition of collective expulsion (Article 19). In this context, it is worth to emphasize that nowadays the new technologies, the globalization of our economy, the profiling activities oblige us to give to privacy, traditionally associated with home, correspondence protection as well as sensitive data, another dimension and to recognize new subjective rights in order to achieve our capacity for self-determination. Data protection legislation appears in that perspective as a historical answer to the risks created for our self-development by an information society and thus is directly derived from the privacy concept. Ambient intelligence and the profiling activities authorized by modern technologies oblige us to renew our legislation in different directions. Traditionally data protection legislations consider only the relationship between data controllers and data subjects considered as a liberal subject, the relationship submitted to the Data Protection Authority control. From now, we have to consider the technology itself insofar as the danger resides in the software algorithms, the infrastructure and the functioning of terminals. The potentialities of the technology, the design of the ICT systems, the logic behind the algorithms and their societal impacts have to be taken into consideration[474]. It is to be expected that in the future one may observe such data protection challenges posed by the increased processing of personal data as: a) generalization of data processing in law enforcement; shift towards dataveillance, proactivity and profiling; b) increasing processing of personal data versus the limitation principle (as much of data as is needed).

474 Costa L., *Virtuality and Capabilities in a World of Ambient Intelligence: New Challenges to Privacy and Data Protection*, Springer 2016.

References

AAS K., 'Crimmigrant' *bodies and bona fide travellers: Surveillance, citizenship and global governance*', in: „*Theoretical Crimminology*", Volume: 15 issue: 3, 2011. pp. 331–346.

Ackleson J., *Securing Through Technology? "Smart Borders" after September 11th*, in: *Technology and Terrorism*, D. Clarke (ed.), Routledge New York 2017.

Amoore, *Biometric borders: Governing mobilities in the war on terror*, in: "Political Geography" 25 (2006). pp. 336–351

Aputtzo M. S. Erlanger, *Patriot Act Rises in France, and is Ridiculed*, in: „*International New York Times*" January 16, 2015.

A War on Terror? The European Stance on a New Threat, Changing Laws and Human Rights Implications, Wade M. Malijević A. (Eds.), New York, Dordrecht, Heidelberg, London 2010.

Balibar E., *Politics and the Other Scene*, Verso, London New York 2002.

Besters M., Brom F.W.A., *Greedy Information Technology: the digitalization of the European migration policy*, in: "*European Journal of Migration and Law*", Volume 12, Issue 4, 2010, pp. 455–470.

Bernal P., *The EU, the US and Right to be Forgotten*, in: *Reloading Data Protection. Multidisciplinary Insights and Contemporary Challenges*, S. Gutwirth, R. Leenes, P. de Hert (eds.), Dordrecht 2014.

Bignami F., *European versus American Liberty: A comparative privacy analysis of antiterrorism data mining*, in: "Boston College Law Review" Vol. 48 (3) 2007, pp. 609–98.

Bigo D., *Security and immigration: Toward a critique of the governmentality of unease*, in: „Alternatives" 27 (2002).

Bigo D. - Carerra S. - Gonzalez G. - Fuster E. -Guild P. - de Hert P.- Jeandesboz J.-Papaconstantinou V., *Towards a New EU Legal Framework for Data Protection and Privacy Challenges, Principles and the Role of the European Parliament*, European Parliament Study, Brussels, 2011.

Boehm F., *Information Sharing and Data Protection in the Area of Freedom, Security and Justice. Towards Harmonized Data Protection Principles for Information Exchange at the EU level*, Springer Berlin Heidelberg 2012.

Boehm F., *EU PNR: European Flight Passengers under General Suspicion-the Envisaged European Model of Analyzing Flight Passenger Data*, in: „Computers, Privacy and Data Protection: an Element of Choice, S. Gutwirth Y. Poullet, P. de Hert, R. Leenes (eds), Springer Dordrecht Heidelberg New York 2011.

Bolstrom N., *Superintelligence: Paths, Dangers, Strategies*, Oxford University Press United Kingdom 2014.

Boyd D. and Kate Crawford, 'Critical Questions for Big Data'. "*Information, Communication & Society*" 15 (5):2012.

Broeders D., Schrijvers E., van der Sloot, B.van Brakel R.de Hoog J., Hirsch Ballin E.,*Big Data and security policies: Towards a framework for regulating the phases of analytics and use of Big Data*, in: "Computer Law & Security Review" 33 (2017) Elsevier, Amsterdam

Brouwer, E. *Digital Borders and Real Rights*, Brill/Nijhoff Leiden Boston 2008.

E. Brouwer, *Legal Boundaries and the Use of Migration Technology*, in: „Migration and the New Technological Borders of Europe", H. Dijstelbloem and A. Meijer (Eds.), Palgrave Macmillan, New York 2011.

Brouwer E., *The Other Side of the Moon: The Schengen Information System and Human Rights: A Task for National Courts*, in: *CEPS Working Documents*, No. 288, April 2008.

Butler, J., *Precarious life: The powers of mourning and violence*, London: Verso 2004.

Buzan B. Waever O. De Wilde J., *Security. A new framework for analysis*, Lynne Rienner Publishers, London 1998.

Caplan J. (ed), *Written on the Body: The Tatto in European and American History*, London: Reaktion Books 2000.

Cohen, J. E. 2012. *Configuring the Networked Self*. New Haven: Yale University Press.

Connorton Patrick M., *Tracking Terrorist Financing Through SWIFT: When U.S. Subpoenas and Foreign Privacy Law Collide*, in: "Fordham Law Review" Volume 76, Issue 1, pp. 283–322, available at: https://ir.lawnet.fordham.edu/cgi/viewcontent.cgi?article=4298&context=flr (Accessed: January 2020)

Costa L., *Virtuality and Capabilities in a World of Ambient Intelligence: New Challenges to Privacy and Data Protection*, Springer International Publishing Switzerland 2016.

Craig P. & de Búrrca G., *EU Law: Text, Cases and Materials*, Oxford University Press 5th ed. United Kingdom 2011.

De Hert, Paul, and Serge Gutwirth. 2013. *Anthologie de la vie privée: Compilation d'articles, de législation et de jurisprudence concernant la protection de la vie privée et des données à caractère personnel pour la Belgique jusque 1998.* Bruxelles: Academic and Scientific Publishers (ASP) & Commission Protection de la Vie Privée.

De Schutter, Olivier. 2001. Vie privée et protection de l'individu vis-à-vis des traitements de données à caractère personnel. *Revue trimestrielle des droits de l'homme,in: "Revue trimestrielle des droits de l'homme"* - no. 45, pp. 137–183 (2001)

Edley C., *The new American dilemma: Racial profiling post-9/11*, in: *The war on our freedoms: Civil liberties in an age of terrorism*, R. Leone, & G. Anrig (Eds.), New York: Public Affairs 2003.

EDRI, "SWIFT Found In Breach of Belgian Privacy Laws", *EDRI-gram*, 4.19, 11 Oct 2006.

Els J. Kindt, *Privacy and Data Protection Issues of Biometric Applications. A comparative Legal Analysis*, Springer Dordrecht Heidelberg New York London 2013.

Marischka C (2009) *Frontex: Im Netz des EU-Sicherheitssektors: Let them eat batons*. Jahrbuch Komitee für Grundrechte und Demokratie, Kőln: pp. 39–51.

Mironenko Enerstvedt O., *Aviation Security, Privacy, Data Protection and Other Human Rights: Technologies and Legal Principles*, Springer International Publishing AG Switzerland 2017.

Engbersen G., *The Unanticipated Consequences of Panopticon Europe. Residence Strategies of Illegal Immigrants*, in: V. Guiraudon and C. Joppke (eds) *Controlling a New Migration World*, Routledge London 2001.

Embedded, Everywhere a Research Agenda for Networked Systems of Embedded Computers, United States National Research Council. 2001, Washington, D.C.: National Academy Press.

European Data Protection Coming of Age, Gutwirth, S., Leenes, R., de Hert, P., Poullet, Y. (Eds.), Springer, Dordrecht; New York 2013.

Ewald F., *Insurance and risk*, in: G. Burchel, C. Gondon and P. Miller (eds), *The Foucault Effect: Studies in Governmentality*, Chicago IL; University of Chicago Press,1991, pp. 191–210.

Foucault M., *Discipline and Punish: the birth of a prison*, London, Penguin 1991.

Foucault, M., 'The Subject and Power'. In *Essential Works of Foucault: 1954–1984*, edited by P. Rabinow. New York: The New Press 1997.

Fundamental rights implications of the obligation to provide fingerprints for Eurodac, Fundamental Rights Agency 05/2015, Vienna.

Fundamental rights and the interoperability of EU information systems: borders and security, European Union Agency for Fundamental Rights, Vienna 2017.

Fusco S. J., R. Abbas, K. Michael, A. Aloudat, Location-Based Social Networking and Its Impact on Trust in Relationships, in: „IEEE Technology and Society Magazine 31 (2), 2012, pp. 39-50.

Gonzalez Fuster G., *The Emergence of Personal Data Protection as a Fundamental Rights of the EU*, Springer 2014.

Giddens A., *The Nation-State and Violence*, Cambridge: Polity Press 1985.

Gilliom, J. 2001. *Overseers of the Poor: Surveillance, Resistance, and the Limits of Privacy*. Chicago: University of Chicago Press

Grabbe H., The *Sharp Edges of Europe. Extending Schengen Eastwards*, in: „*International Affairs*", Volume 76, Issue 3, 1 July 2000, Pages 519–536.

Greenfield, A., *Everyware – The Dawning Age of Ubiquitous Computing*. Berkeley: New Riders 2006.

Guiraudon V. and Joppke C.(eds) *Controlling a New Migration World*, pp. 242. Routledge London 2001.

Guild E., *Moving the Borders of Europe*, inaugural lecture delivered at the official ceremony of the assumption of the professorship of the CPO Wisselleerstoel at the University of Nijmegen 2001, pp. 101–119

Gutwirth S. Leenes R. de Hert P., *Reforming European Data Protection Law*, Springer, Dordrecht 2015.

Hall G. Kevin, *Security Will Tighten on Mexican Border: U.S. Plans New Safeguards*, in: "Miami Herald" (6 March 2002).

Harris R., *The collected speeches of Margaret Thatcher*, Harper Collins Publishers, London 1997.

Hildebrandt M. and Katia de Vries, *Privacy, Due Process and the Computational Turn: The Philosophy of Law Meets the Philosophy of Technology*, United Kingdom: Routledge 2013.

Hoofnagle Ch., 'Big Brother's Little Helpers: How Choice Point and Other Commercial Data Brokers Collect, Process, and Package Your Data for Law Enforcement' (2004) 29 N.C.J. Int'l L. & Com. Reg., pp. 595–637.

Hustinx P. (2008): Round Table: "*Liberty and Security in Integrated Management of EU Borders*" in: European data protection Supervisor "Annual Report 2008", p. 70

Huysmans J., *A Foucaultian view on spill-over: Freedom and security in the EU*, 2004, in: „Journal of International Relations and Development", October 2004, Volume 7, Issue 3, pp. 294–318.

Ignatieff M., Will the Quest for Security Kill the Human Rights Era?, in: "International Herald Tribune" 6 February 2002.

Kesby A. G., *The Shifting and Multiple Border and International Law*, in: 27 "Oxford Journal of Legal Studies" 101, 2007, pp. 101–19

Knyrim, R., and G. Trieb, 'Smart Metering under EU Data Protection Law', in: "*International Data Privacy Law*", March 2011, Vol. 1, No 2, pp. 121–128.

Kosta E., *Consent in European Data protection Law*, Martinus Nijhoff Publishers, The Hague 2013.

Kuster B. Tsianos V.S., *How to liquefy a Body on the Move: Eurodac and the Making of the European Digital Border*, in: *EU Borders and Shifting Internal Security. Technology, Externalization and Accountability*, Springer International Publishing Switzerland 2016

Lichtblau E. & Risen J., *Bank data sifted in Secret by U.S. to Block Terror*, in: "New York Times", June 23, 2006, at A1.

Lindwer, M., D. Marculescu, T. Basten, R. Zimmermann, R. Marculescu, S. Jung, and E. Cantatore, 2003. 'Ambient Intelligence Visions and Achievements: Linking Abstract Ideas to Real-World Concepts', in: *Design, "Automation & Test in Europe Conference & Exhibition"* Vol. 1. Los Alamitos, California: IEEE Computer Society.

Lőhr T (2008) *Frontex-europäischer Grenzschutz im rechtsfreien Raum?*, in: Grundrechte Report 2008, Kőln zur Lage der Bürger- und Menschenrechte in Deutschland.

Lyon D. (ed.), *Surveillance as Social Sorting: Privacy, Risk, and Automated Discrimination*, Routledge New York 2002.

Mach Z., *Symbols, Conflict and Identity, Essays in Political Anthropology*, New York: State University of New York Press 1993.

Manners I, *Normative Power Europe: A Contradiction in Terms?*, in: "Journal of Common Market Studies", Vol. 40, Issue 2, June 2002, pp. 235–58

Matthew R. Van Wasshnova, *Data Protection Conflicts between the United States and the European Union in the War on Terror: Lessons learned from existing system of financial information exchange*, in: "Case Western Reserve Journal of International Law" Vol. 39, Issue 3, 2007–2008, pp. 827–865

Migration and the New Technological Borders of Europe, Huub Dijstelbloem, Albert Meijer (eds.), Palgrave Macmillan, United Kingdom 2011.

Nagel C., *Geopolitics by any other* name: Immigration and the politics of assimilation, in: „Political Geography" 21(8), 2002, pp. 971–987

Neeman, A. Radiation in passenger screening: busting the myths, in: "*Aviation Security International*" 21, 2015, pp. 21–32

Nardell, Gordon Q. C., *Levelling up: Data privacy and the European Court of Human Rights* in: *Data protection in a profiled world*, eds. Serge Gutwirth, Yves Poullet, and Paul De Hert, Dordrecht: Springer 2014.

N. Yue Liu, „Bio-privacy. Privacy Regulations and the Challenge of Biometrics", Routledge Taylor&Francis Group, New York 2012, P. 3.

Quinlan, T., "Discrimination: the questionable effectiveness of screening based on race, religion, national origin or behaviour", in: "*Aviation Security International*" 21 (2015), pp. 36–39

Rasmussen R.,'*Is International Travel per Se Suspicion of Terrorism? The Dispute between the United States and the European Union over Passenger Name Record Data Transfers*', in: Wisconsin International Law Journal 28 (2008), pp. 551–90

Reading V., *The European Data Protection Framework for the twenty-first century*, in: "International Data Privacy Law" 2012, vol. 2, No. 3, pp. 119–129

Reding V., *Protecting Europe's Privacy*, in: "International New York Times", 17 June 2013.

Rijmpa Jorrit J., *Brave New borders: The EU's Use of New Technologies for the Management of Migration and Asylum*, (in:) *New Technlogies and EU Law*, M. Cremona (ed.), Oxford University Press 2017, United Kingdom.

Rijmpa J., *EU Border Management after Lisbon Treaty*, „Croatian Yearbook of European Law and Policy"5 (2009), pp. 121–149.

Rizer A., *'Dog Fight: Did the International Battle over Airline Passenger Name Records Enable the Christmas-Day Bomber?'* Catholic University Law Review Volume 60 Issue 1, Fall 2010, pp. 79–104.

Rosen J., *The right to be Forgotten*, in: 64"Stanford Law Review" 88, February 13, 2012, pp. 88–92.

Michael L. Rustad & Sanna Kulevska, *Reconceptualizing the Right to be Forgotten to Enable Transatlantic Data Flow*, in: "Harvard Journal of Law & Technology", Volume 28, Number 2 Spring 2015, pp. 351–416.

Scheer D., *For Young Eyes Only-Europe's new High-Tech Role: Playing Privacy Cop to the World*, in: "Wall Street Journal", Oct. 10, 2003, p. A1

Schmitt E., *Traces of Terror: Immigration*, Ashcroft Proposes Rules for Foreign Visitors, in: "International New York Times", June 6, 2002.

Scott J., Seeing like a State: How Certain Schemes to Improve the Human Condition Have Failed, New Heaven: Yale University Press 1998.

Shaffer Gregory C., 'Globalization and Social Protection: The impact of EU and International Rules in the Ratcheting up of U.S. Data Privacy Standards', in: "Yale Journal of International Law" (2000) 25 Issue 1, pp. 2–80.

Slobogin Ch., *Privacy at Risk: The New Government Surveillance and the Fourth Amendment*, Chicago University Press 2007.

Slobogin Ch. and Schumacher Joseph E., '*Reasonable Expectations of Privacy and Autonomy in Fourth Amendment Cases: An Empirical Look at Understandings Recognized and Permitted by Society*', in: 42 „Duke Law Journal" 727 (1992–1993).

Solove Daniel J., *'Digital Dossiers and the Dissipation of Fourth Amendment Privacy', in:* "Southern California Law Review" Vol. 75, July 2002, pp. 1083–1168.

Solove D. and Schwartz P., *Information Privacy Law* 3rd edition, Wolters Kluwer Law & Business, Aspen Publishers 2009.

Solove D., 'Privacy and Power: Computer Databases and Metaphors for Information Privacy', in: 53 „Stanley Law Review", 2001, pp. 1393–1462

Ståhlbröst A. Padyab A. Sällström A. Hollosi D., *Design of smart city systems from a privacy perspective*, IADIS International Journal on WWW/Internet Vol. 13, No. 1, pp. 1–16 ISSN: 1645-7641.

Savage Ch., *Surveillance and Privacy Debate Reaches Pivotal Moment in Congress*, in: "International New York Times", January 10, 2018, p. 7.

Scheer D., *For Young Eyes Only-Europe's new High-Tech Role: Playing Privacy Cop to the World*, in: "Wall Street Journal", Oct. 10, 2003, p. A1

Scott J., *Seeing like a State: How Certain Schemes to Improve the Human Condition Have Failed*, New Heaven: Yale University Press 1998.

Shaffer Gregory C., '*Globalization and Social Protection: The impact of EU and International Rules in the Ratcheting up of U.S. Data Privacy Standards*', in: "Yale Journal of International Law" (2000) 25, pp. 1–88.

Ståhlbröst A. Padyab A. Sällström A. Hollosi D.., *Design of smart city systems from a privacy perspective*, IADIS International Journal on WWW/Internet Vol. 13, No. 1, pp. 1–16

Tohidipur T, Fischer-Lescano A (2008–2009) "*Europäisches Grenzmanagment: Handlungsrahmender Grenzschutzagentur Fontex*", Jahrbuchőffentliche Sicherheit. Verlag für Polizeiwissenschaft, Frankfurt, pp. 505–516.

Torpey J., *The Invention of a Passport: Surveillance, Citizenship and the State*, Cambridge University Press 2000, p. 35; *Migration and the New Technological Borders of Europe*, H. Dijstelbloem A. Meijer (ed), Palgrave and Macmillan, New York 2011.

Tucker P., *The Naked Future: What Happens in a World That Anticipates Your Every Move*, Penguin Publishing, New York 2014.

Tzanou M., *The EU as an emerging 'Surveillance Society': The function creep case study and challenges to privacy and data protection*, in: Vienna Online Journal on International Constitutional Law, 2010, pp. 407–427

Tzanou M., *The War Against Terror and Transatlantic Information Sharing: Spillovers of Privacy or Spillovers of Security?*', in: „Utrecht Journal of International and European Law", Vol. 31, No. 80, February 2015, pp. 87–103

Whitman James Q., *The Two Western Cultures of Privacy: Dignity versus Liberty*, in: "Yale Law Journal" Vol. 113, Issue 6, April 2004, pp. 1151–1221

van der Ploeg I., *Biometrics and the Body as Information: Normative Issues in the Socio-technical Coding of the Body*, (in): Lyon D. (ed.), *Surveillance as Social Sorting: Privacy, Risk, and Automated Discrimination*, Routledge New York 2002.

van der Ploeg I. and I. Sprenkels, *Migration and Machine-Readable Body: Identification and Biometrics, in: Migration and the New Technological*

Borders of Europe, H. Dijstelbloem, A. Meijer (eds.), Palgrave Macmillan, London 2011.

I. van der Ploeg and I. Sprenkels, *Migration and Machine-Readable Body*, in: Dijstelbloem H., Meijer A. (eds) *Migration and the New Technological Borders of Europe. Migration, Minorities and Citizenship*, Palgrave Macmillan, London 2011.

Weisman J. and Stainhauer J., *Patriot Act Faces Revisions Backed by Both Parties*, in: "International New York Times", April 30, 2015.

Internet sources

- AI Principles, at: https://futureoflife.org/ai-principles/ (Accessed: September 2018)
- Anderson, Chris. 2008. 'The End of Theory: The Data Deluge Makes the Scientific Method Obsolete'. "*Wired*" May 23rd. https://www.wired.com/2008/06/pb-theory/ (January 2020)
- *Biometric-based technologies*, in: „OECD Digital Economy Papers" No. 101 (2004), OECD Publishing, Paris, p. 11, at: http://dx.doi.org/10.1787/232075642747 (Accessed: September 2017)
- Case C-131/12, Google Spain SL. v. Agencia Española de Protección de Datos (May 13, 2013), http://curia.europa.eu/juris/document/document.jsf?text=&docid=152065& doclang=EN, (Accessed: January 2018)
- Cedric Burton, Christopher Kuner and Anna Pa-teraki, The Proposed EU Data Protection Regulation One YearLater: The Albrecht Report, Bloomberg BNA Privacy & Sec. L.Rep. (Jan. 21, 2013),available at https://www.wsgr.com/eudataregulation/pdf/011713.pdf (Accessed: September 2019)
- *China's A.I. Advances Help Its Tech Industry, and State Security* by Paul Mozur and Keith Bradsher, in: "International New York Times" Dec. 3 2017, at: https://www.nytimes.com/2017/12/03/business/china-artificial-intelligence.html (Accessed: September 2019).
- *China: Voice Biometric Collection Threatens Privacy Police, AI Giant Collaboration in Legal Gray Area,* October 22, 2017, at: https://www.hrw.org/news/2017/10/22/china-voice-biometric-collection-threatens-privacy (Accessed: September 2018).
- Clarke R. "Profiling: A hidden challenge to the regulation of data surveillance". *JL & Inf. Sci.*4 (1993), available at: http://www.rogerclarke.com/DV/PaperProfiling.html (Accessed: January 2020)
- Completing the adoption of an EU PNR Directive, at: https://www.europarl.europa.eu/RegData/etudes/ATAG/2016/580886/EPRS_ATA(2016)580886_EN.pdf (Accessed: March 2020).

- Communication from the European Commission to the European Parliament and the Council Towards a reform of the Common European Asylum System and enhancing legal avenues to Europe, Brussels, 6.4.2016 COM(2016) 197 final, at: https://ec.europa.eu/home-affairs/sites/homeaffairs/files/what-we-do/policies/european-agenda-migration/proposal-implementation-package/docs/20160406/towards_a_reform_of_the_common_european_asylum_system_and_enhancing_legal_avenues_to_europe_-_20160406_en.pdf (Accessed: March 2020).
- *EU Passenger Name Record (PNR) directive: an overview*, at: https://www.europarl.europa.eu/news/en/press-room/20150123BKG12902/eu-passenger-name-record-pnr-directive-an-overview (Accessed: March 2020).
- Eurodac Annual Statistics April 2017, at: http://www.statewatch.org/news/2017/jun/eu-elisa-eurodac-stats-prel.pdf (Accessed: May 2019)
- EUROJUST: Consolidated Annual Activity Report 2016, at: http://www.eurojust.europa.eu/doclibrary/corporate/CAAR/Consolidated%20Annual%20Activity%20Report%202016/EUROJUST-CAAR2016_EN.pdf (Accessed: June 2018).
- *European Parliament examines SWIFT II agreement*, Justice and home affairs - 02-07-2010, at: http://www.europarl.europa.eu/sides/getDoc.do?type=IM-PRESS&reference=20100205BKG68527&language=EN
- European Parliament, *"European Parliament votes down agreement with the US"*, Press Release, 11 Feb 2010, at:http://www.europarl.europa.eu/sidesgetDoc.do?type=IMPRESS&reference=20100209IPR68674&language=EN (Accessed: May 2018)
- French antiterrorism laws approved by the Parliament in 2015, at: www.assemblee-nationale.fr/15/ta-pdf/0164-p.pdf (Accessed: March 2020)
- G. W. Bush, *"Anti-Terrorism Technology Key to Homeland Security,"* Remarks at Argonne National Laboratory (22 July 2002), at: https://georgewbush-whitehouse.archives.gov/news/releases/2002/07/20020722-1.html (Accessed: January 2020)
- International Emergency Economic Powers Act, 50 U.S.C. §§ 1701-07 (2000), at: https://fas.org/sgp/crs/natsec/R45618.pdf (Accessed: January 2020)
- Dave Lee, *What Is the "Right To Be Forgotten"?*, BBC (May 13, 2014), http://www.bbc.com/news/technology-27394751 (Accessed: May 2018)
- *Executive summary EDPS Opinion of 7 March 2012 on the data protection reform package*, t at: https://edps.europa.eu/sites/edp/files/publication/12-03-07_edps_reform_package_summary_en.pdf (Accessed: January 2020)

- European Parliament examines SWIFT II agreement, Justice and home affairs - 02-07-2010, at:http://www.europarl.europa.eu/sides/getDoc.do?type=IM-PRESS&reference=20100205BKG68527&language=EN (Accessed: May 2018)
- European Parliament, "European Parliament votes down agreement with the US", Press Release, 11 Feb 2010, at: http://www.europarl.europa.eu/sidesgetDoc.do?type=IMPRESS&reference=20100209IPR68674&language=EN (Accessed: March 2020)
- *EP's report on the Proposal*, at: https://www.europarl.europa.eu/RegData/etudes/ATAG/2016/580886/EPRS_ATA(2016)580886_EN.pdf (Accessed: March 2020).
- *EP Second Report*, at: https://www.europarl.europa.eu/doceo/document/A-8-2015-0248_EN.html?redirect (Accessed: March 2020)
- European Union Committee-Second Report EU Data Protection law: a 'right to be forgotten'?, 23 July 2014, at: https://publications.parliament.uk/pa/ld201415/ldselect/ldeucom/40/40.pdf (Accessed: May 2018)
- European Union Article 29 Working Party, Press Release on the SWIFT Case, (Nov. 23, 2006), available at http://ec.europa.eu/justice-home/fsj/ privacy/news/docs/PRSwiftAffair_23 11 06 en.pdf (Accessed: February 2020)
- European Commission: smart cities, at:https://ec.europa.eu/info/eu-regional-and-urban-development/topics/cities-and-urban-development/city-initiatives/smart-cities_en (Accessed: September 2018)
- *European Commission, Report on the joint review of the implementation of the Agreement between the European Union and the United States of America on the processing and transfer of Financial Messaging data from the European Union to the United States for the purposes of the Terrorist Finance Tracking Program*, Brussels, 16 March 2011, at: https://ec.europa.eu/home-affairs/sites/homeaffairs/files/news/intro/docs/commission-report-on-the-joint-review-of-the-tftp.pdf (Accessed: January 2020)
- European Commission, Report on the second joint review of the implementation of the Agreement between the European Union a the United States of America on the processing and transfer of financial messaging data from the European Union to the United States for the purposes of the Terrorist Finance Tracking Program, SWD(2012) 454 final, Brussels, 14 Dec 2012, at: http://ec.europa.eu/dgs/home-affairs/ pdf/20121214_joint_review_report_tftp_en.pdf (Accessed: March 2020)
- European Commission Decision of 28 June 2006 laying down the technical specifications on the standards for security features and biometrics in passports and travel documents issued by Member States, at: https://ec.europa.eu/transparency/regdoc/rep/3/2006/DE/3-2006-2909-DE-F-0.Pdf (Accessed: September 2019).

- De Conca, S. GC et al v CNIL: *Balancing the Right to Be Forgotten with the Freedom of Information*, the Duties of a Search Engine Operator (C-136/17 GC et al v CNIL), European Data Protection Law Review Volume 5, Issue 4 (2019), pp. 561–567, at: https://doi.org/10.21552/edpl/2019/4/17 (Accessed: February 2020).
- Eurodac Annual Statistics April 2017, at: http://www.statewatch.org/news/2017/jun/eu-elisa-eurodac-stats-prel.pdf; http://ec.europa.eu/dgs/home-affairs/news/intro/docs/commission-report-on-the-joint-review-of-the-tftp.pdf (accessed: March 2020)
- EUROPOL Annual Review 2016–2017, at: https://www.europol.europa.eu/europol_review (Accessed: July 2018).
- *European Union Serious and Organised Crime Threat Assessment 2017*, at: https://www.europol.europa.eu/newsroom/news/crime-in-age-of-technology-%E2%80%93-europol%E2%80%99s-serious-and-organised-crime-threat-assessment-2017 (Accessed: July 2018).
- European Union Article 29 Working Party, Press Release on the SWIFT Case, (Nov. 23, 2006), available at http://ec.europa.eu/justice-home/fsj/privacy/news/docs/PRSwiftAffair_23 11 06 en.pdf (Accessed: January 2020)
- Final report of COWI (European consulting group) of January 2009 preparing an external evaluation of Frontex provided for in Article 33 of the Council Regulation (EC) No 2007/2004 of 26 October 2004 establishing Frontex, p. 48, available at: http://www.statewatch.org/news/2009/may/frontex-eval-report-2009.pdf (Accessed: July 2018).
- Financial Times (2007) Travelers from US face EU crackdown, 7 August, at: https://www.ft.com/content/f490402c-4518-11dc-82f5-0000779fd2ac, (Accessed: May 2018)
- "From Tampere 20 to Tampere 2.0: Towards a new European consensus on migration", Philippe De Bruycker Marie De Somer Jean-Louis De Brouwer (eds.), European Policy Center 2019, at: http://odysseus-network.eu/wp-content/uploads/2019/12/Publication-Final-3.pdf (Accessed: March 2020).
- Frontex: http://eur-lex.europa.eu/legal-content/EN/TXT/?uri=celex:02004R2007-20140717, (Accessed: July 2018)
- General Approach of the Council, at: https://ec.europa.eu/commission/presscorner/detail/en/PRES_12_172 (Accessed: March 2020).
- General data protection regulation: https://gdpr.eu/ (Accessed: January 2020)
- Gurzu A., Cyberthreats could turn smart cities into dumb ones, in: „Politico", 8/27/19, at: https://www.politico.edu/article/cyber-threats-could-turn-smart-cities-into-sumb-ones-copenhagen/ (Accessed: September 2019)

- Henry Stimson Center, U.S. Homeland Security: A Look at the Financial Year 2003 Homeland Security Budget Request, at: https://www.files.ethz.ch/isn/31134/FollowingtheMoney.pdf (Accessed: December 2019)
- Howe N., Artificial Intelligence Paves The Way For Ambient Intelligence, in: "Forbes magazine" May 14, 2015, at: https://www.forbes.com/sites/neilhowe/2015/05/14/artificial-intelligence-paves-the-way-for-ambient-intelligence/#5ed8f28d776f (Accessed: June 2018)
- Legislative Train Schedule. Towards a new policy on migration, at: http://www.europarl.europa.eu/legislative-train/theme-towards-a-new-policy-on-migration/fiche (Access: January 2020)
- International Emergency Economic Powers Act, 50 U.S.C. §§ 1701–07 (2000), at: https://fas.org/sgp/crs/natsec/R45618.pdf (Access: September 2019)
- Italian Appeals Court Acquits 3 Google Executives in Privacy Case by Eric Pfanner, at: „The New York Times" December 21, 2012, at: https://www.nytimes.com/2012/12/22/business/global/italian-appeals-court-acquits-3-google-executives-in-privacy-case.html (Accessed: February 2020).
- Lichtblau E. and Risen J., *Bank Data Is Sifted by U.S. in Secret to Block Terror*, in: "International New York Times", June 23, 2006; at: https://www.nytimes.com/2006/06/23/washington/23intel.html
- Marx, G. T. 2013. 'Technology and Social Control – The Search for the Illusive Silver Bullet Continues', Encyclopedia of the Social & Behavioral Sciences, 2nd edition, at: http://web.mit.edu/gtmarx/www/techsoccon.html, (Access: September 2018)
- Micah Zenko, Bush *and Obama Fought a Failed 'War on Terror.' It's Trump's Turn*, in: "International New York Times", Aug. 25, 2017, https://www.nytimes.com/2017/08/25/opinion/trump-afghanistan-war-on-terror.html (Access: May 2018)
- *Obama's Remarks on Health Care and Surveillance*, International New York Times, June 7, 2013, at: https://www.nytimes.com/2013/06/08/us/obamas-remarks-on-health-care-and-surveillance.html (Access: January 2020)
- *Obama Administration Unveils "Big Data" Initiative: Announces $200 Million in New R&D Investments*, at: https://obamawhitehouse.archives.gov/the-press-office/2015/11/19/release-obama-administration-unveils-big-data-initiative-announces-200, (Access: January 2020 2018).
- Opinion of the European Data Protection Supervisor on the proposal for a Directive of the European Parliament and of the Council on the retention of data processed in connection with the provision of public electronic communication services and amending Directive 2002/58/EC (COM(2005)

438 final), at: https://eur-lex.europa.eu/legal-content/EN/TXT/PDF/?uri=CELEX:52005XX1129(01)&from=EN (Accessed: January 2020)

- *Opinion of the European Data Protection Supervisor on the Final Report by the EU-US High Level Contact Group on information sharing and privacy and personal data protection*, in: OJC 128, 6.6.2009, pp. 1-12 at: https://eur-lex.europa.eu/legal-content/EN/TXT/PDF/?uri=OJ:C:2009:128:FULL&from=EN (Accessed: January 2020)
- PlanIT in Portugal: https://www.urenio.org/2015/01/26/smart-city-strategy-planlt-valley-portugal/, (Access: June 2018).
- *President George W. Bush address to a Joint Session of Congress and the American People*, September 20, 2001, at: https://www.washingtonpost.com/wp-srv/nation/specials/attacked/transcripts/bushaddress_092001.html? (January 2020)
- *Privacy Bridges. EU and US privacy experts in search of transatlantic privacy solutions,* in: 37th International Privacy Conference, Amsterdam 2015, at: http://privacybridges.mit.edu/sites/default/files/documents/PrivacyBridges-FINAL.pdf (Access: February 2018).
- Privacy Implications of Emerging & Future Technologies / Birnhack & Ahituv, PRACTIS, Dec. 2013, at: https://poseidon01.ssrn.com/delivery.php?ID=431123081119072010 1160060241021040690160170500810650390 90094002091122114086004108022107096017002029 1270370660060031240 900201180600090440290351050870180140941161060290470770031 140000 920690661230291200950800020190700240 100140711050221030680271261 02088&EXT=pdf (Access: September 2018).
- Office of Homeland Security, *"Securing America's Borders Fact Sheet: Border Security"*, in: http://www.whitehouse.gov/news/releases/2002/01/20020125.html (Accessed: October 2019)
- Opinion 5/2007 on the Follow-Up Agreement Between the European Union and the United States of America on the Processing and Transfer of Passenger Name Record (PNR) Data by Air Carriers to the United States Department of Homeland Security Concluded in July 2007, At 5, at: http://ec.europa.eu/justice home/fsj/privacy/docs/wpdocs/2007/wp138_en.pdf (Accessed: October 2019)
- Opinion of Advocate General Jääskinen § 19, Google Spain SL v. Agencia Española de Protección de Datos (May 13, 2014) (Case C-131/12), at:http://curia.europa.eu/juris/document/document.jsf?text=&docid=138782&doclang=EN, (Accessed: January 2018).
- *Privacy Bridges. EU and US privacy experts in search of transatlantic privacy solutions,* in: 37th International Privacy Conference, Amsterdam 2015, at:http://privacybridges.mit.edu/sites/default/files/documents/PrivacyBridges-FINAL.pdf (Accessed: February 2018).

- Privacy Implications of Emerging & Future Technologies / Birnhack & Ahituv, PRACTIS, Dec 2013
- Proposal for a Directive of the European Parliament and of the Council on the use of Passenger Name Record data for the prevention, detection, investigation and prosecution of terrorist offences and serious crime, (COM 20011/31 final), Brussels 2.2.2011, at: https://eur-lex.europa.eu/legal-content/EN/TXT/HTML/?uri=CELEX:52011PC0032&from=EN (Accessed: March 2020).
- Processing of Personal Data:https://www.coe.int/en/web/conventions/full-list/-/conventions/treaty/223/signatures (Accessed: September 2019)
- Proposal for a Council Framework Decision on the use of Passenger Name Record (PNR) for law enforcement purposes, (COM 654 2007 final), Brussels 6.11.2007, at: https://eur-lex.europa.eu/legal-content/EN/TXT/HTML/?uri=CELEX:52007PC0654&from=EN (Accessed: March 2020).
- Rana el Kaliouby, *We know how You feel*, in: "The New Yorker", January 2015, at: https://www.newyorker.com/magazine/2015/01/19/know-feel (Accessed: January 2018)
- Reality of Masdar smart city: https://www.archdaily.com/tag/masdar-city/, (Accessed: June 2018).
- Regulation (EC) 604/2013 L 180/31 (recast, ‚Dublin III Regulation'). See for an overview: http://ec.europa.eu/dgs/home-affairs/what-we-do/policies/asylum/index_en.htm (Accessed: January 2018).
- Report of the High Level Advisory Group on Future of European Home Affairs Policy: (2008), at: http://register.consilium.europa.eu/doc/srv?l=EN&f=ST%2011657 %202008 %20INIT, p. 11. (Accessed: March 2018)
- *Obama's Remarks on Health Care and Surveillance*, in: "International New York Times", June 7, 2013; at:https://www.nytimes.com/2013/06/08/us/obamas-remarks-on-health-care-and-surveillance.html (Accessed: March 2020)
- PlanIT in Portugal: https://www.urenio.org/2015/01/26/smart-city-strategy-planlt-valley-portugal/ (Accessed: September 2019)
- Press Send for Brexit: E.U. Seals U.K. Withdrawal by Email by HYPERLINK "https://www.nytimes.com/by/matina-stevis-gridneff" Matina Stevis-Gridneff, "International New York Times Jan. 30, 2020, at: https://www.nytimes.com/2020/01/30/world/europe/eu-brexit-decision.html?searchResultPosition=2 (Accessed: January 2020)
- Reality of Masdar smart city: https://www.archdaily.com/tag/masdar-city/
- Second Report EU Data Protection law: a 'right to be forgotten'?"23 July 2014, at: http://www.publications.parliament.uk/pa/ld201415/ldselect/ldeucom/40/4002.htm, (Accessed: September 2015).

- Shead S., *Stephen Hawking and Elon Musk backed 23 principles to ensure humanity benefits from AI, "Business Insider"*, Feb. 1, 2017, at: https://www.businessinsider.com/stephen-hawking-elon-musk-backed-asimolar-ai-principles-for-artificial-intelligence-2017-2?IR=T (Access: September 2018)
- SmartSantander proposes a unique in the world city-scale experimental research facility in support of typical applications and services for a smart city, at: http://www.smartsantander.eu/ (Access: June 2018)
- *The European Agenda on Security*, at: https://ec.europa.eu/home-affairs/sites/homeaffairs/files/e-library/documents/basic-documents/docs/eu_agenda_on_security_en.pdf (Accessed: March 2020).
- *The Stanford Encyclopedia of Philosophy* edited by E. N. Zalta, Fall 2014, at: http://plato.stanford.edu/archives/fall2014/entries/statistics/ (Accessed: September 2018).
- The End of Theory: The Data Deluge Makes the Scientific Method Obsolete'. "*Wired*" May 23rd. http://archive.wired.com/science/—discoveries/magazine/16-07/pb_theory, (Access: September 2018)
- Tanaka, W. 2012. 'Cities of the Future: Songdo, South Korea – A New Approach – The Network: Cisco's Technology News Site'. *Cisco's The Network*, at: http://newsroom.cisco.com/feature-content?type=webcontent&articleId=630153, (Accessed: September 2018)
- *The cyber threat against the Danish energy sector*, Threat Assessment by the Center for Cyber Security, September 2018, at: fe-ddis.dk (Access: September 2019)
- "Towards a European Public's Prosecutor's Office (EPPO), Study for the LIBE Committee 2016", at: http://www.europarl.europa.eu/RegData/etudes/STUD/2016/571399/IPOL_STU(2016)571399_EN.pdf (Accessed: July 2018).
- Transcript of Secretary of Homeland Security Tom Ridge at the Center for Transatlantic Relations at Johns Hopkins University 2004, at: http://www.dhs.gov/dhspublic/display?theme1⁄444& content1⁄43994&print1⁄4true> (Accessed: September 2019)
- Travelers from US face EU crackdown, Financial Times (2007) 7 August at: https://www.ft.com/content/f490402c-4518-11dc-82f5-0000779fd2ac (Accessed: January 2020)
- NSA collecting phone records of millions of Verizon customers daily, in: "The Guardian" 6 June 2013, at: https://www.theguardian.com/world/2013/jun/06/nsa-phone-records-verizon-court-order (Accessed: January 2020)
- Office of Homeland Security, *"Securing America's Borders Fact Sheet: Border Security"*, at:http://www.whitehouse.gov/news/releases/2002/01/20020125.html (Accessed: March 2020)

- President George W. Bush address to a Joint Session of Congress and the American People, September 20, 2001, at: https://georgewbush-whitehouse.archives.gov/infocus/bushrecord/documents/Selected_Speeches_George_W_Bush.pdf (Accessed: March 2020)
- Press Release, European Commission, *International Agreement on Passenger Name Records (PNR) Enters into Force*, (May 28, 2004), available at: http://ec.europa.eu/comm/externalrelations/us/news/ip04_694.htm (Accessed: March 2020)
- Press Release, European Court of Justice, The Court Annuls the Council Decision Concerning the Conclusion of an Agreement Between the European Community and the United States of America on the Processing and Transfer of Personal Data and the Commission Decision on the Adequate Protection of Those Data, (May 30, 2006) (citation omitted), available at: http://curia.europa.eu/en/actu/communiques/cp06/aff/cpO60046en.pdf (Accessed: January 2020).
- Press Release, European Commission, EU and US Reach Agreement on the Continued Use of Passenger Name Record(PNR)Data(October 6, 2006), http://www.eurunion.orgNews/press/2006/20060086.htm (Accessed: March 2020)
- *Privacy Bridges. EU and US privacy experts in search of transatlantic privacy solutions*, in: 37th International Privacy Conference, Amsterdam 2015, at: http://privacybridges.mit.edu/sites/default/files/documents/PrivacyBridges-FINAL.pdf (Accessed: January 2020)
- *Retailers race against Amazon to automate stores* by Nick Wingfield, Paul Mozur and Michael Corkery, in: International New York Times, April 1, 2018: https://www.nytimes.com/2018/04/01/technology/retailer-stores-automation-amazon.html (Accessed: September 2018)
- Regulation (EC) 604/2013 L 180/31 (recast, ‚Dublin III Regulation'). See for an overview: http://ec.europa.eu/dgs/home-affairs/what-we-do/policies/asylum/index_en.htm (Accessed: January 2020)
- Savage Ch., *Congress Approves Six-Year Extension of Surveillance Law*, in: "International New York Times" January 18, 2018, at:https://www.nytimes.com/2018/01/18/us/politics/surveillance-congress-snowden-privcy.htmlrref=collection%2Ftimestopic%2FNational%20Security%20Agency&action=click&contentCollection=timestopics&region=stream&module=stream_unit&version=latest&contentPlacement=6&pgtype=collection (Accessed: January 2020)
- Smart city Santander: http://www.smartsantander.eu/
- SIS II - 2016 Statistics, eu-LISA, at: http://www.eulisa.europa.eu/Publications/Reports/SIS%20II%20-%20Statistics%202016.pdf (Accessed: January 2018)

- Tanaka, W. 2012. 'Cities of the Future: Songdo, South Korea – A New Approach – The Network: Cisco's Technology News Site'. *Cisco's The Network*, at: http://newsroom.cisco.com/feature-content?type=webcontent&articleId=630153 (Accessed: January 2020)
- Transcript of Secretary of Homeland Security Tom Ridge at the Center for Transatlantic Relations at Johns Hopkins University 2004, at: http://www.dhs.gov/dhspublic/display?theme1/444& content1/43994 (Accessed: December 2019)
- *„Using Amazon Rekognition to Identify Persons of Interest for Law Enforcement"* by Chris Adzima (AWS AI Blog), June15, 2017, https://aws.amazon.com/blogs/ai/using-amazon-rekognition-to-identify-persons-of-interest-for-law-enforcement/ (Accessed: February 2019)
- Visa statistics: Schengen States receive 15.2 million applications for short-stay visas in 2016, at:https://ec.europa.eu/home-affairs/news/visa-statistics-schengen-states-receive-152-million-applications-short-stay-visas-2016_en (Accessed: January 2018)
- Wheeler T., *Can Europe lead on Privacy?*, in: "International New York Times" April 1 2018, at: https://www.nytimes.com/2018/04/01/opinion/europe-privacy-protections.html (Accessed: March 2020)
- Wikipedia, Offender profiling, at:. https://en.wikipedia.org/wiki/Offender_profiling (Accessed: September 2018).
- Savage Charlie, *Congress Approves Six-Year Extension of Surveillance Law*, in: "International New York Times" January 18, 2018, at: https://www.nytimes.com/2018/01/18/us/politics/surveillance-congress-snowden-privacy.html?searchResultPosition=1 (Accessed: September 2019)
- SIS II - 2016 Statistics, eu-LISA, at: http://www.eulisa.europa.eu/Publications/Reports/SIS%20II%20-%20Statistics%202016.pdf
- SWIFT Supports Calls for Debate to Move Beyond Data Privacy to Security and Public Safety (Nov. 9, 2006), at: https://www.google.com/url?sa=t&rct=j&q=&esrc=s&source=web&cd=2&cad=rja&uact=8&ved=2ahUKEwj5y8_0ivnmAhXAwcQBHTYGCpMQFjABegQIBRAC&url=https%3A%2F%2Fwww.swift.com%2Fnode%2F14941&usg=AOvVaw3lCogiq08F564CGS42FL6y (Accessed: Oktober 2019)
- Proposal for the Regulation of the European Parliament and of the Council establishing an Entry/Exit System (EES) to register entry and exit data and refusal of entry data of third country nationals crossing the external borders of the Member States of the European Union and determining the conditions for access to the EES for law enforcement purposes and amending Regulation (EC) No 767/2008 and Regulation (EU) No 1077/2011, at: https://ec.europa.

eu/home-affairs/sites/homeaffairs/files/what-we-do/policies/securing-eu-borders/legal-documents/docs/20160406/regulation_proposal_entryexit_system_borders_package_en.pdf (Accessed: January 2020)

- *„Using Amazon Rekognition to Identify Persons of Interest for Law Enforcement"* by Chris Adzima (AWS AI Blog, June15, 2017, at: https://aws.amazon.com/blogs/ai/using-amazon-rekognition-to-identify-persons-of-interest-for-law-enforcement/ (Accessed: March 2020)
- White House Press Release: *Obama Administration Unveils "Big Data" Initiative: Announces $200 Million in New R&D Investments*, at:https://obamawhitehouse.archives.gov/the-press-office/2015/11/19/release-obama-administration-unveils-big-data-initiative-announces-200 (Accessed: January 2020)
- *'Why Can't Europe Just Forget The Ridiculous Idea of a 'Right To Be Forgotten'* by Mike Masnick in TechDirt, at: https://www.techdirt.com/articles/20120129/23085517583/why-cant-europe-just-forget-ridiculous-idea-right-to-be-forgotten.shtml (Accessed:Oktober 2019)
- Visa statistics: Schengen States receive 15.2 million applications for short-stay visas in 2016, at:https://ec.europa.eu/home-affairs/news/visa-statistics-schengen-states-receive-152-million-applications-short-stay-visas-2016_en (Accessed: January 2020)
- *Yitu Technology won first place in prestigious global facial recognition benchmark test*, at: https://www.prnewswire.com/news-releases/yitu-technology-won-first-place-in-prestigious-global-facial-recognition-benchmark-test-300513646.html (Accessed: December 2020).
- Zimmermann J., co-founder of La Quadrature du Net: *„France in the Era of Mass Surveillance! We must resist!"*, at: https://www.laquadrature.net/en/france-in-era-of-mass-surveillance-we-must-resist (Accessed: January 2020).
- *Report from the Commission to the European Parliament and the Council- 30th Annual Report on the Protection of the European Union's financial interests — Fight against fraud – 2018 COM/2019/444 fina*l, at: https://eur-lex.europa.eu/legal-content/en/ALL/?uri=CELEX:52019DC0444 (Accessed: March 2020).
- *Best Practice Operational Guidelines for Automated Border Control (ABC) Systems"*, at: https://frontex.europa.eu/assets/Publications/Research/Best_Practice_Operational_Guidelines_for_Automated_Border_Control.pdf (Access: March 2020).

Case law

- *Airey v Ireland* [1979] Series A No. 32, App. No. 6289/73, § 32.
- Analysis of Joined Cases: C-203/15 Tele2 Sverige AB v Post-och telestyrelsen and C-698/15 Secretary of State for the Home Department v Tom Watson and Others by Global Freedom of Expression, Colombia University, at: https://globalfreedomofexpression.columbia.edu/cases/joined-cases-tele2-sverige-ab-v-post-och-telestyrelsen-c-20315-secretary-state-home-department-v-watson/ (Accessed: March 2020).
- *Amann v Switzerland* [2000] RJD 2000-II, App. No. 27798/95.
- Digital Rights Ireland and Schrems case 498/16, at: http://curia.europa.eu/juris/document/document.jsf;jsessionid=239E641DD87C6B5BB6CDC4CFC7536040?text=&docid=198764&pageIndex=0&doclang=en&mode=lst&dir=&occ=first&part=1&cid=560500 (Accessed: March 2020)
- *Bensaid v United Kingdom* [2001] RJD 2001-I, App. No. 44599/98, § 47.
- *Leander v. Sweden, supra* note 138, at para 48;ECtHR.
- *S. Marper v. United Kingdom* (Application nos 30562/04 and 30566/04), 4 December 2008, ECtHR (2008)1581.
- *Cemalettín Canli v Turkey* [2008] App. No. 22427/04, § 33.
- CJEU, Case C-362/14, Schrems v. Data Protection Commissioner, Reference for a preliminary ruling from High Court of Ireland made on 25 July 2014.
- C-131/12, Google Spain SL. v. Agencia Española de Protección de Datos.
- CJEU, Case C-362/14, Schrems v. Data Protection Commissioner, Reference for a preliminary ruling from High Court of Ireland made on 25 July 2014
- CJEU, Case C-362/14, Schrems v. Data Protection Commissioner, Opinion of the Advocate General Bot on 23rd of September 2015
- Case C-291/12, Schwarz, Judgment of 17 October 2013.
- Case C-301/06, *Ireland v. European Parliament and the Council,* (2009) ECR I-593 (ECLI:EU:C:2009:68)
- Judgment of the Court (Grand Chamber) of 10 February 2009. Ireland v European Parliament and Council of the European Union. Action for annulment - Directive 2006/24/EC - Retention of data generated or processed in connection with the provision of electronic communications services - Choice of legal basis. Case C-301/06.
- Commission (Plenary) *Friedl v Austria* [1994] RJD 31.
- C-503/03 Commission v Spain, judgment of 31.1.2006
- Federal Administrative Court: Judgement BVerwG, 10.07.2001, Az. 1 C 35.00.
- *Gaskin v the United Kingdom* [1989] Series A No. 160, App. No. 10454/83.

- *Halford v United Kingdom* [1997] RJD 1997-III, App. No. 20605/92, § 42).
- Italian Google Case judgment in original language version: Sentenza n. 1972/2010. Tribunale Ordinario di Milano in composizione monocratica. Sezione 4 Penale.
- Joint cases Case C-317/07 and C-318/04, European Parliament v. Council of the European Union (C-317/04) and European Parliament v. Commission of the European Community (C-318/04), 2006 E.C.R. I-4721.
- Katz v. United States [1967] 389 U.S 347
- *Khelili v Switzerland* [2011] App. No. 16188/07.
- *Malone v the United Kingdom* [1984] Series A No. 82, App. No. 8691/79.
- *M.G. v the United Kingdom* [2002] App. No. 39393/98.
- *M. S. v Sweden* [1997] RJD 1997-IV, App. No. 20837/92, § 51.
- *Peck v the United Kingdom* [2003] RJD 2003, App. No. 44647/98.
- *P.G. and J.H. v the United Kingdom* [2001] RJD 2001-IX, App. No. 44787/98.
- *Schmerber v. California* (1966) 384 U.S. 757.
- *Segerstedt-Wiberg and Others v Sweden* [2006] RJD 2006-VII, App. No. 44787/98
- *Tyrer v United Kingdom* [1978] Series A No. 26, App. No. 5856/72.
- *Niemietz v Germany* [1992] Series A No. 251-B, App. No 13710/88.
- *Rotaru v. Romania* [2000] RJD 2000-V, App. No. 28341/95.
- United States v. White [1971] 401 U.S. 745.
- United States v. Miller [1976] 425 U.S. 435, 437.
- California v. Greenwood [1988] 486 U.S. 3.
- Smith v. Maryland [1979] U.S 735.
- *X and Y v the Netherlands* [1985] Series A No. 91, App. No. 8978/80, § 23
- *Z v Finland* [1997] RJD 1997-I, App. No. 22009/93.

Documents

- Agreement between the European Union and United States of America on the Processing and Transfer of Passenger Name Record (PNR) Data by Air Carriers to the United States Department of Homeland Security, U.S.-E.U., Oct. 27, 2006, 2006 O.J. L 298) 27(EU).
- *"A Secure Europe in a Better World"*-European Security Strategy, Brussels, 12 December 2003.
- Belgian Privacy Commission (CBPL), Opinion N°17/2008 biometric data.

- Commission Decision of 28 June 2006 laying down the technical specifications on the standards for security features and biometrics in passports and travel documents issued by Member States, at: https://ec.europa.eu/transparency/regdoc/rep/3/2006/DE/3-2006-2909-DE-F-0.Pdf
- Commission Decision on the Adequate Protection of Personal Data Contained in the Passenger Name Record of Air Passengers transferred to the United States' Bureau of Customs and Border Protection 2004/535/EC, art. 1, 2004 O.J.(L 235) 11, 13 (EC).
- *Communication from the Commission to the Council and the Parliament, Transfer of Air Pas*senger Name Record (PNR) Data: A Global EU Approach, *COM* (2003) 826 final (DEC. 12, 2003).
- Convention No. 108, the ECHR standard; Recommendation R (87) 15 of the committee of ministers to member states regulating the use of personal data in the police sector, adopted on 17 September 1987.
- Council of the European Union, *Processing and protection of personal data subpoenaed by the Treasury Department from the US based operation center of the Society for Worldwide Interbank Financial Telecommunication (SWIFT)*, 11291/2/07 REV 2, Luxembourg, 28 June 2007.
- Council Framework Decision 2008/977/JHA of 27 November 2008 on the protection of personal data processed in the framework of police and judicial cooperation in criminal matter, OJ 2008, L-350/60; the processing refers to automatic and non-automatic processing of personal data: Article 2 (a) FDPJ, OJ 2008,, L-350/60).
- Council Decision 2004/927/EC providing for certain areas covered by Title IV of Part Three of the Treaty establishing the European Community to be governed by the procedure laid down in Article 251 of that Treaty (2004) OJ L396/45.
- Council Decision 2009/371/JHA, OJ 2009 L 121/37 on the establishment of Europol.
- Council Directive 95/46/EC, art. 2(d)-(e), 1995 O.J. (L 281) 1, 11–12 (EC).
- Council of the European Union, Processing and protection of personal data subpoenaed by the Treasury Department from the US based operation center of the Society for Worldwide Interbank Financial Telecommunication (SWIFT), 11291/2/07 REV 2, Luxembourg, 28June 2007.
- EDPS welcomes a "huge step forward for data protection in Europe", but regrets inadequate rules for the police and justice area, Press release 25 January 2012.
- European Parliament resolution on the interception of bank transfer data from the SWIFT system by the US secret services (P6_TA-PROV(2006)0317).

- Homeland Security Act (H.R. 5710) 107th Congress, 2d sess., 13 November 2002.
- ICAO, Doc 9303, *Machine Readable Travel Document*, Seventh Edition, 2015.
- *"The National Security Strategy of the United States of America"*, September 2002
- Regulation (EC) 1987/2006, OJ 2006 L 381/4 ('SIS II Regulation') and Council Decision 2007/533/JHA, OJ 2007 L 205/63 (' SIS II Decision')
- Regulation (EU) 603/2013, OJ 2013 L 180/1.
- Regulation (EC) No 810/2009 of the European Parliament and of the Council of 13 July 2009 establishing a Community Code on Visas (Visa Code), OJ L 243/1 § 32.
- Report of the High Level Advisory Group on Future of European Home Affairs Policy: (2008), at: http://register.consilium.europa.eu/doc/srv?l=EN&f=ST%2011657 %202008 %20INIT
- Tom Ridge, statement on the Department of Homeland Security, House Select Committee on Homeland Security, (15 July 2002).
- Tucker, P. 2014. *The Naked Future: What Happens in a World That Anticipates Your Every Move*. United States General Accounting Office. 2004. 'Report to the Ranking Minority Member, Subcommittee on Financial Management, the Budget, and International Security, Committee on Governmental Affairs, U.S. Senate'. United States General Accounting Office
- United States Department of Homeland Security. 2008. 'Privacy Impact Assessment for the Future Attribute Screening Technology (FAST) Project'. United States Department of Homeland Security.

Studies in European Integration, State and Society

Edited by Magdalena Góra, Zdzisław Mach and Katarzyna Zielińska

Vol. 1 Józef Niżnik: Democracy versus Solidarity in the EU Discourse. 2012.

Vol. 2 Grzegorz Żuk: Europe in Polish Public Discourse. 2013.

Vol. 3 Zdzisław Mach (ed.): Local Community, Power and European Integration. 2017.

Vol. 4 Janusz Węc: Germany's Position on the System Reform of the European Union in 2002–2016. 2018.

Vol. 5 Krzysztof Kowalski / Łucja Piekarska-Duraj / Barbara Törnquist-Plewa (eds.): Narrating Otherness in Poland and Sweden. European Heritage as a Discourse of Inclusion and Exclusion. 2019.

Vol. 6 Marek Aleksander Cichocki / Tomasz Grzegorz Grosse (eds.): The Many Faces of Crisis. An Analysis of Crisis Management from an Economic and Political Perspective. 2019.

Vol. 7 Marek Aleksander Cichocki (ed.): Contemporary States and the Crisis of the Western Order. 2019.

Vol. 8 Marta Kołodziejczyk: The use of technology for the management of the EU/US Immigration and Asylum Policy- possible risks for fundamental rights protection. 2020.

www.peterlang.com

www.ingramcontent.com/pod-product-compliance
Ingram Content Group UK Ltd.
Pitfield, Milton Keynes, MK11 3LW, UK
UKHW041826031026
15587UKWH00002B/585

9 783631 808191